Virgil Chittenden Hart

Western China

A Journey to the great Buddhist Centre of Mount Omei

Virgil Chittenden Hart

Western China
A Journey to the great Buddhist Centre of Mount Omei

ISBN/EAN: 9783743313651

Manufactured in Europe, USA, Canada, Australia, Japa

Cover: Foto ©Thomas Meinert / pixelio.de

Manufactured and distributed by brebook publishing software
(www.brebook.com)

Virgil Chittenden Hart

Western China

WESTERN CHINA

SCENES ON THE UPPER YANG-TSZE.

(1) *Lukun Gorge.*   (2) *Chang-Chou Pagoda.*

WESTERN CHINA 

A JOURNEY TO THE GREAT BUDDHIST
CENTRE OF MOUNT OMEI

BY

REV. VIRGIL C. HART, B.D.

FELLOW OF THE ROYAL ASIATIC SOCIETY

ILLUSTRATED

BOSTON
TICKNOR AND COMPANY
211 Tremont Street
1888

University Press:

JOHN WILSON AND SON, CAMBRIDGE, U. S. A.

TO THE

REV. ERNEST FABER, F.R.A.S.

AN EMINENT SCHOLAR,

*For many years an honored member of the Rhenish Mission at
Canton,*

And to ARTHUR MORLEY, M.D., *and* REV. H. O. CADY,

My fellow-travellers on my West China trip,

*I most cordially and heartily dedicate these pages, which will
recall to them familiar scenes, genial intercourse,
and most delightful experiences.*

CONTENTS.

CONTENTS.

LIST OF ILLUSTRATIONS.

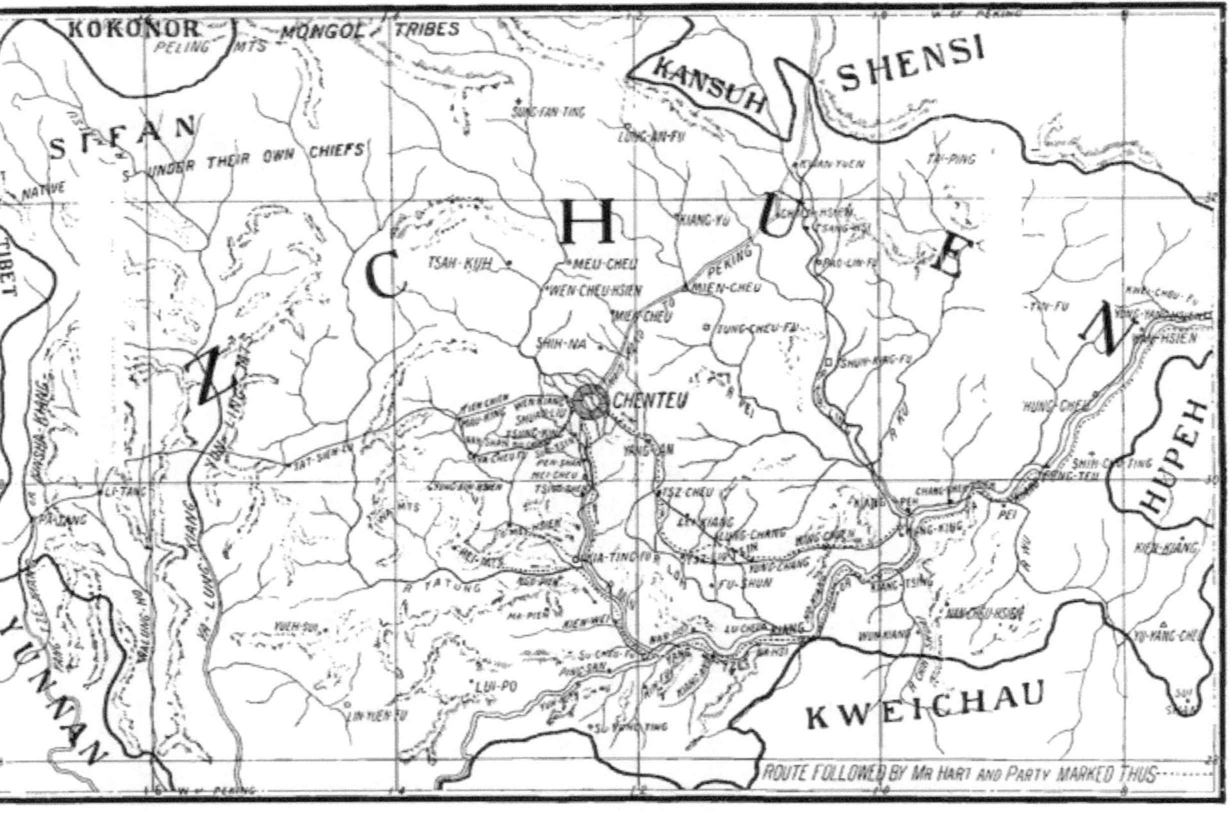

MAP OF WESTERN CHINA, SHOWING THE ROUTE TRAVERSED BY MR. HART.

WESTERN CHINA.

CHAPTER I.

HANKOW is a very populous town, six hundred and fifty miles from the mouth of the Yang-tsze River. It is the centre of the black-tea trade, and the largest port above Shanghai. It was opened to foreign trade in 1860, and until 1877 was the highest open port on the Yang-tsze; since then, Ichang, four hundred miles farther west, has also been open to foreigners.

Hankow is situated upon the north bank of the Yang-tsze and the east bank of the Han, which here joins the larger river. The great provincial city of Wuchang faces Hankow on the south bank of the Yang-tsze, while across the smaller river is the city of Hanyang. The population of these three cities is at least eight hundred thousand, and together they make the most important inland commercial centre of China.

The resident foreign population is about one hundred and seventy; but in the summer the "English Tea-tasters" bring the number up to two hundred and fifty or more, and at this season the largest sea-going vessels run up to Hankow to load with teas for the United States, England, and Russia. These foreign residents are mostly English and Russian tea-merchants, the latter having extensive manufactories of " brick tea," for use in Siberia and other parts of Russia.

Branches of the London and Wesleyan Missions and the Protestant Episcopal Mission of the United States are established here. The first two came with the opening of the port, and have maintained a strong staff of able laborers : the present leaders are Rev. Griffith John and Rev. David Hill, — heroic teachers of Christianity, bravely working among the millions of this great valley.

Here, late in the evening of April 11, 1887, the writer, with Rev. Ernest Faber and Rev. H. O. Cady, was in the small saloon of an antiquated steamer, the " Kiangtung," anxiously awaiting the signals for departure.

At ten o'clock a large party of Hankow friends came on board to speak words of encouragement, and bid us God-speed in our dangerous journey and undertaking, — which was the re-establishment of the American Methodist Episcopal Mission at Chungking, which had been so tragically closed by the great riot in July, 1886.

The day had been stiflingly hot, with a breeze from the southwest as from a heated furnace ; and at evening the sickly puffs, which reached us at rare intervals, were laden with noxious gases from a mountainous pile of refuse which had been dumped upon the bank near our anchorage during the winter, and was now being loaded in boats for the rural districts.

At length the machinery groaned, the wheels revolved, and we felt that another link with Western civilization and catholic Christian sympathy had been broken.

We awoke at daylight to find the boat anchored and everything enveloped in a thick fog, which did not lift until after eight o'clock. Our American ark, which has seen nearly thirty years of perpetual service, was at great disadvantage in contending with the swift current, and our speed was not such as to reflect credit oh a wealthy steamship company or soothe the jealous anxiety of the chief engineer, who is usually very sensitive about the time he makes.

Captains, as a rule, are non-committal about the speed and the weak points of their boats. If they make a poor run, it is always owing to " a slight head-wind," " a nasty current," " a double sea," and so on.

The distance from Hankow to Ichang is one hundred and sixty miles as the crow flies, but on account of the great bends, it is three hundred and sixty by the river. The captain told us that the trip would take from five to ten days, all depending upon the quantity of water and the frequency of fogs, — never a word about the good or bad qualities of his worn-out tub. After breakfast I noticed that although the engine wheezed and the hull quaked as if the boat were doing its best, the peasants walking on the bank easily outstripped us, and I began to doubt if ten days could bring us to Ichang.

At this moment the engineer came on the front deck, and I asked him our present rate of speed, and if we had the prospect of continuing it. In my innocence I had fired a bomb, and was somewhat startled by the pyrotechnic explosion which followed. He gave me a cynical look, and turned his eyes to the shore as if to see which way we might be going, and tried to smile as he said : " She is doing well — quite four knots. Why, last year, when the water was high and I had crowded her all I could, I found her falling astern when I came on deck."

As the engineer was a frank man, I could but believe him, and soon went to my room in disgust, drew the curtains, shut the door, and tried to lose myself in sleep. There is a story that on one occasion when the water was high and the " Kiang-tung " was hugging the shore, she was found to be falling astern. All hands were called and ordered to grasp the long grass which fringed the shore, and thus pull the boat along ; by this means a point was rounded.

It is the custom of the people living on the shore to crowd down to the water's edge and beg for empty bottles and cans, or anything which the officers and sailors will give them. It is curious to watch the nimble motions of the women with their crippled feet under these exciting circumstances. They outstrip the steamer, stand upon some outjutting, tumble-down point of the bank, and frantically call for a *yangping*, " foreign bottle." When an object is thrown they rush down the oozing bank, thirty feet or more, followed by a pack of ragged boys and girls, and all go plunging about searching for the coveted treasure.

Where this custom prevailed the people were civil, and addressed us with some degree of respect ; but where the shore was too abrupt for near approach, the air was rent with shouts of " foreign devil," while mud and clay were hurled upon the boat from every available point.

If these were mischievous outbursts of sarcasm, aimed at the Steamship Company for competing with the native junks for the carrying trade of this rich commercial region, one could almost pardon these rustics if they were to sink the old boat; but I fear that the ludicrous phase of this subject has not occurred to them, and that the dwellers in this part of Hupeh have little respect for foreigners, — certainly politeness is an unknown quantity to them. I found that this was not an unusual occurrence, as the people here had always been abusive in this way. It is strange that the officials permit a native company, carrying the great Dragon flag, to be thus insulted, although the officers are foreigners and there are occasional passengers so unfortunate as not to wear the pigtail and petticoats. If this practice continues on the upper Yang-tsze, where only rocks are at hand, woe to the passenger who shall attempt to enjoy the beauties of the scenery in the gorges from the saloon deck!

This portion of China has often been described. The geologist, botanist, archæologist, and ethnologist have crossed and recrossed this rich alluvial basin, teeming with millions of people, and filled to plenteousness with the rich and varied products of a never-impoverished soil.

A casual glance at its topography reveals to the traveller that it was not always in its present condition. There are too many small lakes, too many water-courses running hither and thither, too many canals and dikes, while the river banks are too low to indicate any great age. I have little doubt that a comparatively short time has elapsed since the blooming garden through which we now wind was covered by a vast sheet of water. The mariner may have sailed directly from Hankow to Kincheu, a distance of one hundred and forty miles, and from Tien-Mun, on the north of the Han, to Siang-yang, south of the Tungting Lake. Here was a great overflowing reservoir, sending its swirling floods eastward by the so-called Great, or Long, River.

The channel is very tortuous, winding toward every point of the compass within a few leagues, and on our course making one bend of thirty miles. This constant change of position gave us excellent views of the prominent green hills to the south, while the cities and market-towns were so numerous as to lend a certain picturesqueness to the otherwise monotonous plain, as well as to show the wealth and populousness of this part of Hupeh.

The largest market-town, a possible rival to Hankow, is Shashi; it extends some miles along the north bank of the river, the important city of Kincheu being just behind it. Thousands of up-river junks anchored along the shore give an appearance of thrift not seen elsewhere above Hankow.

English diplomacy was certainly outwitted when Ichang was substituted for this natural commercial centre; it is the terminus for most of the upper Yang-tsze traffic and most favorably situated for easy commercial intercourse with Hunan and regions north and east, aside from its close proximity to the large and interesting city of Kincheu. Both town and city are noted for their hostility to foreigners, who seldom visit them without encountering abuse, or even violence, from the natives. The China Inland Mission has a feeble station here, and the Protestant Episcopal Mission maintains a branch of the mission at Hankow.

Between Hankow and the Tungting Lake, a distance of about one hundred miles, we had observed large fleets of junks, but from that point to Shashi the river was almost deserted, as the fleets find easier and shorter channels in the smaller streams. The Tungting is the largest lake in China, and has several rivers flowing into it; it joins the Yang-tsze at the populous city of Yoh Chao, and as the lake is the centre of a great timber traffic, many rafts come through the lake into the river and ultimately reach all parts of Central China.

The crops and the methods of tillage are the same as in the lower Yang-tsze valley. Rapeseed in full bloom is seen in all directions, and fills the air with fragrance;

in the distance are mulberry orchards, the trees laden with large, dark, tender leaves, while here and there are fruit-trees white with blossoms.

The river abounds in fish, but few nets are cast; probably the canals and lakes are well supplied, and the fish are more easily taken there. At Salamis bar, and for some miles, the river was covered with oil, indicating that oil-wells are near at hand.

Four-wheeled wagons are drawn along the banks by water buffaloes. These wagons are surmounted by rough racks; the wheels are made from heavy planks pegged together, the outer rim being strapped with rough iron; and as these wagons move they groan and squeak, as does all the machinery in China. A wheelbarrow of a peculiar construction, such as I have not seen elsewhere, is used here for clearing ditches and rough places. It has a small wheel not more than a foot in diameter, placed two or three feet in front of the large wheel and supported by shafts.

About forty miles below Ichang we leave the great delta or valley; beautiful hills slope to the river, while lofty mountains tower in the far distance. We are upon the borders of the mountain land, and shall not see another large valley until we reach that of Chenteu, seven hundred miles to the west. The hills are well wooded, cultivation being mostly confined to the narrow ravines. Farm-houses built of mud, with thatched roofs, are seen on the tops and scattered over the sides of the low hills.

Ten miles below Ichang we came abreast with the gorge of the " Tiger's Teeth." Upon the south side of the river a famous natural bridge spans a foaming torrent, while two curious and interesting caves are pointed out a short distance above.

The forms of the mountains near Ichang are very

curious and interesting. Lofty summits are seen in the distance in all directions, while near the river are lovely cones and pyramidal peaks. As far as it has been explored this region has great interest for the botanist and geologist, while the entomologist must find it a veritable paradise.

As everywhere in the mountainous districts of China, so here are magic streams, fairy dells, and wonderful caves, which are the scenes of mythical and legendary tales without number; many of these have great interest for the student of folk-lore. In one of these curious caves there are many chambers and wonderful formations of rock produced by the action of water in past ages. The people tell of a strange race, having white faces and red hair, who came down the rapids in ancient times and took possession of these caves and pillaged all the neighboring land. From whence they came and to what race they belonged was never known, but when they were satisfied with their booty they vanished into the land of mystery.

Since leaving Shashi the lost shipping has reappeared, and we meet every variety of boat coming from the upper Yang-tsze, rowed by from ten to thirty men, and laden with coal, salt, drugs, charcoal, silk, and other commodities; while all along the shores an equal number of boats are sailing or being "tracked." Fishing-boats also appear; and on the banks, where the currents run swiftly, men are stationed at intervals, swinging hand nets of a peculiar make. Two bamboos are bent into the form of a snow-shoe, and a pouch net is attached to the large end; a cross piece is firmly tied three feet from the small end, and is grasped by the fisherman with one hand. The net is plunged into the swift current and swept along by it in a partial curve, and then

SCENERY BELOW ICHANG.

brought gracefully to the bank at the rate of about one sweep per minute.

Ichang is situated upon the north bank of the river, and is one hundred and twenty-nine feet above the sea level. The annual rise and fall of the river here is about sixty feet; in some months it is flooded, but in the spring is quite a distance from the water. Although it was dark before we came to anchor, our arrival caused an excitement, and a line of battle junks lying near the shore saluted us with a fierce cannonading, on account of a military officer who was on board. The amount of powder burned and the din and display made in the reception of a third-grade official made me wonder what would be done should the Emperor himself arrive.

We had come on a feast night, and all the shore was alive, while the sampan men were wild with excitement. The river was studded with red lights for several miles; they swept past us in all directions, bobbing up and down with the waves, and circling round and round with the currents; and the poor drowned souls might certainly see their way out of Tartarus then, if ever. These lights are made by putting half an ounce of oil in a little four-cornered paper box about four inches in width, in the middle of which is placed a tiny, lighted wick, showing a red, smoky flame.

The trade at Ichang is increasing, and were there proper steamers running here at regular intervals they would undoubtedly take the freights now sent to Shashi and Hankow by native boats. Were there a through line of boats to Chungking, and Shashi made an open port, the up-river traffic would be greatly increased. There is already much excitement over the proposal to open the river to Chungking during this year. A steamship company has been formed, and a steamer is expected at Shanghai at an early date. But the treaty is not very clear, and the Chinese officials will find some means of thwarting the enterprise or delaying action until some outside pressure is brought to bear on them. An official commission will be sent to visit the region and report upon the feasibility of the project. The report will be adverse, and a thousand unforeseen obstacles will be reported to the ministers at Peking.

The foreigners residing in Ichang are an English consul, a physician, two missionary families, two Catholic priests, a commissioner of customs, and a few customs men. Scarcely any buildings have been erected in foreign style, the Imperial custom-house being in an old tumble-down temple, with the commissioner's office in the rear. The Roman Catholics have an extensive establishment and a large school, in connection with which are ten students of divinity. The Scotch Presbyterians established a mission here in 1877 ; they have a few converts, a chapel in the native city, and two day schools.

Although Ichang is a prefect or *foo*, and has about forty thousand inhabitants, besides a large boat population, the streets are not crowded, and one sees few evidences of activity or wealth. At the same time, the beauty of the scenery, the many delightful excursions in the neighborhood, and the communication with the outside world by means of steamers makes a residence here endurable, at least. Objects made of the fossil " pagoda stone " are sold in Ichang ; they are nicely carved, but if the buyer is not an expert he may purchase the imitations, which are numerous.

We were detained nine days in Ichang, all of which time was spent in hiring a boat and making it ready for our journey. The Sz-Chuanese boatmen regard all foreigners as treasure-houses, and begin by demanding of them three times the price they would ask of a native for the same service; thus boat hiring is a tax on one's leisure, diplomacy, and patience.

Our teacher, or interpreter, was despatched at once to find a boat suited to our needs and bring back a report as to price. This report is sure to be made in the interest of the captain of the boat, and that of the teacher as well; for he considers his services indispensable, and will not 'fail' to act accordingly.

He returned to say that the officials were taking all the good-sized boats to convey machinery to Chenteu. We make a mental discount on this statement. He then adds that he has found a boat at two hundred and sixty-eight dollars which can be made ready in a few days; possibly by waiting some days another boat can be found at less price, but he is very doubtful about it.

Of course the captain knew that we had not come thus far to turn back, and that time, which meant nothing to him, was of value to us; and the few dollars which we could save on his price by haggling with him was a fortune to him, and probably half the worth of his whole craft. These boatmen, after bringing down an official from the West, will wait from two to six months for an official to go up, or will return without a freight. Their expenses in port are simply the cost of the rice they eat, and on the voyage up they frequently pick up travellers who will pay their board and five cents a day to the boatmen, who do the work of beasts.

We knew that our teacher had simply given us the " opening mouth price," which means little, and went ourselves to see the captain and the boat. We were politely and frigidly received by an emaciated opium-smoker, who could be agreeable or otherwise, as his interests demanded.

The boat was seventy feet long and eleven wide, perfectly flat and turned up at the stern. It was not new, nor old; had recently been oiled; partitions were out and doors down; but it was profusely carved and grotesquely decorated. About one half of it was enclosed and divided into four rooms, leaving the half toward the bow open ; here, at night and in rainy weather, bamboo mats are spread to protect twenty-five sailors, who lounge about with or without clothing as their fancy or the weather may determine, and who use bedding or not as their simple tastes may indicate.

In the centre of this open deck, extending its whole width, is a pit four feet wide and three feet deep, in which are a furnace, kettles, coal, bricks, store-room, and pantry. This is presided over by a diminutive being with sore eyes and small pigtail, with just sufficient intellect to boil a pot of tea and steam a caldron of rice and jump on deck in trying times to " holler " with the best on board. Here he stands full sixteen hours a day, washing, wiping, rattling chopsticks, fanning, blowing, scraping kettles, punching the fire, and wiping his eyes,—an indispensable being, the glory of every craft !

After inspecting mast, boards, ropes, and the numerous odds and ends proper to a fully equipped junk, to see that everything requisite was there, we came to the real business of our bargain. The captain demanded eight days to prepare for a journey of less than a month, and said that he must have thirty sailors for tracking and rowing, aside from those he could pick up on the way to pull us up the rapids. We then came to the price, and the " cutting down " which is the custom all over China. He fell at last to two hundred and fifty-two dollars, and from that we could not move him.

We left to seek another boat, and found one grimy and dirty, with a large hole through the side. The captain already knew what we required, and as we stepped upon the front deck he uncoiled his long, coarse, and glossy black queue and met us with a freezing salutation. He was of the bull-dog type, with high cheek-bones, a long jaw, and an evil eye, — a man who would turn pirate or rob a shipwrecked crew for half an inducement. After many tiresome preliminaries he said, " You can have this boat for four hundred and twelve dollars." In very polite language we replied that we should prefer to buy a boat and crew. A grim smile came over his face as we rose and left him.

We found no boat better than the first, and having spent an entire day in further negotiations we took it at two hundred and five dollars. An imposing document was then drawn up, in which each point of our agreement was distinctly mentioned; but when the captain signed he reduced the number of sailors to twenty-seven, and we afterward found, as is usual in Chinese documents, that a mental reservation had been made here, for the number of sailors must have included the cook, wife, child, and the dog, since we could never muster, all told, more than twenty-five.

To this reduction we stubbornly objected, but he knew our necessity and was unyielding. Another half-day was spent in unavailing efforts to bring him to our terms, and then the papers were signed and we had our boat for Chungking, — a distance of four hundred miles.

The unnumbered objections, quibbles, and evasions practised by that meek, emaciated captain are too numerous to be recorded. I have described somewhat minutely this business affair, which should have been concluded in an hour, that my readers may have a faint idea of the difficulties attending the transaction of business with a people who are quick-witted, disposed to take every advantage of the necessities of others, and without the least conscience in keeping or breaking a written engagement, unless the arm of power be at hand. I am describing the ordinary Chinaman under ordinary circumstances.

The time drew near for our departure, and we were snugly settled on board, flattering ourselves that the trifling annoyances incident to the preparations for such a journey would now give place to a series of magnificent day-dreams and lovely night-visions amid the glories of gorges and thundering cascades. But the star of felicity had not yet risen above the horizon.

A Sz-Chuanese woman, who had been instrumental in bringing down from Chungking to Kiukiang a number of orphan girls after the riot, was attached to our party on her way home. Between Hankow and Ichang she gave birth to a son; and a foreign lady who was on board, and took some interest in the woman, told us that she found her in bed while the infant was lying on the iron deck, nearly dead. When she remonstrated with the mother, she replied that it was of no account as she had three sons at home.

At Ichang the woman was taken by our cook to a native hotel, and the next morning the child was found dead. Before the inhabitants were astir the cook and the teacher conveyed the little body to the most convenient receptacle, which I doubt not was the swift, muddy river. The hotel-keeper was furious, and demanded large sums of money from the cook, besides some slight humiliations of *kotows*, or very low bows, and a purifying mass. He was satisfied in some way, and the woman sought refuge elsewhere.

When we were ready to leave, our captain refused to receive so unfortunate a person on his junk. At length the affair was settled, as we thought; but at two o'clock in the morning we were aroused, and a peremptory demand made upon us for her removal. Where? was now the question, for these boatmen are the most superstitious people in the world, and nothing (except perhaps an extra fifty dollars) could have induced the captain to allow the woman to enter his junk. Reports from the shore convinced me that the city would soon be convulsed with excitement if some drastic measures were not taken at once, and possibly Her British Majesty's consul would be dragged from his bed to face a howling mob.

My teacher, who was the son of a Honan official, and formerly connected with a newspaper in Penang, was the only person whom I dared to trust in this emergency. Thanks to this true son of Han, before daylight the poor bewildered woman was led to a farmhouse a stone's throw from the main street, where, for a mere pittance, she could remain a few weeks. I went with the consul to see the woman and verify the statements of the teacher, and after placing sufficient funds in the hands of this gentleman for all emergencies, — unless it were to pay an indemnity for any disaster that should come to the community through her presence, — I returned to the boat believing that our troubles were ended.

Alas! there was our most important servant, the cook, now twisting and groaning, now in spasms, and again in a flood of tears, with his head tightly bound up in a white cloth. Dr. Morley, of Hankow, had joined our party, and was called on for a diagnosis. We could only learn from the sufferer that his heart was paining him frightfully, and he must go on shore and could not make the trip with us. My own boy had been ill for some days, and was lying by the hatch beneath which the cook's boxes were stowed. Surmising the cause of the sudden illness I gave my boy orders to allow no one to approach the hatch in my absence; I then gave the cook some paternal advice and went off to the hills on the opposite shore. These simple precautions proved effectual. It was as I suspected; the cook had been seized with a sudden fancy for the woman we had left, and, forsooth, his heart was bursting with grief! but we must have a cook, and it was our duty to save the virtuous Sz-Chuanese from a scandal.

CHAPTER II.

After many delays the old sail was hoisted with much ado, and in the twilight we sailed across the little river, only to anchor about two hundred yards from the spot we had left! Not half the crew had crawled out from the opium dens; the captain and his confederates had not yet loaded a sufficient number of iron kettles to peddle by the way; and the bales of cotton which were to be smuggled into Sz-Chuan were not yet on board, while rice and even ropes were taken on at the last moment.

It makes the Anglo-Saxon blood boil to see men sit in indolence to the last possible moment, then, after two or three finishing smokes, and a last cup of tea, deliberately taken, rise with great effort to perform a trifling act.

Max Müller says that nothing puzzles the mere savage more than our restlessness; our anxiety to acquire and possess, rather than to rest and enjoy. The same remark largely holds good with the more civilized Chinaman.

An Indian chief is reported to have said to a European: " Ah, brother, you will never know the blessing of doing nothing and thinking nothing; and yet, next to sleep, that is most delicious. Thus we were before our birth, thus we shall be again after death." I feel confident that if our captain thought anything, his thoughts must

have run in some such channel. But let us be merciful;
life at its best must be somewhat of a burden to these
half-fed, badly used sons of toil.

Late at night the last article was on board, and our
maudlin crew were snugly rolled together, heads and
feet, before our cabin doors; and with the first glimmer
of a beautiful dawn there was a tearing down and stow-
ing away of awnings and awning frames, a screeching of
orders from every quarter, while we heard alongside the
splash and swash of two huge *yiulos*, or immense oars,
handled by twenty men. We were off in company with a
fleet of freighting junks, which we were destined to see
each morning and evening, and at every rapid or town,
for many days to come. Rarely we led them, but were
generally far behind, coming up to the rapids only in
time to take the fifth or even tenth turn with the extra
trackers required for the ascents.

At length we are in the Ichang gorge, with the cool
and gentle April breeze in our faces; its grandeur cannot
be painted with word or brush. The wide river has narrowed to two hundred yards, and flows as quietly as the
Hudson; while on either side tower cliffs of limestone,
slate, conglomerate, and granite, to the height of fifteen
hundred to three thousand feet. At this season there
are few eddies, and the regular current flows in graceful
curves, while the water is fortunately low and not rising.
The gorge is ten miles in length and displays the grandeur of the Omnipotent Power with overwhelming force.
These walls are filled with geologic wonders, while from
their thin but rich covering of soil a myriad species of
trees, shrubs, and plants spring forth. Looking above,
one soon grows dizzy in counting the strata of rocks
piled one upon another. The majestic walls and columns, with block upon block placed in order, are as the

work of demigods in imitation of the work of the great World Builder. Here and there are clefts a thousand feet high and a hundred feet wide. Pretty cones stand up, carpeted with grass and shaded with firs, — a mass of living green; these tiny parks, with their lovely climate, furnish a home to numerous exultant birds and insects. These treasure palaces are built too high and too broad for easy comprehension, and these glories of Nature so richly strewn fatigue the eye and exhaust the mind, even as a festal board too bounteously spread satiates desire and destroys the relish of the appetite.

Looking backward, the mighty stream is hidden from view by grim, projecting walls, and sweeps on in silence, vexed now and then by some bolder rocks which refuse to move from their everlasting foundations, even after ages of angry surging. Looking onward, a lofty curtain screens the winding flood from view as it struggles for broader freedom.

Yonder a tiny silvery stream issues from a dark gorge; not two yards in width it pours itself in a sparkling stream over a shelving rock, makes a leap of a hundred feet, and divides itself, as by magic, into two streams, again subdivides into four, and falls, half liquid and half spray, a score of feet, when it gathers itself again into two parts, and finally plunges, a unit, into a basin by the river's brink.

On the more sloping shelves small patches of wheat, barley, and peas are seen, carried as high up as the rude art or enterprise of the native can take him. Trees of many kinds twist their roots over rough and smooth rocks, into narrow fissures where a handful of earth has lodged; flowering shrubs cling to every crevice; while ferns and blossoms hang from the damp, over-jutting bowlders.

Everything we see around us has a fascinating interest. Even the clumsy junks, rowed by fifty men or more, rushing into view as by magic, and lost as quickly, seem in some way to be a part of Nature's lineaments. The men are screaming as they row; one stands in their midst with his hands on his hips; he looks daggers at this file and then at that; he stamps his feet and yells, and pitches their screaming on a higher key; each man bends to the oar with all his force until the long, clumsy timbers bend and creak; now comes a lull, and the great sweep turns the boat to the middle of the current.

We spent our first night above the gorge at Hwanglin temple.

The cultivation of the poppy commences at Ichang, but owing to the ruggedness of the country its cultivation does not become general until the first rapid is passed. Above this point, eighteen miles from Ichang, the country assumes a quite different form; the mountains recede and are less rugged, and a large variety of grains and fruits are grown upon them in all available places and in more favored situations even to their tops. Huge blocks of granite in all shapes lie scattered and piled in heaps along the shores, while the river's bed and solid croppings are limestone. From whence they came and by what forces were brought, are questions for geologic investigation. They strike one as queerly out of place, children driven by cruel fate from their distant home and stranded hopelessly on the shore to be washed and worn by rising and receding floods.

For four or five miles above the first rapid navigation is difficult and dangerous, on account of the swiftly rushing counter-currents, which are very numerous near the banks, while rocks rise above the water in the middle of the stream. A wide, smooth, deep current usually flows in the centre at about eight knots an hour.

We are near the right bank, and have eighteen men on shore at the end of three hundred feet of bamboo rope. The boat veers first to one side, then to the other, rocking backward and forward, while a man sits by our cabin door, beating a small drum as though his life depended upon the number of strokes per minute. All is confusion on board, while the half-naked men on shore pull like mules, jumping from rock to rock like cats. One, more agile than the others, clambers upon sharp, rocky peaks to dislodge the entangled rope, ready at a moment's notice to cast aside his shirt, his only garment, to plunge into a boiling " rush " and loosen the rope from a sharp jutting reef. The men catch a word and repeat it in chorus for a minute, then give a long and heavy groan, and end with a short, sharp " chuck, chih."

A man called the " whipper " follows the straggling team, whose duty it is to urge them on at the difficult places ; he carries a bamboo stick and applies it to the rope at a proper time, never or seldom striking a man. He sometimes rushes ahead, kneels down and " kotows " to the team, beats the ground, runs back and flies along the line as though he would flog every one; but his frantic movements end in a few blows on the taut rope, and several sharp yells which are caught up by the frantic team, while a few taps on the drum brings all this exuberance of energy to an abrupt end.

In the centre of the prow of the boat is fastened a long stick of timber which extends back into the boat from ten to fifteen feet and even further out beyond the prow, where it tapers to the size of a large oar. It turns from side to side as if on a pivot, and is managed

by means of ropes. It is called a " sweep," and its use
is to turn the boat in the rapids and swift currents
where the rudder is not of sufficient power.

A sailor, who is a very important personage, is near
the " sweep," and not only governs that by signs with
his uplifted hands, but also, at the same time, directs
the crew or head man on the shore. When a thousand
feet or more of rope is out he makes these signs to command a start or a stop, or to increase or lessen the
speed. We have also a mammoth yiulo on each side
of the boat; these are used in rounding bends or
cliffs where there are no accessible paths on the shore,
as well as in crossing the river and its estuaries. Our
men are all Sz-Chuanese, and their language, while sufficiently intelligible, is somewhat peculiar.

There is a fascination in this reckless, excitable life,
in which conventionalities are forgotten, and these toiling thousands live in almost archaic simplicity. I begin
to feel the spirit of *abandon* creeping over me, and am
quite at home in my new surroundings. The constant
sway and rock of the boat soothes me; the sudden
jerks at the mast and the terrific uproar of the frantic
men wake me from my day-dreams; while the danger
from breaking ropes and spinning whirlpools is sufficient
to keep up a gentle nervous excitement.

I had wondered why we had so much bamboo rope on
board, for our house is covered with immense coils of it,
while every boat we see is piled with stacks of rope and
cable. At the rapid I saw the need for this, when a
thousand and more feet were dragged out by a hundred
men, and drawn over sharp rocks, or through holes worn
a foot deep by constant friction. Here also are immense depots for ropes of all sizes and lengths, while
half the population are making them. Hemp or coir

rope is not used, as it would be more costly and less serviceable.

Agents of the " Life Saving Association " are seen at all dangerous points. The entire length of the Yang-tsze is patrolled and guarded by its boats; at convenient stations are its houses, in which are an overseer, bedding, clothing, medicine, and coffins, with a fleet of boats at hand. This purely benevolent institution is the result of the efforts of an official of the present or the preceding dynasty, who was wrecked near Chinkiang, where the central office is located. An annual report is made, showing the number of persons saved from drowning, number of bodies recovered and buried, medicine and clothing dispensed, and the amount of money received and spent. We also met a so-called gun-boat, — a mere cockle-shell, not able to carry more than three or four men, which indicates the safety and peacefulness of the upper Yang-tsze. The amount of traffic seems very unimportant, — not half that of the Poyang Lake or Grand Canal.

We reached the Tatung rapid about noon on the 25th, and as there were several junks ahead of us we waited two or three hours for our turn to pass. The boat in front of ours parted her cable in the middle of the rapid, and drifted down a half-mile or more. Our captain went on shore and drummed up about fifty men and boys, — as hard-looking a set as could be found " within the four seas," — whom he promised the smallest wages, and paid grudgingly when the work was done.

Our hauling line is lengthened and lowered to the foot of the mast, to which, as well as to the cross timber, a very long cable is made fast and thrown out; then, all being ready, we swing into the foaming flood. Our two teams of seventy-five men and boys yell and pull: the boat advances inch by inch, swaying and trembling as the billows strike her; the ascent of three hundred feet is made in half an hour, and we congratulate ourselves on the achievement.

Meanwhile we had found it pleasanter to walk along the shore and rest in the shade of the bowlders while the boat was drawn up. There is an abundance of granite here, somewhat veined with hornblende. The trumpet tree was in full bloom, and the gentian in flower, but the wheat-fields were not very promising.

At evening, in rounding a rocky point, the floods broke upon us with such force that our rope snapped, or our men lost their footing and let go, and we experienced the sensation of describing some eccentric circles. Poor tired fellows! They had worked hard all day, pulling and screaming, wading streams, and clambering over rocks like a pack of greyhounds; as soon as their supper of rice and coarse vegetables was eaten they stretched themselves upon the deck and were soon in the land of dreams.

Now all is quiet while I write my journal for the day, except the tireless, rushing flood, which eternally thunders around the bowlders a few rods ahead and boils over to the opposite bank in great whirlpools. The night is perfect; the great stars are placid as the blue vault itself, and the new moon has just disappeared behind the high black crags. For here the queen of heaven drops not "down behind the sky," but behind the Lukan gorge, which towers fifteen hundred feet above us. We are alone with the mountains and river; a few temples, like white specks, are perched on distant peaks; no boats are near, no splash of oars, no voice of man or beast is heard, no rustling wind; there is no sound save the solemn, rhythmic roar of pent-up waters.

On the morning of the 26th we found that one of the worst rapids was just before us. A strong west wind detained us at our anchorage, for it is impossible to track through the gorges, and with a head wind the men cannot make progress against the swift current with oars and pikes.

With Mr. Faber I climbed the nearest hill to the height of a thousand feet. For about three hundred yards the bank was strewn with rugged granite blocks, climbing over which we found a path leading in circles, past a few poor hamlets, up a steep defile. After searching we spied a narrow trail and plunged into a thicket in which grew some stately pines, while in the more open spaces there were peach and apricot trees laden with half-grown fruit, and pumalo-trees in luxuriant bloom. After a time we lost our way and struggled toward a well-wooded wady; for some distance dark-green orange-trees and the thick-leaved pepa pushed up into the light, borne down by creepers; the honeysuckle concealed the sides of the ugly bowlders; the firs and arbor-vitæ shaded little grottos in which were some tiny streams, and near them a variety of young ferns had begun to unroll their tender fronds.

Higher up the mountain was barren, and we had difficulty in scaling the pulverized rocks. At length we saw a single house upon a ridge, and going there found two men and a boy scratching about among a handful of stunted vegetables and buckwheat. They were as much startled at sight of us as though beings from the moon had fallen before them; but a word in Chinese allayed their fear, and they gradually came near to us. My silver watch-chain excited their curiosity, and they inquired as to its use; when they caught sight of the watch their admiration exceeded all bounds, and they

decided that by its aid I could see one thousand li, or
three hundred miles! When I explained to them that
it was a watch, and in motion, they were entirely incredulous, and gave me a look that plainly said, "You
cannot fool us so easily." After some persuasion the
middle-aged man allowed me to place it at his ear;
it was well worth our climb to see the broad grin which
broke over his sunburnt face when he heard the tick.
Then the old man of seventy came up, and finally the small,
coy grandson, who naturally listened more than once.

They followed us as we descended the opposite side of
the mountain, and directed us to a cold spring flowing
from a rock; when the lad observed our awkward mode
of drinking he ran to an oil-tree and plucked a couple
of large leaves, from which he deftly fashioned cups
with great dexterity. I then tried to shape the cups,
with no success; at this the little fellow laughed, and
no doubt congratulated himself that in some things he
could excel the man with the "living clock."

At last our boat was off, and after an hour of yelling,
pulling, backing, and swinging, and the breaking of a
rope, we reached the entrance to the famous Lukan
gorge, a picture of which makes the frontispiece to
Captain Blackistone's attractive book. But we now saw
something which he did not see, — telegraph poles.
What strange objects in this weird place! Why should
modern science intrude upon this enchanted region?
Why cannot modern inventions be left to commonplace
locations? The brown donkey tethered under the ledge
we have just passed is much more in harmony with
sleepy China than is the "lightning wire."

We had a fair breeze, and in two hours had passed the
gorge, having rushed through a world of grandeur without having time to analyze its beauty. At five P. M. we

SCENES ON THE YANG-TSZE.

(1) *Mouth of the Lukan Gorge.* (2) *Temple near Chungking.* (3) *Entrance to the Wind-box Gorge, Kwei-cheu-foo.*

were at another rapid, close by the small town of Tsin-tan, which lies scattered over lovely hills on the left bank.

On April 27, by great exertions, we made five miles in thirteen hours, passing from Tsin-tan to the city of Kwei-cheu. At this season there are three rapids at the first town and two at the last. In the course of these five miles we had our full share of excitement and incident. We waited an hour to see a clumsy junk hauled over one rapid; we were closely wedged between two ragged rocks when crossing the river; our right yiulo was broken; the men lost their hold upon the rope and we drifted down a rapid, to be swept back by a return current, — a sufficient variety in five miles.

Tsin-tan is clean and attractive for a Chinese village, and is built on a rock. The people live by pulling boats up the three rapids, fishing, and cultivating a few acres of sterile soil. Half the town is given up to opium saloons for the accommodation of boatmen and passengers. The farmers and water-carriers here bear their burdens differently from those on the lower Yang-tsze. A frame of bamboo is made to fit over the shoulders, and is held in place by a strap under the arms. A large circle, also of bamboo, is attached to this frame just behind the neck; into this a tub, crock, or basket is fitted, as the burden may require. A heavy club, with a handle at one end and a spike at the other, is carried, by which the weight is supported when rest is needed. Long lines of men and women are seen scaling the dangerous ledges and carrying heavy loads up and down the mountains in this manner. The ordinary carrying pole is little used.

Just above Tsin-tan we entered the Mitan gorge, and as the precipitous sandstone ledges come straight down to the water's edge there is no opportunity for tracking; and we were detained until a breeze would take us through. This gorge is short, but very grand in its effect. At the western end, on the left bank, are several caves which were dug out and inhabited by the aborigines, called *Man-tsz*, "barbarians." These are now deserted; but north and west of Chenteu, the capital of Sz-Chuan, there are numerous tribes living under almost identical conditions.

Every three or four miles are seen from three to five round white towers, erected in conspicuous places; they are called *yien-tung* or *yien-tui*, which means " smoke towers." They are signal stations, and originated in the time of the Cheu dynasty, five hundred years before the days of Confucius, who lived in the sixth century B. C. At that time a system of these stations was maintained throughout the empire, by means of which news was quickly carried from point to point, as well as signals given when important events occurred. The sign used was a fire which was made of wolf-ordure, and tradition says that the smoke from the towers always rose straight into the heavens. These towers of the past are religiously maintained, even where the electric wire is stretched above them; slowly, but surely, however, modern science is supplanting the rude methods of ancient greatness.

The air is stifling with heat, even when pure; but at evening, when at anchor and surrounded by junks which almost touch us, the fumes from the opium-pipes and the various unpleasant odors from the cooking all around us force us to close our windows and endure a condition of semi-torture. The cook in the nearest junk is scarcely four feet from my head: he washes and scrubs, fires and fans, while coolies are sprawling on the deck in every direction; one, entirely nude, lies within a foot of the furnace and steaming rice-kettle. These rascals, almost beasts in their habits, work like beavers all day; we will not complain if they eat four meals a day and drink tea each time the old tea-jar comes in view.

The morning of the 28th dawned with a glorious sunrise; the air was delicious, and the trees and plants clothed all our world in the freshest of verdure. I sent my teacher to the city with letters to a half-dozen different localities; he was charged ten cents for mailing the package, with a promise of " wine money " to the postman at Ichang. Whenever we mail a letter in China we write on it a promise of " wine money " to be given to the letter-carrier, the amount varying with the distance. This, like all Chinese customs, has a *raison d'être;* it is a healthy inducement to honesty and despatch, and without it there is much doubt as to whether the letter would be delivered.

My teacher brought back two and three quarter pounds of luscious cherries which had cost four cents, a quantity of fresh eggs at four and a half cents a dozen; and from an old woman who hobbled down the mountain side we bought a basket of tender bamboo sprouts for one cent, and had a delicious dish from them. The fine mandarin fish is sold at two cents a pound; and these items serve to indicate the small cost at which one can live on " the fat of the land."

Kwei-cheu is a walled city, well supplied with officials, but it has no trade and not more than six thousand inhabitants. In the evening Dr. Morley astonished the Chinese by leaping from his cabin window into the swift current, diving from rocks, and swimming against the stream. He received an enviable amount of praise, but I content myself by remarking that he is young and venturesome.

We have now reached the Sieh rapid, — called Yeh by Blackistone,—and as ten boats precede us we must take our turn, as but one boat can possibly pass at a time. The Chinese, so ingenious in many ways, seem to be far behind themselves in overcoming the difficulties at the rapids. A post on which to wind the cable, on a prominent point above the rapid, would be a great improvement; while a capstan and wheel would take the boat up in half the time consumed in the present method.

This rapid is called " the forth-bursting." Just here a sudden curve in the river confines it to half its usual width, and it then rushes forth over a ledge of rocks. It is the most dangerous fall we have seen; the water seems to be at least two feet higher in the centre than at the sides of the stream, and whirls along at ten miles an hour. Two days ago the river rose ten feet, but fortunately for us has since fallen quite as much.

These sudden or even continued floods, which occur from March to August, are due to violent or continuous rains in the province of Sz-Chuan, — which is the most cloudy and rainy district of the empire, — and not to the melting of snow and ice in Thibet, as many have supposed.

While awaiting the movement of the fleet I went on shore and picked my way to the foot-hills, leaping from one piece of red sandstone to another for a quarter of a mile. A little river came thundering down the ravine, whirling its jasper-green waters over beds of beautifully tinted stones, worn round and smooth. Above the rapids a little town is perched upon its banks. Ascending the first foot-hill on the east of this stream we came to a colliery, where we found several abandoned shafts and a number of seams of coal in process of excavation. These seams were horizontal with the bank, about two feet wide and six high, and only worked to the level of the entrance. I explored one of the shafts for about fifty feet, but found nothing but darkness within. The coal is a fair quality of anthracite, and is drawn from the pits in bamboo baskets placed on low sleds. A number of men were pulverizing the fine coal and mixing a generous proportion of earth with it, after which they added water enough to make a paste, which they moulded into bricks and thus sent it down the river. At the anchorage the price of coal was seventeen cents for one hundred and forty pounds.

With some difficulty I rounded the collieries by following a sort of natural tunnel, and suddenly found myself on the verge of an Alpine-like valley which hugged the little stream for some miles. For a better view, and in order to test a new aneroid, I climbed a sandstone cap five hundred feet high; once there a second cap led me still up, until the aneroid registered 1,050 feet above the river; the mercury standing at 100° at nine A. M. From this height a bold, rugged cone came into view, and I began its ascent; the way was difficult, but Nature supplied many shrubs and plenty of long grass to which one could cling, and my boots were strong. The beaten track was the hardest to climb, being too dry to afford a good foot-hold. As in the journey of life we often find ourselves rising faster by a rough and thorny path than by more attractive ways, so here I found it better to take the rough one every time. A few flowering shrubs smiled upon me, and their sweet fragrance pervaded the heated air; lizards of various kinds were here and there, on decayed logs and stones, and their bright eyes meeting my gaze for a moment, they darted out of sight; locusts and cicadas encouraged me by piping in their shrillest tones, until a fortress of bowlders covered with thorns and briers prevented my further ascent.

I had now reached an elevation of fifteen hundred feet, and descending two hundred, I again took an upward trail around a red sandstone cliff which was barely the width of my foot in some places. A fresh breeze was now blowing up the sheer precipice, and with the aid of my umbrella acting in some sort as a balloon, I climbed to the top without accident, and was proud to find that I was eighteen hundred feet above the river and two thousand above the sea. Descending, I struck down through groves, fields, and orchards of pear and peach, and in some places was forced to be on the alert to avoid the farm dogs, which are as cunning as foxes and bold as lions.

We next sail through the Wu-shan gorge, which is very picturesque and quite unique in some ways. The mountains are cultivated in places in the narrow pass, but for the most part precipitous ledges rise straight up from the water's edge, to the height of seventy-five feet. They are of gray sandstone, flat, or nearly so, on top, while the smooth face is cut into irregular channels by the little rills of water in time of heavy rains, and the friction of the pebbles which are washed down. In some instances these fissures were quite four feet deep and two wide; during severe storms they make a charming effect, — hundreds of little white falls plunging into the yellow river within a distance of a few rods.

It is impossible to conceive how the poor villagers hereabouts can live and thrive as they seem to do, unless the fishing is good. I saw fishermen standing in every available point upon the rocks, regularly swinging their hand-nets. Blackistone says that he saw fishermen all along the river, but never saw one catch anything; the same writer says that the porpoise does not go above Ichang, but Mr. Faber saw one above Chungking.

CHAPTER III.

Whenever we are to ascend a dangerous rapid, — and nearly all are so considered by the native Itinerary, and probably are at certain seasons of the year, — a boatman brings out an old rusty four-barrelled blunderbuss, rams the barrels full of powder, picks in fuses, and stations himself at the side of the boat for the most serious business connected with the ascent. As the boat strikes the first fierce breakers, one barrel is discharged into the water; the gun is then dropped upon the deck, and the sailor tugs for a while at the ropes; when we have swung around, and ploughed and plunged sufficiently with little progress, he drops his work, whatever it may be, fires another fuse and explodes the half-ounce of powder into the foam; the third and fourth chambers are likewise emptied if the business is continued long enough.

This may seem a curious and useless custom to those unacquainted with the Chinese ideas of demonology, but once having mastered this branch of their intricate religious system, it will appear to be the most natural and necessary proceeding. Malicious spirits are in and around all dangerous places, and ready to do all manner of mischief. They can be frightened by terrific sounds; ergo, in passing all such spots the Chinaman naturally yells, beats a gong, explodes fire-crackers or powder in any form. At worship, at weddings, funerals, in times of severe sickness, the greater the noise the more likely the demons are to hide themselves. The water is crowded with such demons, and they are either frightened or propitiated by the boatman. During the day several reports of cannon were heard, and immediately after each one a beautifully constructed paper boat came in sight and passed down on its religious voyage. It was yellow, about fifteen feet in length and three or four wide; six men stood on the bow in the attitude of command, — three in blue, two in white, and one in yellow; it carried a red lantern and had several ornaments in red; it whirled round and round in the great eddies, but did not capsize. At all this cost the poor villagers try to appease the wrath of the dragon king.

The results of these superstitions are various; the following circumstances which came under my own observation may interest my readers.

Some years since I was startled by an aged teacher who had been in the church several years. He rushed into my study, exclaiming, "A great calamity has befallen me!" After many questions we elicited the following story from the frightened man.

A near neighbor of his had just lost a small child from scarlet fever, and had brought the dead body into the teacher's house and laid it on his bed, and then proceeded to destroy the crockery and furniture of the house. He did not mourn for these losses; but to have the dead child placed in his bed was a great sin against him unless he had caused the child's death, while it would be a terrible calamity to have brought about the sickness and death of the child. At length we learned the reasons which led to this desecration of his home.

In the fourth moon of the present year he had decided to build a small board house on a vacant lot in the city of Kiukiang ; but a neighbor of his on the east, who wished the lot to remain as a playground for the children of the precinct, and a place for drying clothes, did not approve his plan. He proceeded to influence the minds of all the neighborhood against the teacher, and his most effective accusation was that " Christians bear a wonderful talisman by which they can repel evil influences and inflict terrible calamities on others." He assured the neighbors that if this Christian were allowed to build his house, three or four of their children would die during the present summer.

When the teacher was ready to begin to build, this man told him that if he commenced work from the 1st to the 11th of the month, those who lived on the east would be injured ; if from the 11th to the 22d, those on the west would suffer.

He waited until the 18th, and began to build. His house faced the south, and could not be objected to on the score of disturbing the *fung-shui*, or " luck" (for during this year all houses should be built to face the south or north).

When his house was nearly completed it happened that an infant in the third house to the west sickened with scarlet fever. The father of the child called a *ti sin*, " astrologer ; " the characters " yin mao shen " for the present year are baneful ones in the cycle. The astrologer brought a compass and placed it in the front door of the house in which the sick child lay, and declared after investigation that the southwest corner of the teacher's house was in direct line with the character " mao " upon the face of the compass as it pointed from the door of the house where the child was. He decided that the new house was the source of malignant vapors. After this step the next in order was to call a sorcerer to exorcise the evil influences. He decided that the dirt should be dug away from that corner-stone and a charm written upon it to counteract the evil influences. A request was made to this effect, and granted. A cock was quickly caught, and the blood from his comb was mixed with wine, and with this mixture enigmatic characters were scrawled upon the stone. In about three hours' time his neighbor returned, saying the ceremony was insufficient and there must be another. An adept in such matters came; he ordered all the pillar stones to be dug about, charms written upon them, a quantity of money-paper and fire-crackers burned, and the litany read.

The same day a rice-cake seller strolled into the house of the sick child, and told the people that devils were tormenting it; that the soul of the child was crushed beneath one of the pillars of the Christian's house. He ordered the pillars to be hewn and charms written upon them, declaring that after this ceremony there would be great peace.

But upon the 26th the child was worse, and an astrologer was again called. He ordered eight cash of great virtue to be folded in red paper in two packages of four each. He wrote charms upon them and buried them under the second outside pillar on the west and the second pillar of the second row upon the east. The following day the carpenter came to finish the work upon the house, but was forbidden; he might come the next day; the following day they decided he must wait seven days. Upon the 29th the neighbor came and said that he had been advised to remove three layers of tiles in the west centre of his house. This was done. Next day it was necessary to remove the first pillar stone that was laid ; this was done, and a board placed underneath the pillar. About two hours later the man came and said he had been advised to have the house torn down, and if it were done his child would surely get well. This was a little too much for a Chinaman to endure, but the teacher proposed that the man who advised this should come and promise that the child would get well if this were done, and further, agree to defray half the expense of rebuilding the house; but the man did not come. The next day the child died, and the father brought it and placed it upon the teacher's bed.

When this news was brought to the teacher's school-room he was beside himself with fear, for there also came rumors that preparations were being made to drown him. He hastened to us for protection, after having been refused admittance to the magistrate's *yamen*. As he was a member of our church, we concluded to go with him and ask the magistrate to hear his story, and send a guard to remove the child from his house and protect his property. After some hesitation this was done, and not long after the new house was completed without further trouble.

After this long digression let us return to our journey. The numbers of temples upon the picturesque peaks near the river seem very disproportionate to the sparse population, to whom it must be a heavy tax to support all the mummery of their religion; but they do not complain of this.

From an almost perpendicular cliff issued a large stream of green water, only about three feet above the surface of the river, yet in its fall there was much noise and the water was dashed into foam. Such torrents were frequent, as were also those rushing out of narrow

cañons, pouring their jasper-colored streams into the
river with such force as to change its color for some
distance. I picked my way up one of these little cañons, along the smooth side of the torrent, holding on
by jutting rocks and pulling myself along by twigs
growing in the crevices. Fortunately I found a rock
in a cool, shady spot about fifteen feet above a deep,
clear pool; from this spot I could see five distinct falls
and pools, the highest of which was not more than
sixty feet.

The gorge was narrow and dark, quiet and cool; the
great world was shut out, and the only sound was the
plash of the waters on the smoothly worn stones. The
highest fall was grand enough to excite the imagination,
and the smaller cascades and curiously wrought forms
of the solid rock beautiful enough to tax the descriptive
powers of a Wordsworth or a Bryant. The river rolled
on at my feet, the cliffs and mountains towered to the
sky above me, and hushed in awe I murmured, "Many,
O Lord my God, are the wonderful works which Thou
hast done!"

At Wu-shan-hsien two secretaries came on board to
copy our passports, as it is the first city in the province
of Sz-Chuan. It is small and unimportant, exporting
a little hemp and lumber, and importing cotton and
foreign goods from Hankow.

On May 2 we made an early start, and at the breakfast hour were waiting our turn to be pulled up the rapid
preceding Wind-Box gorge. This is the shortest regular
gorge, but quite famous; the cliffs are imposing, though
not equal in grandeur to those of Wu-shan. The river
narrows to one hundred or one hundred and fifty yards,
and flows in a smooth, regular current, except in time
of floods. The wind came in gusts, and through care-

lessness in handling the boat we were several times in dangerous positions.

We reached Kwei-cheu-foo early in the afternoon, going up on the south side of the little sand-bank below the city, celebrated for its brine well or spring. The salt water seems to be on its surface, and is dipped up in buckets. The island is above water only from January to May, and the manufacture of the salt is confined to those months. There is sufficient brine to supply about one hundred and twenty pans, and about one million five hundred thousand pounds are made. A great part of this is sent down river and usually sells for three cents a pound. This is an enormous amount from one well, and gives an easily acquired revenue to the hungry officials.

A large quantity of coal is mined not far from the east gate, which sells at ten cents for one hundred and thirty pounds. It is broken up, mixed with water and dirt, moulded into bricks, and exported to Hupeh. This city is further celebrated for its vermicelli, which is considered the best in the empire; it is very small and white, is in great demand, and brings about six cents a pound at the factories.

Kwei-cheu is surrounded with walls, and has four gates; the circumference of the city is not far from two miles, and it is said to have forty thousand inhabitants. There are two fine mosques here and about five hundred Mohammedan families; also a Roman Catholic church, said to date from the time of Kanghsi, A. D. 1662. Three priests and one hundred families belong to this communion.

The telegraph office has ten operators, the chief of whom told me that the average work was ten messages a day!—one operator for each message, and the office open from eight A. M. to nine P. M. Telegraphing in China is both amusing and provoking. At Nanking I wished to send a despatch to Chinkiang, a distance of forty-five miles. I entered the office at eight A. M., to find two operators in bed in the public room. It required some persuasion to induce the younger man to get up. I asked him to put the message in Chinese, the price being but half that for English. When he had written it I found he had used enough superfluous characters to make it more expensive than in my own tongue; this being remedied, I asked him how soon I should get a reply. He stared at me and said, " Do you want an answer ? " Now this was certainly amusing, as my message read, " What time does the steamer ' Fuh-Wo ' leave Chinkiang ? " At length he told me it would come " about one o'clocks." I presume he wished to say in one hour; but it did not come while I remained, and I gravely doubt its having come at all.

All boats passing Kwei-cheu are compelled to pass a customs inspection, and it is noted for its irregular tax, called *li-kin*, which is a provincial tax enforced by the Viceroy and levied on all goods. It grew out of the distress in the late rebellions, and has never been remitted. The regular tax, the *shui-li*, goes to the central government. The detention occasioned by this examination by two sets of officials often amounts to two days, so we considered ourselves fortunate to be passed in thirty-six hours.

If the Roman tax-gatherers were as low, ill-bred, and " cheeky " as these men, they merited the hatred they received. The fat, jolly chief of the li-kin staff estimated that about fifty junks were examined daily ; this would make the daily trade up and down the river amount to three thousand tons, not including the local traffic, which is very considerable in some places.

We had provided ourselves with a quantity of pictorial literature, — illustrated Scriptures, stories of Biblical personages, and small illustrated books. These were from the recently organized Chinese Book and Tract Society, which is under the efficient management of the veteran Dr. Williamson. They are edited by my esteemed companion, Ernest Faber, who has used the best material; while the pictures are the finest that could be obtained, and the typographical work almost perfect. We sold about six hundred books to the crowds who came and went, commenting upon the beautiful pictures; and if the brass coins we received had been placed in a row, they would have stretched across the river. Book-peddling is pleasant or disagreeable according to the humor of the crowd: a drunken loafer will sometimes bring a following of roughs or little boys and give great annoyance; but here the people were in good nature, pilfered no more than usual, and cheated in paying quite in the regular way.

My first impressions on the morning of the 4th of May were somewhat confused. There was a compound racket from screeching men, roaring currents, and pouring rain. I threw my windows open just in time to see four boats floating down stream, in a tangle of ropes and poles; men excited, some pulling ahead with boat-hooks, others pushing back; but down they went a few hundred yards and were brought up by running into the bank.

I have not seen an anchor since leaving Ichang. The boats are moored to the shore by means of stakes and stones; for a short stop a stake is driven into the sand or mud through a hole in the boat's prow.

The rain ceased at two P. M., by which time the necessary papers had been sent from the custom-house. The skipper's gong sounded twice, and our lazy crew fell to packing away the awning. Thirty-six hours is a long detention at so dead a city as Kwei-cheu-foo.

The gullies, which had been dry before the rain, were now full of foaming torrents, and tracking was very difficult. We saw two boats with broken ropes, which had lost the results of an hour's hard work in a moment.

Blackistone speaks of meeting disasters here, and having to send back for carpenters. After twenty-six years I saw a boat undergoing the same sort of repairs at the identical place he mentions. There are very few serious disasters in going up the river; occasionally a hole is knocked through the bottom of a boat by running on the rocks, or a rudder is crushed in narrow passes; but there is always an opportunity to land or lighten the cargo, and repair damages without beaching.

Farming is carried on under disadvantages in this region, where the inclination is so great that walls of stone must be built around every little garden patch to keep the soil from tumbling into the river. I saw a couple of men clearing a field full five hundred feet above us, and all the stones which were not required for wall were given a little toss, and landed on the river's bank.

Neuralgia is bad enough on shore, but far worse on a boat. I had recourse to the Buddhist Prayer-book to drown the affliction, and found the translation of a page or two a very good narcotic. Rain fell in torrents until dark.

On May 5 the morning sky was cloudy, with a few threads of silver in the east, and a strong west wind made our progress very slow. We made excursions on shore, and found the country more open and the soil of a better quality than farther below, which doubtless accounted for the fineness of the wheat, as the climate is no better here than in other places, and the method of tillage quite the same; but the grain, which was now ready for the sickle, was tall and stocky, and much better than I had seen in any part of China.

Irish potatoes are much grown in Sz-Chuan, and are of excellent quality, free from insects and blight. When or how they were introduced into Western China is unknown; but on Mount Omei, eleven thousand one hundred feet above the sea, the priests raise excellent potatoes by the American method, keeping them free from weeds and in regular hills. The potato is now the chief winter vegetable used on this sacred mountain.

A large area of the land passed to-day has just been cleared of a poppy crop, and young maize plants are in process of setting. Seed-corn is seldom planted or sowed as in America, but is started in small patches, and transplanted when six or eight inches in height, setting one or two plants in a place. Ngan-pin is a small town ten miles above Kwei-cheu-foo; it has some very pretty temples; one has two towers with porcelain pinnacles. The rapid is somewhat dangerous, and unusual precaution is necessary. The "whipper" was thrown into a frightful rage by some sarcastic remark made by the "sweep-pilot." He set up a most demoniacal howl, jumped up and down, and shook his fist from the rocks; he would walk a few rods with bowed head, and then, overmastered by his feelings, would jump into the air as if shot, and utter the most dreadful curses. I feared a scene when he came on board; but the magical rice bowl and the sound of the chopsticks subdued him to lamb-like docility. I have never seen a severer or more degrading occupation than tracking a junk up this river, nor one that was less remunerative. Three dol-

lars per month without board cannot be a great inducement to prolong life above threescore and ten; yet
there is no lack of adventurers, for the boats going
down are covered with sailors, who expect to find their
way up at the end of a thousand feet of rope.

The 6th of May was a lovely day, with a clear air and
cool breeze, and the pagoda of Yung-yang-hsien was distinctly seen ten miles distant. On the right bank we
have high red sandstone cones, half denuded of their
soil, and the smooth, bare rocks shine like molten glass
where the water oozes from spongy grass-tufts. No
doubt these same barren hills were terraced and richly
cultivated a few hundred years ago. On the left bank
is a series of red sandstone terraced pyramids, from
six to eight hundred feet high, and partially cultivated;
but they will be as bare as their cousins across the river
in a few hundred years.

We had been running with a strong, fair breeze to
Tung-ling Point, and looked ahead at the broken current
with no little degree of satisfaction, expecting to make
quick work of one rapid with full set sail. Our skipper
took the opposite bank from the other boats as an
experiment, but when he reached the foot of the rapid
he suddenly changed his mind and lowered the side for
a retreat; but he was not in time, as a swift back current caught us and carried us quickly abreast of the most
dangerous part of the rapid, and then a reverse whirl
sent us broadside into the foam. The men leaped to
one side of the deck, but not in time to save us from
keeling over until the water poured in at our cabin
windows and doors. The shock was so severe that the
cargo shifted to one side, and everything in the cabins
and stern-rooms was thrown into confusion. We were
standing at the front windows watching the progress of

events, when in came the water, and over went tables, chairs, boxes, trunks, baskets, and drawers with eatables ; cutlery, crockery, bottles, and empty tins went flying to leeward. Boxes of ferns, which Mr. Faber had petted assiduously, leaped into space ; ink-bottles were smashed, citric acid haplessly scattered, phials shivered into fine fragments, and even the doors broken down. The teachers and servants were having a feast, and when extricated from bowls, rice, tea, beds, books, shoes, hats, etc., they scarcely had courage to stand erect. The cook-house by the rudder was a picture of perfect despair, and the cook more distressed than all. After the boat reached still water I found him clinging to its side, surveying the remnants and fragments of all his former glory. The oven was shattered, and lying in the centre of the room, ashes, charcoal, and flour were delightfully mixed, and his breakfast a ruin. The rudder room was nearly demolished ; the old gold-washed god was cast down from his throne and hung dangling by the side of the boat ; tablet and incense-holder, with many other articles, were in wild disorder. There were a few barrels of water in the hold. Mr. Faber had a sprained thumb and a cut upon his arm, and my teacher was wounded in the leg ; such experiences are happily infrequent.

I had a walk of some five miles along the sides of the pyramids with the telegraph wire above me. There are a few farm-houses perched upon these shady heights, and the inmates were too frightened to speak, but not so the dogs ; they are not easily scared, and defend their precincts with great zeal. Shady ravines were on every hand and well watered, while little falls were discernible even on the highest points. What a natural park lies here by this grand old river !

Yung-yang-hsien is an attractive city, and has some

imposing edifices, the chief of which is the Kiangsi guild, the Wan-sheu-kung. The trade of Sz-Chuan is largely in the hands of merchants from other provinces, and in this respect Kiangsi stands first. The architecture of the temples is more pleasing than in Central China. A most attractive monastery stands on the opposite bank of the river, upon a bold bluff near a stone bridge; it is connected with the adjoining bluff by an artificial way, while between the temples and pavilions rolls a small river. The traveller will see four characters carved upon the smooth rock, "A spirit bell of great antiquity." These temples strike one as far above the average Chinese building in symmetry, and have several beautiful cupolas covered with green glazed tiles, which glistened in the early morning sun.

The monastery is noted for possessing the head of that celebrated warrior, Changfei, of the third century. He was the bosom friend of the famous Kwanyü who championed the cause of Liupei, afterward king of Shu. He is reported to have been a butcher in early life, but the days of martial strife aroused him and he cast in his lot with the above-named heroes about A. D. 184, and achieved many brilliant victories. After all his exploits, and the attainment of great honors, he perished at the hand of an assassin, A. D. 220. His head is supposed to be enclosed in a shrine here, and is worshipped; while his body is at Pao-ling-foo, northwest of Chungking, and is also enshrined as a god.

Above Yung-yang-hsien there is a gradual transformation of the mountains; the river is wider, with fewer rapids, and the ravines are of greater extent; while two or three rivers of some importance join the Yang-tsze on the north. There are more trees, and farming is more general.

Fortresses and castle-like towers are seen upon the high and rugged points. This part of Sz-Chuan has suffered much from local outbreaks, bandits being able to move with great secrecy among the mountains. In times of trouble the people of the scattered hamlets and villages provision these walled stockades, and at the first signal of the approaching enemy escape hither with their scanty portable effects.

The sweet notes of the oriole are heard in the groves, and many species of birds seen, but few of them are songsters. The winter crops are nearly all gathered, the young cotton plants are already up in some fields, while the farmers are busy sowing seed in others.

The sandstone is a veritable paradise for snails; the sides of the rock in sections are half covered with cast-off shells, and the sand is full of them, but only in two or three varieties. We came near a ledge of low rocks where a disabled junk was breaking up; the crew was busy transferring the cargo of cotton to the shore in sampans. No one noticed the wreck except to make a passing remark, or laugh at the misfortune; this is the usual sympathy given to the unfortunate by the masses in this land. Quantities of loose cotton were floating down stream, to be gathered in due time by strolling peasants. Bales of cotton weighing two hundred and fifty pounds each form quite four fifths of all cargoes going up the river at this season. Chickens, eggs, and other eatables demand better prices than below.

The approach to Wan-hsien is peculiarly beautiful; the river is broader and the country more fertile. The town lies on either side of the West or Hemp stream, which is generally called the Small river. We reached the lower end of the town at dusk and passed it early the next morning without stopping. It presented at night more the appearance of a foreign city than any purely native place I had seen in China. Lights were scattered profusely in every direction, along the shore, among the shipping, and over the sides of the hills within the city walls. The buildings present an uncommonly good appearance, and everywhere we could see signs of activity and prosperity. It is a commercial centre for half a score of other cities. Many boats discharge a part or all of their goods here and reload, for either up or down the river.

Chenteu, the capital of the province, is easily reached from this point in sedan-chairs or by ponies. Nearly all officials from the East go by chair, the journey being made in thirteen days, or about the same time as from Chungking, thus saving a most tedious journey of about twenty days by boat from here to the latter city. I met two officials at my hotel in the capital, who had taken chairs at Wan-hsien. I have no doubt that in time steamers will bring goods directly from Hankow to this point, here to be reshipped by rail to inland towns, to Chenteu, and possibly to Chungking. The navigation by steam from Kwei-cheu-foo would be mere play; all that is needed is the power to make from twelve to fourteen knots, as the worst rapid is not above ten knots. There is plenty of water for boats drawing four or five feet at any season. I have no doubt, from all I can gather, that Wan-hsien will be a great commercial centre in the coming age of progress.

Mr. A. Wylie visited this city in 1868, and I have just found his remarks, which I quote in full : —

" In the forenoon of the following day we were at the district city of Wan, and this was the first place in which we had seen signs of business activity since leaving Ichang. Here the accumulation of shipping, the large and wealthy stores, and

PAGODA ROCK.

See page 65.

See page 65.

the general aspect of the place and people all bore witness to its commercial importance. There is a very large suburb on both sides of the Si-ho, ' West river.' This river rises to the northwest, and has a very picturesque appearance as it passes the city, in a channel scooped out of the rock. The clear water falls down a cascade into a deep pool, and then, flowing under a natural bridge formed of a huge block of sandstone, emerges from a fissure by a shorter fall into another basin below; and so, by a variety of tortuous bends, finds its way into the Kiang. Probably no artificial bridge would withstand the force of this current in flood-time; so a pathway is formed across by a series of piers about a foot square, and something like two feet apart; being, in fact, a line of stepping-stones, firmly fixed to the bottom."

Wan-hsien, like Yung-yang, is noted in history. It was the home of Li-peh-tai, the great poet of the Tang dynasty. He studied and wrote in a secluded and romantic retreat upon a cliff overlooking the city on the west. He lived from A. D. 699 to 762. Mayer says he was " the most widely celebrated among the poets of China, — a distinction earned no less by his erratic genius and romantic career than by his powers of versification. He was remotely connected by descent with the sovereigns of the Tang dynasty." He was called from his seclusion to the capital, pampered and petted; the Emperor even feasted him with his own hand, and required his favorite and proud concubine to attend him with writing materials; he also commanded the chief eunuch and privy counsellor to divest him of his boots when intoxicated with wine. The poet at length offended the concubine with his cutting satire, and was expelled from court. He led a wandering, aimless life for a time, and was accused of taking part in seditious uprisings, and banished to the borders of Yun-nan.

One of the largest cities of refuge on the river is seen upon a lofty crag on the north of Wan-hsien. Immediately after passing the city our pilot ran plump upon a sand-bank. Dark clouds began to cover the heavens, and distant thunder gave us fair warning to look out for a deluge, for when it thunders up here it means floods of rain. It soon came, and with such violence that our men tied up to the first convenient rock, spread their mat-house, and soon fell to their opium-pipes, half suffocating us with their fumes.

After the storm hundreds of little rivers came thundering down the ravines, tumbling in wild disorder into the Yang-tsze; some were a few yards wide, falling straight down from fifty to one hundred feet with deafening roar. While waiting for a fleet to work around a boat which had come to temporary grief upon a rock, I watched with peculiar pleasure the pranks of a hurrying stream, the aggregate perhaps of hundreds of little rills, as it swept down a sandstone cliff. It circled, leaped, frothed, and spouted up spirals of spray, until at last, with the energy of a little giant mad against restraint, it made one grand plunge and rolled its chocolate-colored foam into the placid bosom of the great stream. Its angry spirit was tamed as by magic, and its intoxicated importance as entirely gone as is that of many frothing upstarts when they are lost in the great world of thought.

Just above, upon a mountain of sandstone, rises a wall-like cliff to the height of two hundred feet and not more than three hundred wide, which stretches back at right angles to the river until lost to view. Its top is green and wooded, and out of its verdant glades peep a number of whitewashed temples, — a picture not to be forgotten.

On the 9th of May we ascended the Hu rapid, but not until a strong current sent us bumping along among a colony of rough bowlders. We passed a small river just below, and a little town embowered amidst banyans and other widespreading trees. Several mills are located on the little stream. The temptation was too great, and we scaled over an acre of sandstone blocks, climbed a high hill, wended our way along a back street, past a fine temple and some ponds, and through gardens and grave-yards, until we touched this Japanese-like village, shaded by numberless trees festooned with many creepers or "coiled in the clasp of huge dark-stemmed grape-vines." Behind this clean and prosperous village an almost circular arched bridge, fifty feet in diameter, spanned the torrent; it is built of granite in the very finest workmanship. There were several flour-mills below the bridge; the wheels were turbine, the whole wheel lying horizontal in the water. While the flour produced is dark and rather coarse, it is a vast improvement on the ordinary stuff coming from the cattle mills.

The sallow complexion of the people, their emaciated forms, and languid movements attract our attention everywhere along the river. I do not see a beautiful face or figure, nor a rosy cheek; a dead leaden color is on all faces, old and young, male and female. I look at the broad swift river, I feel the cool clear breeze, I gaze at the high green hills, the flowing rivulets, and the widespreading trees overhanging the hamlets. Upon the mountain sides are houses and hundreds of workmen; approach those busy laborers and you will see this deathlike pallor on all faces.

The climate seems the acme of perfection, — a long pleasant summer, with a cool agreeable autumn and bracing winter; yet there is a want of energy and life among the people. There is plenty of food and of excellent quality for China, — rice, wheat, millet, peas, beans, corn, oils, and fruits of many varieties, — all within the means of the humblest laborer.

I enter a large field near a hamlet, by the side of a luxuriant growth of ripening wheat. The field is clean, not a weed visible; but close together and four feet high stand stalks with large dry heads, brown and decaying now, for their bright flowers faded a month ago. These decaying stalks speak; they tell me why the death-pallor is upon all faces, from the shrivelled form of age to the bow-legged child sitting in the cottage door. O seductive viper, curse of millions! Who shall dare to stand up in the presence of this fast-fading, degenerating people, and say the evil is not widespread and fatal?

Traverse the fairest portions of all the provinces: not cities alone, but the quiet, out-of-the-way places are all saturated and besmeared with the black paste, even to the gods. The Abbé Huc more than thirty years ago wrote in the following strain about the opium-smoker, and my own observation confirms all that he then said : —

" With the exception of some rare smokers who — thanks to quite exceptional organizations — are able to restrain themselves within the bounds of moderation, all others advance rapidly toward death, after having passed through the successive stages of idleness, debauchery, poverty, the ruin of their physical strength, and the complete prostration of their intellectual and moral faculties. Nothing can stop a smoker who has made much progress in the habit; incapable of attending to any kind of business, insensible to every event, the most hideous poverty, and the sight of a family plunged into despair and misery, cannot rouse him to the smallest exertion, so complete is the disgusting apathy in which he is sunk."

I had a long, wearisome stroll on the right bank, — the gullies being full of water, and the steep banks hard to climb, on account of the fine sand on their sides. In one instance I was pulled up by the coolies with their small tracking ropes. When we came to our anchorage at dusk, our botanist, Mr. Faber, was missing. A messenger with pole and lantern was despatched, but after half an hour returned without tidings. It was already dark, and we had anxious fears for his safety, and started out with poles and lantern to search for him. We made the hills and ravines echo with our patent whistle, but no response came. We tramped through wheat and poppy fields along dangerous ravines until we reached the outskirts of a hamlet, where the dogs were barking in concert not far from us; we aimed for that particular spot, and were rewarded by finding the object of our search standing quietly in a poppy field, awaiting the rising of the moon.

The market-towns are large and generally located upon the sides of hills, with small streams flowing through or near them. The country is becoming daily more interesting and more productive. Here, as in other parts of the province, there are regular market days every third day. I am told that the towns are quiet enough on the ordinary days, as the greater portion of the population will be at a fair ten miles away, or in the fields; but on the days of the fair there is a grand revolution, and the streets which were empty yesterday are full of excited crowds.

The *chai*, or cities of refuge, are very numerous and some of them most picturesque, perhaps none more so than that on the left bank thirty miles below Chung-hsien, called Shih-pao. There is a small town around this peculiar rock, with a large temple facing the river, and behind the temple, in connection with it, is a nine-storied wooden tower which reaches to the top of the fortress rock. It is one of the most striking works of art we have yet seen.

The graves are works of art, being differently constructed from those in Central China, and far more costly. They are largely built of stone, profusely carved, lettered, and gilded; some are painted, and are very effective at a distance. The carvings consist largely of human figures, flowers, and birds, and are better executed than in other sections of China.

There is little to record for the 11th of May; the same old worn-out routine, crossing and recrossing the river, tracking and poling, shying a sand-bank or ledge of rocks here, and rounding an island of silted gravel there. I wandered aimlessly over finely wooded hills, through open fields, and watched men and women as they set out the young rice-shoots and cut with sickles the golden wheat. The women showed some sign of fear at my modest intrusion, but when they heard me speak with the men they were emboldened to draw near; they are not a whit uglier than their sisters in more fashionable centres. The birds did their best to cheer me with their songs, and before my return to the boat my languor and bilious headache had quite vanished.

It was the morning of the 12th before the beautiful city of Chung-hsien came into view. It has an un-Chinese look as if dropped down here from Siam or some other tropical land; it is full of shade-trees, and several towers and high temples rise from the midst of dense foliage. The façades are richly carved and fantastically painted and gilded. There is little shipping visible, and to avoid a dangerous reef of rocks, the junks ascend the river on the opposite side.

We sought anchorage here on our way down to escape the fury of a heavy storm, and an official presented the hsien's card before we were anchored. Late at night, when all were in bed, there was heard a fearful din of gongs and a demand for passports, but we did not give them up.

A few bags of rice were purchased by our skipper, and our cook took the opportunity to spend a thousand cash for chickens and lard. I have often wondered what becomes of all the lard purchased for the foreign kitchen. Any account would be incomplete without an item for lard; it is brought in a basket, mixed with chickens, cucumbers, beans, a few greens, always some eggs, and half-a-dozen odds and ends; but you will look in vain to find any in the larder two days later. While the boat was tied to a bowlder we strolled up into the bamboo groves above us, leaving the crew lounging about. Those fortunate enough to have clothes were busy searching the seams and rents for vermin; the pilot was most assiduous and showed great skill at this business. We reached a lovely glade, shady and cool, and skirted along the foot of the mountain for some distance. Cool springs of water gushed from the solid rocks, and little rills poured leisurely over shelving rifts.

A shattered temple about one hundred and fifty feet above the present surface of the river attracted our attention; on the stone steps leading to the front door were carved several characters, which informed us that in the ninth year of Tung-chi (1870) the water rose to that point. Looking down through the bamboo groves to the rocky shore it seemed almost incredible. That year was noted for a great flood, which swept away whole towns, and in some instances portions of the cities. I noticed very fine temples along the river erected

in honor of the Emperor Yu, who is worshipped as the
Great King Yu. He is said to have controlled the
watercourses of China between the years B. C. 2286 and
2278, and to have been so devoted to his great work
that he gave no heed to clothing or food, and passed his
own door thrice in the time and did not enter, although
he heard the wailings of his infant son within. After
nine years of herculean labors his task was ended and
the empire divided into nine provinces. He is further
honored in mythology as having opened the great
Wu-shan gorge for the accumulated waters of the west.
No wonder the people of this watery region remember
his prodigious work with gratitude, and rear the finest
arches and temples in his honor.

A walk of five miles gave me an opportunity of inspecting the fields and picking up a number of fine
pebbles. In some sections poppies and cucumbers alternate, the very best land being used for them. The
cucumbers are grown in rows two feet apart, and in
hills eighteen inches apart, and trained to poles like
beans. I should think from the looks of the fields that
this district could supply the whole valley. There are
neat lodges in the fields, and the reference in Isaiah i. 8,
" As a lodge in a garden of cucumbers," was brought to
mind; but it looked desolate enough, as there was no
human being in sight. As twilight advanced I was
compelled to cross a small river, and this without dis-
robing; I had to trace its windings for some distance,
and with each step the way became more interesting
and romantic, and I was led more by curiosity than
necessity to follow up the ravine. I managed with a
bamboo stick to leap over the wet and slippery places
until I came to the rim of a giant basin fifty feet in
diameter, full to overflowing with clear sparkling water.

A semicircular sandstone cover extended half-way over it, and not more than twenty feet above the water; in the centre of this cover a stream ten feet wide rolled down into the pool. Through the fissure cut by the stream a beautiful park was disclosed, not more than a couple of hundred yards distant. It was the most lovely picture yet seen, and whetted my appetite still more to taste the mysteries and beauties which lie hidden in the unexplored background.

It was with a pang of regret that I descended to the muddy river and cramped junk. There is a wideness and freedom in Nature congenial to my indolent tastes. A squad of Chinese — a sort of advance guard — stood upon the bank near by, making cabalistic gesticulations as I advanced. A few friendly words, however, put them at ease, and gave them the unexpected opportunity of holding a council over a genuine foreigner.

CHAPTER IV.

Between Chung-Cheu and Fungteu-hsien, a distance of thirty-nine geographical miles, the river is wide, and generally free from rocks and difficult rapids. In one place, a short distance below Kao-kia-tsun, there are rapids nearly or quite the whole width of the river, but not of such violence as where the river is narrower. I have no doubt that in winter the water is not more than three or four feet here, while in summer there is ten times as much. There are few high mountains near the river ; the rock is mostly red sandstone, and there is an abundance of coal of an inferior quality. The hills are nearly all cultivated, even to their tops. The chief products are poppy, maize, wheat, rice, tobacco, beans, peas, and many varieties of vegetables, the first three being the staples. Very few cattle, goats, and sheep are seen. . As soon as the poppy or fluid is gathered, the ground is ploughed and corn set. It is not poor, thin soil which is used for the poppy, as some suppose, but the best, — better even than that used for wheat. The area of land devoted to this now staple and remunerative product has steadily increased for many years, until the valley lands in some sections have been given up to its growth, and consequently the rice and wheat fields are

FUNGTEU-HSIEN AND ITS SACRED MOUNTAIN.

narrowed. The price of rice has risen one third within twenty-five years, owing to this constant poppy encroachment; and we see the two greatest crops grown in many sections of the province,—opium and Indian corn,—turned to uses deleterious to the interests of the people, namely, smoking and drinking. Very little corn is eaten or fed to stock, so extensively is it distilled into alcohol.

The poppy is planted in November and gathered in April, in favorable sections. The seed is sown in hills, in rows about two feet apart, and when the plants are three or four inches high they are thinned out, leaving two or three vigorous plants in each hill. It flowers in February; and when the petals fall and the heads are still fresh, six or eight slits are cut in each one,—lengthwise, usually, though in some places, as in Honan, the slits are oblique. These cuts only penetrate the outside covering and do not interfere with seed ripening. From the incisions made in the morning sufficient fluid exudes for evening gathering, and *vice versa*. This process continues several days,—until the heads are dry. When the seeds are sufficiently matured, the heads are collected and the seeds shelled out by women and children. Thirty catties of seed yield about ten catties of pure oil, which is considered more nourishing, and better for use in lighting, than many other vegetable oils. If the poppy is grown for the apothecary, no incisions are made. I was told that the poppy and wheat require the same amount of cultivation, manure, etc. It is the most remunerative agricultural product in the province, easily grown, and sure of ready sale. The opium raised here is not equal to that grown in the Northern provinces, but finds a ready market in Hupeh, Nganhui, Kiangsi, and some other parts of the empire.

Kao-kia-tsun is a flourishing market-town, and although we passed it at an early hour, thousands of farmers and traders were pouring in from every quarter. Every kind and quality of boat was in requisition, plying up, down, and across the river, filled to overflowing with people, live-stock, and light merchandise. Long strings of men, women, and small boys were seen hastening down the steep sides of the hills, eager to fill the little ferry-boats, which came and went in rapid succession. Each peasant, as a rule, bore some load, or drove a cow or pig. They had new wheat and barley, opium, and other products just harvested. All conceivable odds and ends were brought to these frail canoes, their poor owners hoping to dispose of them during the market hour.

There is no law against excessive loading or unseaworthiness; people crowd in as long as a space for sitting or standing remains, with cattle, pigs, and fowls in the centre; and a boat is used as long as the planks will hold together. If a boat capsizes and a score of unfortunates are drowned, it is merely a day's wonder, and the same carelessness goes on year after year. There is no Press to herald accidents all over the country, to arouse the public conscience or create an opinion.

Fungteu-hsien, or the city of Tophet, is beautifully situated, and has some good streets and shops. It was almost ruined by the great flood of 1870, but is rebuilt on higher land; there is a record in stone of the height the flood attained. The little picturesque mount below the city, separated from it by a bridge, is one of the most interesting points to the traveller in China. It is literally covered to its top—which is about five hundred feet above the river — with large temples and mammoth banyans. More celebrated, however, than its beauty, is the historical notoriety to which it has attained, first from Taoist recluses, and next from the wonderful claims put forward by the Buddhists, who for a long time have held a sort of religious monopoly of the Hadean manifestations here exhibited to the upper world. To this wonderful retreat Dr. Morley and I directed our steps, while the rest of our party entered the city for book-selling.

The road, from bottom to top, is intensely interesting, from the twenty temples which we pass and the ancient stone tablets recording the wonderful events of antiquity. Some of the stone monuments erected a thousand years ago are still standing, and the characters engraved upon them are decipherable. A broad sandstone road leads by easy stages from temple to temple, the stones worn so thin upon the outer edges that in places it was much the same as ascending the side of a smooth rock. Yen-lo-wang, King of Tartarus, is the chief divinity worshipped; but the religious tastes of the Chinese are too varied to permit any one god to hold absolute sway over any celebrated locality, so we find both Buddhist and Taoist gods who hold the destinies of mortals in their keeping—not only in Sheol and Hades, but in Paradise — receiving full honors here. A very peculiar worship was seen in one temple: nine huge serpents coiled to beams, and dangling their heads over the worshippers, receive special homage. The reason is said to be on account of the disappearance of the great serpents once found on the mountain.

The Goddess of Mercy, with a thousand hands and eyes, is popular here, as everywhere throughout China. Before the image of the King of Tartarus were numerous votive offerings, such as eyes, hands with wounds, arms, feet, hearts, lungs, — all being thank-offerings for miraculous cures upon such as had besought help from the god and made vows to him. Votive offerings are in very general use all over China, and many are promised which are never paid. A story is told of a man on a boat which was in great danger of being wrecked, who vowed that if saved he would give a certain saint a taper as large as himself! A fellow-sufferer suggested that he would not remember his promise, when the first man replied, " Did you think me in earnest ? Let me get my feet on dry ground, and I would not give him as much as a tallow candle." But the amount of offerings adorning these temples prove that many such promises are religiously fulfilled. It is not uncommon for a wealthy person to build an entire temple to a god to whom he has appealed in times of distress, and there are cases where the man also devotes himself to the service of the god and performs the most menial offices.

We saw many goddesses of great size, before which were rows of casts of women's feet, — thank-offerings from those who had been cured. I fear that my teacher could tell a story of an eye, a hand, and a pair of small feet, as such objects were afterward seen in his possession.

A cosmopolitan spirit seems to rule here, and subjects to suit all fancies have been depicted. Some of them fail to convey any moral or religious lessons. One panel even represents two English military gentlemen of robust appearance shooting birds; while another has a portly foreigner in the centre, surrounded with a profuse and extremely grotesque decorative border.

We were joined by a number of Taoist priests who looked more like beggars than like men of the long robe, who, without invitation, became enthusiastic guides, pointing out the many objects of interest which were already becoming bewildering, though we had but just commenced our examination of these wonderful shrines. We were exhorted to make the difficult ascent to the temple which crowns the brow of the hill, where we should see a goddess who is a permanent incarnation, none other than the wife of the King of Tartarus.

The legend concerning this goddess runs thus: Twelve hundred years ago, in the glorious days of the Tang, when Buddhism was at its height, a fair maiden came hither from Chungking to pay her vows to the King of Tartarus. While in the act of worship she lost one of her beautiful ear-rings, exquisitely wrought in fine gold with pearls, emblematic at once of the maiden's purity and of the wealth which could purchase such ornaments. Her distress at this loss will be easily understood; and though she feared that the ear-ring had dropped into the incense-burner, yet she searched carefully for it, and was aided by the old priest who was in attendance.

After the maiden had left the sacred mount the priest found the jewel in the hand of the god, and also received a mysterious revelation to the effect that henceforth the fate of this lovely girl would be bound up with the life of Yen-lo-wang himself.

A revelation was also made to the maiden, who told her parents, on reaching home, not only of the mysterious loss of her ear-ring, but that it had been revealed to her that she was to be the spiritual bride of the King of Tartarus, the time of her death being already fixed and near at hand. When the day approached, everything was prepared for the young girl's death as if it were to be her wedding; and she gradually sank into greater and greater weakness, as if passing away from the effect of disease, when suddenly a tempest arose, so terrific in fury that the instinct of self-preservation was the only consciousness that remained with the terror-stricken family, and even the dying girl was forgotten in the midst of their alarm.

When the storm was over, what was the surprise at finding that the maiden's body had disappeared! Then they remembered her words, that shê was to be the bride of the great god of Fungteu, and they went immediately to his temple there to see if possibly these miraculous occurrences could be explained to them.

It is not easy to imagine their astonishment at finding the body in the possession of the priests, who had recognized it by the ear-ring in their keeping. They declared the body to be spiritualized flesh, which must be enshrined in the temple as the wife of the god in the spirit world. The relatives then brought beautiful silk and satin robes for the goddess, and gilded her face to preserve it from contamination; and every year since that long-ago time the descendants of the Chens have made pilgrimages to this shrine, bringing richly colored robes for the goddess, and taking away those of the previous year. They also bring three great sticks, — perhaps bundles of incense, — which require as many men to carry them up the mount, and two wax tapers so heavy that a man is required to bear each one. The wily priests were ready to draw aside the curtain and show us the fair creature, somewhat in the manner of the priests in Rome who exhibit the portrait of Saint Luke painted by himself. My teacher, who is something of a Christian in his way, called for an extra light, as he wanted to see her face; but the ministering priests, just at that moment, became very much interested in an illustrated copy of the Gospel of Saint Matthew, and made a purchase, taking two copies and several illustrated tracts. They cut the novel exhibition short, and gave us a pressing invitation to visit the tea and wine saloons in an upper story, the largest of which could seat two hundred men with ease ; it was open on all sides, affording exquisite views of the city, river, and mountains.

After climbing several flights of winding stairs we reached the top of the tower and a remarkable room which contains images of the Taoist genii, Wang-Fan-Pin and Yin-Chang-Sen, celebrities of the Han dynasty that flourished about two thousand years ago. They are seated at a rustic table, playing chess. One is in the act of making an important move, holding his hand waveringly over the board. An image of a black boy, poor and wan, stands near with his elbow resting on a tree, supporting his chin with his hand and watching the game most intently. The story goes that in the Tsin dynasty, more than eighteen hundred years ago, this boy, a wood-chopper, went up into a certain mountain near by to cut wood, and found these two genii sitting in a grotto playing chess; one of them gave the boy something in the form of a date-stone ; he became oblivious of time, and is said to have watched the game two hundred years or more. At last one of the genii suggested that it was time for him to return to his home ; coming to himself he found his clothes rotted away, and his hatchet consumed with rust. When he made his advent into his native village, like Rip Van Winkle he found that the world had not been asleep in his absence; and finding himself a stranger, lost in such surroundings, he hurried back to the mountain and became a famous Taoist recluse, and is now honored as a god.

I casually remarked to one of the fraternity that the situation was beautiful, and must be cool in summer. "Yes," he said, " and a great resort for the city gentry, who congregate here to drink wine and play games."

Ah! my Buddhist brothers, not wine and chess alone, nor confined to the city gentry; your sunken cheeks, your wrinkled brows, and ghastly looks, your hollow speech, and prematurely aged forms proclaim that Satan's mortgage is upon you; your mental and physical powers have all been poisoned and palsied. The raw opium besmeared upon the hideous mouths and faces of the ferocious giant gods at the entrance to the temples and along the corridors, the cords of poppy stalks piled in the courts, its presence everywhere, with wine, cards, chess, and other indications of more secret vices, symbolize the lustful character of your religious aspirations,—aspirations not above those of the poor coolies, who congregate in dens and brothels all over this land. It is indeed a sickening sight to look upon these ancient temples, these stone monuments, these grand old giant trees, built, set up, and planted by nobler monks. "Men are we, and must grieve when even the shade of that which once was great is passed away."

Williams's Dictionary has the following in reference to Fungteu: "A district on the Yang-tsze River, in Chungcheu in the east of Sz-Chuan, where the fire-wells occur; it is used as a term for hell, or Tophet, the entrance to which is under the Wuh-tsao stone placed there; in it is Fungteuchen, the city of Yen-lo-wang, or Pluto, who is styled the great Ruler of Hades." I was not successful in finding anything more than rumors of such wells as above described. The myth that Hades, or Purgatory, is under or near by this beautiful mount and city is of comparatively recent date, not going back of the tenth or twelfth centuries. It may have grown out of the fact that certain caverns are found near by, which may have been explored with calamitous results, thus giving rise to dread surmises and superstitions; and the Taoists and Buddhists were not slow to seize upon these events and convert them to religious ends. Buddhism is more practical in its aims than Taoism, and never loses an opportunity of appealing to the fears and prejudices of the people for its gain.

I was told that the west gate was formerly sealed, on account of the great number of evil spirits who prowled about the country beyond, supposed to come forth from the caverns to inflict evils upon those venturing to traverse the road near their precincts. A legend relates that during the Min dynasty (fifteenth century) an official from Chungking was appointed magistrate of Fungteu. He came down the river with his flag flying, and went into port, but was amazed to find, anchored near by, a boat similar to his own, with a flag of same grade, thus claiming that the official on board was magistrate of Fungteu. "How can this be?" thought he. "Am I relieved before reaching my post, or has some one imposed upon me?" He sent his card to the boat, and requested an interview, that he might understand the reason of what he saw. He was politely received and informed that the occupant was a magistrate of the district, to be sure, — but of the underground one, or Tophet, not of the visible town!

The mind of the magistrate was quieted, and he no doubt congratulated himself upon establishing official relations with one so intimately acquainted with the affairs of the invisible world, which he was politely invited to visit, and had all needful directions given him as to how and when he could accomplish this wonderful journey. Romance was passing into reality, the mystical and religious becoming clear and political. He no doubt imagined the popularity that he should gain, and the revelations to be made.

As the appointed time for the visit drew near, the magistrate ordered the gate unsealed, which brought forth many protests from the people ; but his commands were enforced, and his chair-bearers and escort started upon what they considered a perilous undertaking, from which they would gladly have run away.

They had not proceeded far beyond the gate when the heavens became lurid, and tinged with yellow in spots. Unseen beings pressed upon them, and became so furious that the chair-bearers ran away in fright, and only one or two of the escort had the bravery to remain with their courageous master. Taking to his feet, he marched to the cavern and sent forward his card, which was received by the magistrate of Yen-Kin (Tophet) where spirits good and bad wait for trial and judgment from its king. He was taken by the spirit guards, blindfolded, and conducted through the dark prisons where untried spirits waited in their foul abodes to be called forth to condemnation and punishment or to be released. At length he was led into the guest-hall of the official he had met upon his arrival at Fungteu, and his eyes were unbandaged. But how changed was Satan now! how august and terrible! The bold mortal was shown over the invisible abodes and entertained as befitted one of his rank and bravery. As he was leaving, the ruler made the reasonable request that any surplus chains he might have should be sent below, as his were badly rusted and insufficient for present uses.

This legend may throw some light upon the so-called " fire-wells," and explain why the Buddhists have been able to make the little mountain a Mecca for those desiring to propitiate the supposed rulers of the world of darkness, whom they believe to be influenced by the priests and the rich offerings made on the altars.

But I must say farewell to this city of so much historical romance, which Captain Blackistone pronounces the prettiest city upon the river. After our sight-seeing we went through the town and sold our whole stock of books. The only evidence I had of the proximity of Fungtcu (Tophet) was that as I sought my boat above the city, a crowd of vagabonds followed me, hooting and throwing mud and gravel.

We passed the city of Feu-cheu on the 16th of May. It is pleasantly situated upon the right bank of the Yang-tsze and left bank of the Kung-tan or Feu-ling. This river flows from the province of Kwei-cheu, and is navigable for one or two hundred miles by light boats and small bamboo rafts. It flows through a mountainous and picturesque country. The boats are destitute of houses or coverings, and the traveller is obliged to seek quarters on shore wherever the boat may stop for the night. There are a few small cities and towns upon its banks. Salt from Upper or West Sz-Chuan is conveyed into Kwei-cheu by this small river, and a variety of merchandise from Shashi and Hankow takes this difficult route. Feu-cheu is a place of considerable importance, quite twice the size of Kwei-cheu-foo. There are a number of fine public buildings covered with green tiles, and many large *hongs*, or warehouses. Boats of small size are seen in both rivers.

The country to the south is rugged, while about the city it is smooth and under fair cultivation. When I say smooth, it means that the omnipresent red sandstone mountains are covered with earth to the depth of eighteen inches in the most favored localities. The heavy rain of last night and this morning filled all the waterways to overflowing; yesterday they were dry, to-day really dangerous for the trackers to ford, and the rush of water is so fierce that the men use all kinds of precautions in crossing, as a misstep would send one rolling over bowlders into the red floods of the river. The streams partake of the color of the soil in the ravines, — some almost yellow, others chocolate, and again a reddish-brown.

We noticed women along the shore shelling the poppy seeds. There are some large salt hongs above the city where salt is stored to be reshipped to the province of Kwei-cheu. The Mantsz caves are seen opposite the city, as well as a number of temples. The rainy season seems to have set in; we have cloudy weather and showers nearly every day, with a very low thermometer; it has not been above 73° to 75° for some days. Coming to anchor above the city at an early hour we took to the fields and gardens, and strolled among the farmhouses and graves until darkness sent us to our boat. The roads were covered with deep mud, but the prospect was so enticing that we counted it a small matter so long as we could stand upright and lift our boots from the miry depths. Half-a-dozen books were sold, and ten cabbages bought. I don't know when my gardening proclivities have been so pleasantly awakened as they were this evening. Irish potatoes in full bloom are no longer a rare sight, for they are everywhere; but to stumble unexpectedly into a cabbage-garden — foreign cabbages, beautiful heads, and worms too — stirred me to the very depths. It was useless to try to suppress my emotions; and ere I was aware of it, my hand involuntarily fell upon the old gardener's shoulder, and I congratulated him upon the success of his noble enterprise! His wife stood by a stone hand-mill near the cottage door, grinding wheat; with one hand she turned the upper stone, and with the other dashed water and wheat into a hole in the top of the stone, while a wheaten paste poured out into a receptacle below. I thought she looked at me with surprise and disgust until she heard me bargaining with her lord for ten cabbages, when something like admiration and genuine satisfaction came over her wrinkled face. It is wonderful what a cheery influence foreign products in the country and foreign merchandise in the city have upon the traveller. The sight of these common products imported from England or France makes the country, and even the people, seem a little nearer and dearer to us. The foreign cloths upon the shop counters, the glass lamps hanging in the hall, the matches upon the wayside stand, Devoe's oil cases scattered about the city, — one and all are avenues of approach to this strange people. There is a sympathy expressed in clothes : a Chinaman with a foreign calico coat or English broadcloth has taken a short step toward international brotherhood.

Our cook, who always looks sidewise and appears meek, — a habit well cultivated, — was sent ashore at the city, two miles below, to replenish our wasted stores. It was ten o'clock ere his plaintive voice was heard from the shore meekly calling for a sampan. There was no boat to be had, and during dreams and semi-conscious moments I heard his meek voice appealing for help above the roar of the rapids. At last, after several frantic efforts, he succeeded in floating his chickens and vegetables to the junk, and was himself pulled on board by a sailor, and with chattering teeth crawled into his nest.

Our next stage was rather difficult, as there are some rocky points, one of which is very dangerous; it is at the head of a large island where there are two strong opposite currents, with dangerous eddies where they divide. Li-teu, thirty li above Feu, is a busy town with some fine public buildings. Lin-shih, about eighty li above Li-teu on the right bank, boasts a very large stone bridge, the best we have yet seen. Three graceful towers relieve its heavy plain masonry. A large green-tiled temple is also an object of attraction, and shows well from the river. Toward evening the fortress called Sien-Nu, "fairy women," was passed. It is a charming mount, green as emerald, on which are some good temples.

This is a land of surprises. There is great variety in the scenery, which gives it an inexhaustible charm, while the sudden transformation in the customs and habits of the people shows the individuality of this Western empire. While on the whole there is the closest affinity in everything truly Chinese, yet under the universal robe of likeness there is no little diversity in taste and modes of expression.

It is not uncommon in Eastern China to see colossal characters carved upon the faces of the cliffs in the vicinity of large monasteries, as spiritual reminders to be ever present with the forgetful monk as he wanders in the precincts of his earthly paradise. Here these mottoes are not seen, but in their stead are little temples hewn out of the solid rock, or built with blocks of sand-stone on some shelving crag, and decorated with carving and fresco. We have passed several to-day, and in one almost perpendicular cliff great niches are cut out, a hundred or more feet above the water. These rock temples are usually faced with hewn stone and appro-priately decorated, and within are giant images made of stone, representing either Buddha or Lao-tsz, and some-times both. In other similar structures I could see the sedate yet kindly face of the Goddess of Mercy. On one was an inscription saying that "In ancient times the water rose to that lotus terrace."

Moderate-sized forests are now frequent, and charming groves of bamboo, the trunks twisted and quaintly interlaced, while the tops are straight, gracefully plumed, and exquisitely colored. Coal abounds, and much lime is manufactured from the occasional limestone croppings near Changsheu-hsien, " Everlasting City."

Since leaving Kwei-cheu it has been a common sight to see men and women carrying large, flanging baskets upon their backs, and in some instances we have seen men bearing wine-casks on top of these baskets. To-day we saw another method of transportation which becomes more general the farther west we go. Cows and bullocks, fitted with saddles or racks, bear great loads of coal or lime in baskets. When rounding a sharp corner in the mountain or descending a dangerous defile, the drivers are considerate enough of their beasts to remove the burdens to their own backs and drive or lead the cattle to a smoother road.

The sky has been covered with clouds and mists for ten days, and the temperature has been low. Thick mists veil the city " Eternal," Changsheu, and only an occasional glimpse is caught of the fortress-like walls which crown the mountain. The city proper is about eight hundred feet above the river, and is built on a broad crest. There is a pretty four-arched bridge across a little stream flowing through the suburbs, and a fine water-fall near the city wall is discernible through the mists.

Bamboo rafts are seen here, of very small dimensions, directed and kept in the current by means of bamboo rakes; a man stands in the forward part of the raft and rakes the water right and left according to the need, while the swift current carries the light craft along at the rate of six or seven miles an hour.

The clouds had rolled away during the night, and the 20th of May dawned as perfectly as heart could wish. The joyful rays of light danced along our cabin floors as the boat twisted and rolled amid eddies and swirls. A marvellous effect had been wrought in us by a simple change from cloud to sunlight; all were happy and disposed to be generous and obliging. Projects were very soon put on foot, widely varied, but equally necessary for health and happiness,—an excursion and a washing of soiled clothing. It is unnecessary to say that John came in for the washing and we for the shore.

It was a joy, indeed, to leap from the clumsy craft upon the hard brown sand, and strike out into vales and over low, well-shrubbed hills, to farm-houses snugly enclosed by fruit-trees and creepers. Where paths existed we walked in them; in their absence we went across corn and tobacco fields. We passed hamlets perched upon hillsides in little glens, where pumalos, oranges, and nectarines shaded the front doors. Children were playing in the mud just as they do in civilized lands, but with much less trouble to their mammas; for they had discarded all artificial covering, and were able to roll in mud and water without any reproof for soiled or torn garments. In one instance only was any fear of us manifested: an elderly dame saw us coming, and called to the young women to shut the doors; they were banged and bolted in a hurry, and we lost sight of youth and beauty, but youth and beauty could see us through cracks and holes.

Tobacco plants are very vigorous, and the untasselled corn is shoulder-high in some places. The cured tobacco leaf is rolled into loose cigars three inches long, and smoked in bamboo pipes which have brass bowls. This method of smoking is nearly universal among the middle and lower classes, and gentlemen often adopt it when the water pipe is not at hand.

A climb to the top of a red sandstone cone and a rest upon the clean green grass under a banyan or upon square ivy-grown stones which had been in the great barricade in the days of trumpets and arrows, gave to both body and mind that pleasurable relaxation which is apt to end in a pensive excursion into the dim past, when the encroaching Mongol, step by step, dislodged the cave-dwellers and the roving hordes of savages, until the very westernmost confines of the empire beheld the " almond-eyed." I peered into the vales to the north and traced the distant slopes and gorges of high mountain ranges until they were wreathed in impenetrable mists.

It had proved anything but a happy day for the captain of our junk, as a strong northwest wind had made it next to impossible for the men to drag the boat around the rocky points. After wearying ourselves with a thousand beautiful sights, we returned by the river bank in search of our delinquent craft, and were not a little annoyed to find her snugly moored, and a broken rudder on shore. Carpenters were called from the nearest town, and before sundown we were again on our way, but at a snail's pace at the best, and often losing ground. By dark, however, we had rounded the dangerous reef, and our men were actively engaged in the one serious pursuit of life,—emptying the rice-bowls, and later came their cards and opium. It was gently hinted that we had better keep our windows closed during the night, as robbers infested the neighborhood; doubtless the boatmen believed this, for they made the night hideous by their use of gunpowder.

We anchored just above Mu-tung-sz, a town of several thousand inhabitants. Although late, Mr. Faber and Dr.

Morley ventured out to sell books. I was not surprised
to see them returning shortly followed by roughs and
an army in blue, the doctor being pelted with gravel
and sand. I have always found the evening a bad time
to mingle with a Chinese crowd; as then the populace,
if the weather be warm, has taken largely to the street
and to wine and tea drinking, the bad boys are home
from school, and roughs through with their day's work,
and ready to engage in any mischief.

The water has risen fast the past few days; the swirls
are larger and more dangerous. It requires no little
patience to submit to a month's incarceration upon an
inconvenient, dirty junk, making an average of twelve
miles a day. It is a shame that travellers to and from
the vast and populous province of Sz-Chuan should be
drawn by human flesh, and under conditions that de-
grade the poor fellows to the level of the mule or
bullock. It would be a boon to thousands of men if
this severe, unnatural work could be done by steam.
It is appalling to think of the unnumbered ages that
poor unfortunate man has been used as a beast, and
for a mere pittance been compelled to haul boats up
this river. The poor fellows must extract some pleasure from the expected bliss at the end of the journey; and many boast, like Goldsmith's negro of his
native land : —

> " The naked negro panting at the line
>   Boasts of his golden sands and palmy wine,
>   Basks in the glare, or stems the tepid wave,
>   And thanks his gods for all the good they gave."

We pass through a narrow but short gorge ten miles
below Chungking, and emerge into a comparatively open
country. The hills are closely set with small trees resembling the oak. The fields wave with luxuriant crops

of corn and tobacco, principally the last, and such mammoth plants I have not elsewhere seen.

The approach to Chungking is, if possible, more beautiful than that to any other city on the Yang-tsze, and as the termination of a tedious journey the traveller hails it with supreme delight. A bend is made to the south two miles below the city, which brings immediately into view Kiangpeh, the small but romantic district city on the north bank of the Kia-ling, which river separates it from Chungking. This is more frequently called the " small river," and unites with the " Golden Sands " at the lower end of the city. In a few moments the higher portions of Chungking burst into view, and by degrees all the high and hooked cape upon which the city stands is before us. Under the hazy atmosphere which presses down upon mountain and valley the greater portion of the year, the view is not particularly bright or cheerful, but somewhat melancholy. The wall is built close to the high river bluffs, leaving little space outside for suburbs. The end of the cape is narrow, and widens to one and one half miles in the centre of the city, and then gradually narrows for some distance. Tier upon tier of hongs rise to the yamens and other public and private mansions, which from the approach appear suspended in mid-air, as no trees or land are seen beyond. Looking up the Golden Sands from our position, a beautiful range of mountains is seen eastward from the city and across the river, from thirteen to eighteen hundred feet high, the farthest and highest one being crowned with a white pagoda called Wenfung, " literary luck," built fifty years ago to regulate the literary fortunes of the city. Just above us as we pass along the right bank of the Golden Sands, stands a fine temple to the Emperor Yu, the great mythological deity of the Yang-tsze. A short distance beyond upon a perpendicular sand-cliff are carved the two gigantic characters, " Tu-san."

There is a legend that Yu took a wife from this locality, and that she dwelt here while he was engaged in the herculean task of controlling the turbulent waters of these several rivers, and opening sufficient waterway from them to the ocean. I am sorry he did not make the gorges a little wider and remove some of the dangerous reefs with a few blows of his ponderous hammer. He must have " eaten a great deal of bitterness " below this point, and one could hardly blame him for stopping his titanic work long enough to take a wife and a short rest upon the beautiful slopes of Tu-san. But two other places in the empire claim the honor of giving him a wife, — Sheu-cheu and Hwaiyuen in the province of Nganhui ; perhaps he had two or three wives. The historical records are silent ; but an incident in his life while engaged in the godlike labor of clearing out the Wu-shan gorge points to this place rather than Nganhui. Before he had completed the work he is said to have passed his own door three times, and quite naked too, and no doubt in need of rest. He heard the wailing of his infant son, but did not stop, the work was so pressing. Now if his cave or house was in this rock, when he sailed down or was pulled up in his *kwatsz*, he could have distinctly heard the moans of his darling son ; and further, the water of the river must have been a hundred feet higher than in these degenerate days. Circumstantial evidence certainly points to this identical spot as Mrs. Yu's home. Nothing would please me more than to decide a great historical fact, so that I might have a peg on which to hang posterior historical events from B.C. 2278 downward.

The city of Chungking is modern, — a mere babe in

CHUNGKING AND PART OF KIANGPEH.

comparison with those far-off mythical days of great achievements. It was in the time of the Shu Han, about A. D. 230, when Changfei, the great warrior, with Liupei, the king, had pacified these Western regions, that the noble Li Yiu was sent to make a dirt wall four and one half miles in extent and to build a city. It was not until A. D. 1400 that the Emperor ordered Tsaiting to build a stone wall around the city. It was to be three and one half miles in length, and, with the natural rock walls upon which it is reared, one hundred and twenty feet high, with seventeen gates, eight of which were to be sealed up; at this time the city became noted for its traffic. Later on, at the beginning of the present dynasty, or the fall of the Min, the city was stormed and all the people slaughtered; and it was not until twenty years later, in the second year of Kanghsi, A. D. 1664, that the Viceroy Li Kwoh Ying repaired the walls. History tells us that the story of this city at that time was a picture of all cities and towns in the province. As the first Emperor of the Tsings took the throne, this greatest and most populous province was nearly depopulated and a barren waste. People from Kwangtung and other provinces were imported to re-populate the ruined districts.

From the above items taken from the provincial topography it will be seen that Chungking is a comparatively small city in extent; and being destitute of suburbs, a very large population must necessarily be packed within the walls. The lower part of the city is densely peopled, but the upper half is taken up largely with public buildings and official residences, which in many instances are empty. Mr. Baber puts the population at one hundred and twenty thousand, which cannot be far out of the way, as it is based upon official records.

CHAPTER V.

WE took peaceable possession of the anchorage in
front of Tsiensz gate at an early hour on the 22d of
May. Ferry-boats were thick as bees flying to and fro
from Kiangpeh, — the Brooklyn of Chungking. The
broad steps leading to the city were thronged with
passengers, porters, and the ubiquitous "boy." We
were snugly stowed between some empty ferry-boats,
and had the pleasurable prospect of a quiet Sunday.
These agreeable anticipations were not destined to long
life. We were scarcely seated when the sharp-eyed
youngsters, who had been collecting in squads, instinct-
ively moved to the empty boats, and took up their
position near our windows, first peering through the
cracks, then slyly opening them an inch or two, and
finally, when unobserved, throwing them wide open.

They seemed really hungry for a good look at the
last foreign importations; it was dark ere they yielded
to fatigue, and they went away then as if disappointed.
It is amazing what efforts the Chinese boy will make,
and what dangers and discomforts he will undergo, in
order to have a good look at a foreigner. These same
little boys had seen many foreign faces before, but here
were fresh ones. They wondered, too, at our sudden
appearance; for only a few months ago the officials had

sent away the missionaries at night, and lo! here was a boat-load of them in broad daylight, and in the most conspicuous place about the city. They probably thought, " These foreigners are strange beings ; we mob and drive them away and burn their houses, only to see others come to take their places." It is pleasant at times to be the centre of attraction ; but after a month of publicity, and being a gazing stock for Celestial eyes, a quiet corner is acceptable, and one is quite willing to be unnoticed and unknown.

The secretaries of the hsien were abroad at an early hour to copy our passports, and inquire into our future movements. A certain Chinaman who had given the Mission no little trouble as a preacher before the riot, and had feathered his nest during and after the *emeute* from the property of the missionaries which escaped destruction by the rioters, came aboard, and meekly waited for an interview.

His story was long and pathetic, especially when he related how an official had slapped him in the face with a shoe because he robbed the Mission! Here he burst into tears, and I closed the interview that he might have the opportunity to retire and compose himself. I learned afterward that this rascal had stolen the chapel furniture and appropriated thirty dollars in rent due the Mission, besides selling much valuable material that was left scattered about after the riot ; and yet he had the audacity to come to us, after we were settled on shore, with a claim for services in protecting the property of the Mission.

Fortunately the morning of the 23d was rainy ; for the Chinese youngster does not like water, and we could move about far more quietly without him. The streets were almost deserted. Our chairs were very narrow, and our heads barely escaped the covers, so we were not altogether comfortable when on level ground, and as we ascended the zigzag streets and interminable stone steps, the coolies swayed the chairs to and fro, keeping time to their slow movements. When ascending a hundred or more steps at an angle of forty-five degrees I tried leaning back, but experience taught me that to bend forward and grasp the front supports was far more soothing to the mind. The aneroid showed the Mission location to be three hundred feet above the river, and it was less than a mile from the gate.

We were heartily welcomed by Mr. Turner of the China Inland Mission, who was living in the central part of the city. His house suffered little during the riot, although it was almost surrounded by the buildings of the Roman Catholics, which were entirely demolished. The fact that Mr. Turner's was a purely native house, and rented from a Chinaman, accounts for his escape from violence. Poor Loh, the Catholic Chinaman who defended his property so manfully last year, and perhaps went beyond his legal rights in self-defence, has paid the penalty in the loss of his head.

There had recently been some excitement in the country, and a few miles of the newly erected telegraph poles had been destroyed. The trouble was caused by a careless lad who persisted in flying his kite over the wires, for what purpose I know not; he may have been a youthful Franklin who was trying to draw lightning from the wires. At all events, he got a severe shock from an official's battery, which not only fired him, but the whole district, and a grand bonfire of poles and destruction of the wire was the result. The people as usual had to bite the dust in the end, and officialdom gloried in its tyranny.

Fung-shui is practically a thing of the past, and any kind of innovation would now be met with silent acquiescence by the people. Why? Has a great change come over the populace? Not in the least; officialdom holds fung-shui in its palm, to make it a bugbear whenever it sees fit to terrify foreign diplomats. The people under the present régime are as grass in Sz-Chuan; and half-a-dozen beggarly "yamen runners," with red hats and rawhides, can clear the busiest street in half an hour. Just before our arrival some evil-minded persons had posted placards near the China Inland Mission, setting forth the prejudices and preferences of the people in rather plain language. They proclaimed missions to be a nuisance, and missionaries and their books unacceptable. They were careful to state that foreigners who came for business purposes would be tolerated. It is needless to say that the officials removed these inflammatory notices before any measures were projected to put their palatable teachings in force. The taotai had also issued a proclamation against certain singers and players who were going the rounds of the country with a travesty on the late riots, and selling a pamphlet called "Beating the golden planks." From what I hear and see, there is no doubt that the city contains a large class of loafers, and many literary men out of employment and so degraded by opium and other vices that they are ready to launch upon any enterprise which will afford them temporary amusement and some plunder.

The first serious business of our Mission was to rent a suitable dwelling. We had been recommended by the former consular agent to a Catholic convert who owns valuable property, and hitherto has rented to the British Government, but for some unexplained reason he had changed his mind and declined an interview.

Our teacher scoured the city for two days, when he reported some houses to let near our old quarters and the Roman Catholic Cathedral. Being anxious to keep in advance of reports and head off any schemes that the officials might have, I went immediately to inspect them. Rambling over damp, mouldy, and decaying residences, to find one fit to live in, is not agreeable, but at last a bargain was struck with the degenerate scion of the Loh family for three hundred dollars a year, including heavy furniture. The taotai was duly notified of our act, and politely requested to issue a proclamation stating to the good people of the city that we were among them again. The lease was signed on the 25th of May, and on the 27th we sat peacefully at our supper-table in the guest-hall of our new home. The same evening a secretary from the magistrate made his bow, and requested to copy our passports. There is nothing more incomprehensible to a foreigner than an official residence, with its gates, folding-doors, halls, side-rooms, balconies, carved and frescoed pillars, lattices, and matted ceilings. What mottoes we find, what queer lounges, beds, tables, and cupboards! Lanterns are scattered everywhere, and always where the foreigner would not have them. The frescos are gaudy, and represent every conceivable subject, from genii walking among clouds, to a moth upon a peach. The roof is a tangled mass of Asiatic glory. The Sz-Chuanese houses excel all others in China in their exterior decorations; the ridges, gateways, and corners are beautifully trimmed with broken bits of blue and white porcelain, which at a distance have a most pleasing effect. For instance, the character for longevity or happiness will be made of colossal size, protected by a round or square frame, then covered with blue porcelain and put upon the centre of the roof or over a high gateway. Whatever else the people of this province are deficient in, they certainly excel in toy-like decoration.

It is doubtful if there has been a riot in China during the past century which had less apparent cause for violence and rapine than had that of 1886, or one in which there was so much destruction of property with so little personal violence and loss of life among foreigners and native Christians. It could not in any sense be called a revolt against Christianity, for the act was one of momentary impulse and aimed at property ; both before and after the sudden ebullition, there was but little violence to Christians. It has been thought by many foreigners — and is certainly not contradicted by some influential Chinese — that the whole affair from beginning to end was conceived and executed in the hsien's yamen. His only pretext, if he made one before the trouble, was personal spite; but afterward he justified the acts of the populace, who were wholly under official control, on the score of the unfair dealings of the missionaries in taking possession by fraud of certain prominent sites for dwellings. Although he had been a party to the transfer of these eligible building lots, he had raised no objections up to that time.

I was informed that just before the riot certain well-known characters were invited to his yamen, where the situation was explained to them, and an indirect intimation given that certain properties could be justly destroyed. It would take but a short time to communicate such official license to a sufficient number of the baser sort to wreck all the property in and out of the city, and they would be sure to be joined by an army ready to go beyond any acts that the astute mandarin had contemplated. It is wonderful indeed that so many men,

women, and children could be safely gathered from
diverse sections of the city into the yamens without
any particular injuries, unless the officials were in col-
lusion with the mob.

It is not our purpose to inquire into the origin of the
lamentable affair; it occurred, and an immense amount
of property belonging to the Catholics and the Methodist
Episcopal Church was destroyed, and about fifty private
dwellings of the Catholic Christians were looted. One of
the strange things is that the libraries and furniture of
the different homes were so well preserved by the rioters;
weeks and months after, things new and old were brought
forth for sale, and it is one of the strangest incidents
that the lion's share of these stolen goods was taken by
people who had been employed in and around the mission. After the missionaries were taken to the yamens,
and before the buildings were formally destroyed by
the tardy mob, these innocent individuals are reported
to have made some productive private raids.

Another strange feature in the plot was that the Catholic missionaries were taken, or went with the British
agent, to the chief official of Eastern Sz-Chuan, and the
Protestant missionaries to the hsien, or lowest. There
is no doubt, from proclamations posted directly after the
affair, and a few months later, that the taotai was easily
won over by the Catholic bishop and his colleagues, and
posted upon their head-quarters for public affairs —
a sort of Catholic guild — the following proclamation,
which was a strong indictment of the Protestants and
defence of the Catholics: —

Proclamation of Hsia, Taotai of Eastern Sz-Chuan.

That important defile [or isthmus] to the city of Yu has
been surrendered by the English and Americans. They

have ratified it in writing, and are now at peace with the people. This affair had nothing whatever to do with Frenchmen. Their churches at every place shall have uniform and ample protection. If any one hereafter shall get up a riot it will be considered a grievous offence against the laws of the Empire.

The curious may still find the following very important edict which was posted throughout the city five months after the riot, when the tribunal had finished its investigations at Chungking. It is an able document for the magistrate, and one which could not fail of making him popular with the people and Catholic Christians. Like the proclamation from the taotai's yamen months before, it makes the English and American missionaries responsible for the trouble, and excuses the people:—

We issue this edict that affairs may have publicity. Be it known of Chungking, that the people and Christians have lived together on the most amicable terms for a long time. This present year, because the English and Americans had undertaken to build houses upon that "important pass" which they had seized upon by fraud, commenced an affair which forthwith brought on the destruction of chapels, schools, hospitals, and residences of the missionaries of all countries, besides the dwellings of many Christians, and very much suffering. This was an outburst of justifiable indignation, yet I cannot pledge you were not paying off old grudges. If there had been impartial investigations into causes, then the branches would have been pulled along, the creepers exhibited, and the roots and stalks involved in the rolling to and fro, implicating altogether I know not how many. By the favor of the Viceroy Yiu, the deputies Lo and Tang were appointed to act in a joint convention with the taotais Hsia and Yi and the prefect Hen. The court had four different consultations with Mr. Ku, lord [bishop] of the French Church, and Mr. Bourne, the English resident at Chungking. After mature deliberation it was agreed that all of the " important passes " should be given up in compliance with the will of the people. Of the vagabonds who got up the trouble, the ring-leaders alone should be seized ; those who were forced into the trouble and those who followed of their own wills, if they are peaceful in the future, shall be graciously pardoned and not punished. Be it known that this is forgiveness for the past only, but a warning for the future. Now the people and the Christians should come to a mutual good understanding. Further, in the settlement of the court all the claims of the Christians who were robbed were considered, and are wholly included in the indemnity, and any persons trumping up false claims will not gain a hearing, for there are no such losses. In this manner the people receive ample protection. [Yes, indeed !] The results of our deliberations have been reported to our superiors, and it is proper that we issue this edict that you may fully understand our decisions.

We expect all military and civil subalterns, severally and unitedly, the overseers and guardians of order of all grades to acquaint themselves with its contents. You certainly know the foreign teachers persuade the people to virtuous actions. Imperial mandates have been frequently given commanding the protection of the Christians ; further, the Christians are surely subjects of China with the common people everywhere, and if not relatives, friends. Now in reference to the recent troubles, it was decided that no matter whether people or Christians, of whatever place or occupation, the former grudges must not be remembered. From this time put away your " ice and coals " [of fire], and give honor to one another with love. Let each one discharge his duty, and remove forever the cause of your troubles. Hereafter in disputes between the people and the Church, wranglings over small affairs, it is permitted the guardians of law and order [small officials] with intelligent men among the Christians to make up such difficulties. If the Christians lean upon the Church for protection and shall cheat and grind the common people, or the common people create trouble out of nothing, and rail at the Christians, and the results become serious, and the people of the place not able to quell the affair, then pleas and rejoinders may be presented to this Court, and there will be a judicial examination according to evidence, that the crooked and straight may be made evident by investigation, and without distinction of Christians or people.

From this time let there be mutual good relations, and conjointly enjoy the blessings of tranquillity.

We further charge the kien and pao [small officials] to be faithful in giving instruction and affording protection. The Christians shall be included in the Associations of the Village Elders, that their persons and property may receive ample protection, and good order be thereby restored. If there be vagabonds who shall foment trouble, it shall be the duty of the subalterns and the " compact " of order to use all their power to capture and send them to the officials for punishment. Bystanders shall by no means shove their hands into their sleeves, but shall use their influence to bring such culprits to trial.

From the issuing of this proclamation, if any dare to hold grudges, and presuming upon their ability act obstinately, such troubles shall be searched out, faithfully examined, and brought to trial, and the sentence shall be strictly carried into execution. If the subalterns are remiss in exercising due protection, they also will be subject to severe inquiry, and certainly no indulgence will be shown. Let each one be scrupulously obedient.

Don't oppose this special Edict.

10th Moon of 12th Year of Kwangsü.

We see by this effusion that the people are really justified for their proceedings; and they well might be excused if the officials themselves had instigated them to break the peace, or at least had assured them that certain measures would be winked at. However, it grew to greater and more serious dimensions than they intended. No doubt their intention was to create a feeling against the missionaries such as would lead to sufficient complications to regain the country sites, and possibly frighten them away from the city.

While Mr. Loh, the Catholic convert who defended his home with such dire results to the heathen, was beheaded, the officials have come off comparatively free, and are either in quite as good positions elsewhere or are "expectants."

One stipulation in our lease was that a gateway should be opened upon the street; but certain objections were evidently raised by some one, for, just as we had finished public services in our guest-hall, Sunday, May 29, a card from the district magistrate was handed in, with a request that he might see me. A servant threw open the great central two-leaved doors, and the portly form of Yuen Chuen, "Sweet Spring," stood directly before them in the outer court. Two secretaries, half-a-dozen menials, and our landlord, with his tasselled hat and several servants, brought up the rear. I made my most gracious bow to the man of flesh, and he twisted himself into all shapes admissible under the circumstances, and after some skilful manœuvring was comfortably seated upon the east side of our capacious hall.

A moment to regain his breath, and a few flutters of the fan were followed by a few questions, such as "Your honorable surname? Your lofty age? Your honored country?" and then His Excellency proceeded indirectly to business. "He had come to look about; had not heard of our taking a mansion until yesterday. He was much surprised at our despatch in renting, etc. It had come to his knowledge that we were about to open a front gate; would we wait a few days until he could make the matter plain to the people and avoid future trouble?" Our landlord endeavored to explain to him that it was his work and not ours; that he was simply opening an old gateway, — one which had never injured the prosperity of those living opposite; and why should neighbors now offer objections? The hsien thought the people would talk and make trouble. His object was, no doubt, to defer the matter until his successor, whom he expected in a few days, should arrive. The landlord urged him to state the matter to the prefect forthwith, with a request that a proclamation be issued informing the people that he was opening his own old gateway. Proclamations are an institution in Chungking, and upon the most trivial excuse an edict is posted; they are as common as handbills on a village board fence in America.

A semi-idiotic grin played over the dreamy physiognomy of " Sweet Spring " as he acknowledged the reasonableness of the landlord's request, but it carried a strong conviction that no steps to further the enterprise would be taken by him. A proclamation from the taotai had been sent us a few moments before the hsien's arrival, and thinking it wise to let him see how his superior looked upon our coming, we asked him to read it. He searched through his large satin boots, and finally drew forth his ancient goggles, and after an extra puff at the pipe and a few grunts, arranged them above his nose. It is not certain that he read more than the first line and examined the seal, for almost instantly he reached for the tea; business was over, as is always understood when the teacups are lifted. This man, who is expected to look after the interests of one hundred and twenty thousand people in the city, and possibly four hundred thousand peasants in the country, is by all odds the most stupid official we have met for many a long day.

My writer explained his awkwardness on the ground of his being a native of the province of Kwei-cheu. The gateway remains unopened.

The proclamation of the taotai read somewhat as follows, and was pasted on a board and exhibited at our front gate for general information :—

"This edict is published to make you acquainted that Rev. Mr. Hart, of America, and others are sojourning in Chungking. Wherever they may have their dwelling, it is reasonable and just that they should be respected. Having issued this edict I expect that soldiers and civilians, all classes, will make its acquaintance. If after its issue there shall be any loafers at the place, sitting or lying around, using uproarious language, or should there be idlers and drunkards making trouble, they shall be punished severely and not pardoned. Let each one tremblingly obey, and by no means dare to rebel against this special edict. 13th year of Kwangsü, 4th moon, 6th day. Be certain to paste this upon the dwelling of the American teachers that all may be notified."

This is the way in which sleepy China governs a parcel of cowed children.

There was a gleam of light on the 2d of June, a sort of lifting up of the obstinate thick clouds and mists which had enveloped us in a wet bath ever since our arrival. It had not been cool nor hot, but a most disagreeable admixture of damp and heat sufficient to cover everything with mould. There is little wind in this province, except perhaps in high isolated places; to pass several days without the least rattling of windows and shutters, with scarcely breeze enough to change the direction of the smoke, is no uncommon occurrence. This is noticeable after a few days, but months of such quiet impress one strangely after coming from a windy quarter, and one longs for a north wind to shake things up and drive the lazy clouds over the mountains to Yun-nan or some other place; but the longing is in vain. The mountains wall the lower sections of the province on every side, shutting out the wind, but permitting an abundance of cloud and rain. I found the boatmen between Chung-king and Chentu afraid of the mildest sort of a breeze, such as sailors in the lower Yang-tsze would delight in and whistle for more. As soon as the water was a little ruffled these men wanted to pull for the shore and lie by. I suppose Fungshen and Lungshen [1] have had considerable trouble to agree over the ruling of wind and water, and the latter is now master of the situation. His namesake, the old Dragon, seems to have a firm grip upon the people, for a more debauched race cannot easily be found outside of Chungking. I am told that they are more tricky than other Chinese, less manly, and will take every conceivable advantage. My experience is not sufficient to settle the problem of their comparative morality. I failed to bring a microscope, and it is now too late to send for one in order to determine such minute quantities.

Taking advantage of the sudden gleam of day, chairs were ordered, and we hastened out of the city to visit the land purchased by our Mission for dwellings and hospital three or four miles distant. This lovely site is upon an isthmus or narrow neck of land half a mile in width. On the west the Kia-ling River is in full sight, and affords some charming views as it ripples slowly on, while to the east the river of Golden Sands bubbles, eddies, and dashes on, bound to be first at the point where they meet, six miles away. The Kia-ling seems in no hurry to make the acquaintance of the bustling Golden Sands, and it is right; for his snapping,

[1] Gods of wind and water.

dirty floods will sadly pollute the clearer snow waters of
the northwestern mountains. On the Kia-ling side our
land bordered upon an almost perpendicular cliff, and
did not require a wall; the great highway to Chenteu,
the capital, bounds the plot in front. A mammoth stone
archway spans the highway, and not half a mile beyond
towers a red sandstone crag called Fu-teu-kwan, which
is enclosed with ramparts and crowned with fortress-
like buildings. It is admirably fitted to enfilade the
approaches to Chungking by land or water, and
proved invaluable to the safety of the city during the
Mohammedan uprisings.

The view from this point is rarely surpassed; the
two beautiful streams flowing from opposite sides of the
province unite in plain sight six miles below. Beyond
the Golden Sands rise tier upon tier of beautiful green
peaks flecked here and there with white temples. On
either river are seen many lovely rural retreats. The
trees near at hand, and the well-cultivated fields bordering upon the city of the dead which covers the narrow
isthmus even up to the city gates, are in quiet contrast
to the rocky ledges and brown roofs. Ferns cluster
upon the damp rocks by the roadside; yellow, white,
and pink flowers lift their cheerful faces amidst the
homes of the forgotten dead; herds of cows followed
by frisking calves feed between the stone graves or
stand upon the higher mounds industriously chewing
their cuds,— a lovely rural scene not to be found in
Eastern China. The people of Chungking, and I suppose all over Sz-Chuan, especially where there are
Mohammedan settlements, use much milk and beef.
Cows with their calves are driven through the city and
into house courts to be milked. The milk is neither
weighed nor accurately measured : a fair-sized teacup

two thirds full costs about one cent. The master of the house or some servant watches the operation to see that no water mixed with bean-curd goes into the cup. There are no suburbs to the west of Chungking, except those of the dead, who are stowed in closer quarters than when living. There is nothing very peculiar about the tombs, mostly mounds a few feet high, surrounded or faced with hewn sandstone; there is now and then an exception where the decorations are good, but not equal to those seen a hundred miles to the east.

The half-finished houses upon the Mission site remain as the workmen left them; the rioters did not think it worth their while to disturb the solid blocks of stone of which the walls were built. All the perishable material has been removed, and Indian corn is now growing over the vacant land. Stones have been put up at convenient distances around the Compound, indicating it to be the property of the pa-hsien. A crowd of peasants gathered at the gateway, and the bolder ones ventured to follow us as we walked over the premises. It is difficult for the oldest missionary to comprehend fully the lurking suspicions of the ordinary Chinaman; they are bred in an atmosphere of distrust; they have little or no confidence in each other, put no trust in the promises of the officials, and why should they in us? It is only after personal experience with missionaries that the common people come to look upon them as different from their own teachers.

There are few temples of more than ordinary merit in the vicinity of Chungking, or any monuments that would attract particular attention. It is a commonplace town, busy and crowded, the streets crooked, narrow, and filthy. As a residence it holds out few inducements to the foreigner, as to climate or immediate surroundings.

Our residence is one of several connected with the family seat of the Lohs, " white horse with black mane." It was erected after the retirement of the elder Loh from public life in the province of Yun-nan, and intended for rent to men of means or officials temporarily out of office. It is a fair representative dwelling such as the higher classes of Sz-Chuan inhabit. It is at one end of the half-dozen half-inhabited houses belonging to the estate, which are closely connected by means of doors and passages, above and below. These comparatively genteel and commodious buildings are probably the result of the honest savings of Mr. and Mrs. Loh while in the Emperor's service in distant provinces, as a certain inscription gently hints. To reach our home from the narrow, stuffy street, we ascend a broad, steep terrace to the great central door, and pass through a broad covered court, or hall, without a floor ; on either side of this court are numerous banner-boards, painted red with gilt characters, such as are carried in procession when in office; a few new and old sedan chairs are packed in the northwest corner ; a beautiful cream-white pony, not much larger than a Shetland, rubs his head against one of the decaying pillars, while a shining black stallion paws the hard earth near by. We turn to the right, the old folding doors are thrown open, and we walk down a dark, damp passage ten feet wide ; at its end we are confronted with strong and lofty doors. Upon these is an amusing picture, the effect of which is nearly spoiled by its dismal position. It is a work of the imagination, representing an official of gigantic stature, with a beautiful female servant holding an immense fan-like shade over his head. His little son stands in front of the maid, holding a cup toward his father with outstretched hands. The scene is supposed to represent an official leading his son to court; the motto on the cup says, " Advance to office and take a drink." The doors are unbolted, and we enter an uncovered passage twelve feet wide, extending the whole length of the front of our house; on the left are the living rooms, school-room, etc., while on the right a street wall towers to the height of twenty feet, defending the house from thieves, and its occupants from much noise and filth. . Turning round I observe above the door just entered two square boards, with very appropriate texts for teachers and pupils, — selections from the ethical teachings of China's great modern philosopher, Chu. The left one as the door is entered is in the place of honor, and reads, "Doing good gives the greatest pleasure," the character for good being written in the centre. Here we have an evangel, the highest and best known to the Chinese, put in the most conspicuous place, that all may read as they go forth to a sordid, pitiless world. The second panel has as its central object the character for beauty or ornament, and above four small characters, as upon the first, saying to the pupils and teachers, " The pursuit of literature gives the highest adornment."

Leaving this classical and unpretentious corner, as we enter the first court the doorposts tell us that " These are halls of the Wu-tung trees, and splendid as phœnixes, and that there are stages of willow bright as parrots." Upon examining the oiled wood panels we find two or three rows of carved characters painted green, and the astounding statement that " Titles and emoluments of office are all within reach; " and " We are leaders of fashion and literary elegance; " and this wish: " May we be still higher in respect and gratified with joyful years of abundance." The artist has done his best to portray the vanity and longings of this family, which is representative of all the wealthy and titled ones. We look above the great doors opening to the "fountain of heaven," and espy a tablet twelve feet by six, the groundwork blue, with square bits of gold foil splashed on irregularly. The end inscription says that Mrs. Loh has been created a lady of the first rank — "Manchurian Crane" — by order of the Emperor. The tablet itself was a birthday gift from her admiring neighbors soon after her return from a foreign province to the old homestead, and presumably after her husband's death. The large gold characters in the centre inform admiring visitors that it is a "birthday congratulation to a gentle lady ; " a patent of nobility conferred upon her by the Emperor. A secret is told us by the side scrolls : " Your taxes from goods and rental of lands ought to be equal to your government salary in Nan," meaning Yun-nan, the province he served. This sentence really says, " You enriched yourself while in government employ." Again, " We rejoice that you are home again as of yore. Now in your new and airy abode, near by the humdrum of a common world, be careful, and know there is much distress in the market-place," — a broad hint from the rejoicing friends that she should remember that there are poor and needy near her living in humble abodes, and that a generous hand would be appreciated.

Entering the guest-hall we are treated to tropes and hyperbole in a lordly fashion : " His was a golden pen streaming light as the sun." " May you rejoice in flowered robes and your halls be opened to the fifth generation ; may royal favors be received, and your blessings be as the abundance of a thousand autumns." Upon the front side panels, the dedicator becomes most extravagant in his metaphors: " A mighty pen he had, like to the nine phœnix towers." " He was a great bell, like to that of a fire-dragon tiger-belfry," — such as are capable of swinging a bell of a million two hundred thousand catties' weight. " Mandarin ducks in the pond and gold fish in the tussel-weed." " Pines and cypresses having hearts, bamboos having skins."

The last two sentences bring up a pleasant picture seen in the grounds of almost any well-appointed gentleman's house. Who has not watched the beautiful ducks plunging from grassy banks to artificial lakes, and the variegated goldfish in the miniature ponds in the rockeries, glancing through the bright light-green tussel-weed ? There are many side-rooms opening into the guest-hall and the interior court, but all are without floors, or windows except in front, and are consequently cheerless, cold, and dark in winter, and damp and mouldy in summer.

On the south side of the court, above the tall and gaudily painted doors, is a narrow board covered with bright frescos. It is a vivid representation of the God of Longevity, seated upon a white crane skimming over the ocean, and on either side are the eight dulia or genii, standing upon great fish and fabulous monsters. The God of Longevity, often called Nan-kih-chuen, is supposed to live in the south polestar, which is reckoned the star of longevity. He is thought to be able to lengthen the life of an individual, and is said to send his spirit crane with some talisman or token. When this is received by a person about to die, his life may be lengthened ten or more years. His eight associates were all Taoists or Ascetics of some note in their day ; they flourished here and there during the past two thousand years; were Taoist cranks, professing to have attained immortality, and believed by the common people to have been spirited away to the skies, where they now live practising their meritorious arts. They are endowed, of course, with supersensuous powers, and are able to revisit the earth, bringing blessings of every conceivable character. We see these demi-gods, both male and female, — as two of them are considered feminine, — painted and carved upon houses, doors, beds, chairs, and all works of art in porcelain, silk, stone monuments, etc.

Above the great guest-hall is another painting, which at first sight would appear to portray different fruits, flowers, and insects merely to please the artistic taste. Not so; every flower, fruit, insect, bird, and animal has a symbolic meaning. There are the great white cranes of immortality, holding in their beaks branches to which are clinging ripe peaches, — a symbol of eternal existence; the deer with a bell is a symbol of high office; the pomegranate with its pink and rosy seeds pressing out, a symbol of a large and happy family; while the grape symbolizes an unbroken posterity; the Buddha's hand (a sort of lemon), the peach, and lotus are all symbols of long life and happiness; the melon, watermelon, and butterfly represent long-continued prosperity; water-chestnuts indicate conjugal felicity; and the swallow is the harbinger of good luck. There are many other similar symbolical objects on the panel, chiefly flowers and insects. An inquiry into the origin of these symbolic ideas and their present influence upon Chinese life would be very pleasant and not altogether unprofitable.

The *lares*, which are sometimes connected with a dwelling, are gathered in the ancestral hall and receive ample attention; the *penates* are gone, even to the kitchen god, and there is no faithful smoke-begrimed image to report our cook's misdoings to the Pearly Emperor on high; so he may " squeeze " to his heart's content. I notice over our cook's door four characters with a pleasant-enough meaning, but not what I fancy a foreign lady would allow to occupy so conspicuous a place, — “ peh-wu-kin-kih,” “just as you please here.” I have been puzzling my head to know what the meek man means; does he intend to say that it is a public place, a communistic hall ? He may mean that he can furnish dishes to suit all tastes, or that the cook has liberty to do as he likes.

I will leave the reader to a quiet soliloquy upon Chinese ways and means; but in all the house there is not a room really suited to living purposes, — all are dark, badly ventilated, damp, and sepulchral.

8

CHAPTER VI.

Two weeks after our arrival in Chungking, Mr. Faber engaged a native boat, for twenty-eight dollars, to take him to Kia-ting-foo, three hundred miles up the Golden Sands and the Min Rivers. He was to go two hundred miles to Su-cheu-foo, and there, leaving the main branch of the Yang-tsze, called the Golden Sands, work his way up to the rivers Ya and Tung, which empty into the Min at Kia-ting-foo ; from thence proceed to Omei hsien and the great mountain near by, for a month's rest in a cooler temperature than could be found in the plain. He was a month on the journey, but made the time profitable in large sales of books and many additions to his valuable botanical collection. It was decided that Dr. Morley and the writer should go overland in sedan chairs to Chenteu-foo, the capital of the province, and from thence by water and chair to Mount Omei, and there join Mr. Faber.

The journey was undertaken for several purposes, the chief of which were to mingle among the people throughout the populous districts ; to test their present temper and attitude toward foreigners ; to obtain as much knowledge as possible of the cities, country, and centres likely to be occupied by our own and other churches· as mission stations ; to disseminate religious literature ; to recruit my own health ; and to satisfy my longing to see the provincial capital and look upon the "Glory of Buddha" on the top of Mount Omei. With such motives we made our arrangements to leave in five weeks from the time we reached Chungking, or at such time as the rainy season would permit. Up to the 26th of June we had incessant clouds and rain; but the rainbow of promise at last spanned the watery elements, and by the morning of the 27th all our preparations were completed. It is needless to say we took an affectionate and reluctant adieu of Mr. H. O. Cady, who was to remain lord of the mansion, and hold at any cost our new position, being the sole representative of the great Methodist Episcopal Church, with her hundreds of earnest young men who are ready to come to the front at the first opportunity.

It was no ordinary responsibility for a missionary to assume the first year of his service; but we are taught that it is a good thing to bear the yoke in youth, and endure hardness. There is nothing which tries the heroic spirit more than a struggle with the Mongolian tongue in the hot days of July and August. He bore the separation like an old soldier, and did good service.

At last our chairs were in fine trim, the finishing touches being long blue cotton awnings stretched fore and aft and tied to bamboo sticks which raised them a few inches above the tops of the chairs. This precaution against the sun is very general in Sz-Chuan, and, as our future experience proved, is of great value. The baskets were well crammed with choice illustrated religious literature, and carefully weighed, that each man should have a fair burden,— eighty catties, or one hundred and six pounds, being the limit.

The magistrate sent an escort of four men for the first stage of sixty miles,— a poor enough looking bodyguard, about as hard a lot as could be picked up, but able to march at the head of the retinue and clear a way through crowded streets. They saluted us upon their bended knees as we took our sedans, and trotted on before us into the narrow street, screaming and swaggering, greatly exalted by the importance of their new mission.

It was seven A. M., 27th of June, when we took up our line of march ; the streets were half submerged in water, and no wonder; for the heavens had poured out watery floods for nearly fifty days. The weather was too oppressively hot to allow of walking with any degree of comfort, so we kept to our close sedans and a continual steam-bath.

The thermometer at nine A.M. stood at 82° in the shade, — a moderate temperature for this latitude, — but the moisture from above and the steam from below makes one most uncomfortable.

When we were once out of the squalid streets and sickening smells, and had passed the gates into the open country, we traversed one of the largest and most interesting highways found in China, — wide, well paved, and busy.

Coming thus from the noisy, begrimed city into the open, green country was a delightful relief, and the eyes wearied not of the manifold beauties of hill and vale. The two beautiful rivers, now greatly swollen, were in full view for some distance ; but by degrees they were widely sundered, and only the regular mountain ranges which wall the Golden Sands on the east indicated to us its winding course.

An hour and a half took us past the Fu-teu-kwan, " Pagoda gateway," and the fortress which commands the approaches to the city. Its quaint form and lofty elevation make it a conspicuous and interesting object. Its abrupt, rocky sides have been chiselled and fashioned by the Buddhist priests. Large, well-modelled stone Buddhas, painted and variously adorned, are seen in the higher niches of the cliff. Buddhas half completed, hewn from solid rock lower 'down, with other carvings of a religious character, consecrate the rock to Buddha rather than to Mars.

Vegetation is luxuriant, of almost tropical growth; the trees are living green, free from insects, and without any kind of blight or deformity. We ride through groves of pine and past fruit-orchards; through endless fields of millet and rice, surrounded with hedges of beans in full bloom, — some with white and pink, and others with clusters of rich yellow blossoms. Massive stone arches span the road at prominent points, dedicated by filial sons, by Imperial edict, to their mothers, who had lived many years of virtuous widowhood, and died beloved and honored by the family. They are perhaps superior in design and execution to those found in some other provinces, but not so different as to call for any particular description. The material employed is largely soft gray sandstone, quarried everywhere and easily worked. The panels and parts on which there are flowers and figures carved in relief are of marble, delicately fitted and highly polished.

Some half-demolished buildings belonging to the Catholics were pointed out to us a short distance from the roadway ten miles west of Chungking; it may have been a college or summer resort.

The scenery becomes more inviting as we advance, and early in the afternoon we ascend an irregular range of hills eight hundred feet higher than the surrounding country. Here we had our farewell view of the " Wenfung " pagoda, east of Chungking, and the old fortress called " Pagoda gateway." There are indigo and tobacco upon the hills, and an occasional field of a peculiar cereal called by the natives *wo-chang-pai*, "goose-palm tare," on account of the peculiar shape of the root and the grain head when grown. The stalk is very thick and reaches about two feet in height, the head being shaped something like the cockscomb, and the berry yellow. It is only used by the very poorest people. Orange plantations are seldom seen on the overland journey, being grown largely along the rivers, and especially upon the Golden Sands, between Su-cheu-foo and Chungking. The oranges are not as sweet as those from Canton, but so plentiful that a dozen may be bought for one cent. There are few signs of want, and the fields are covered with luxuriant crops; the houses are generally of one story, mud walls, whitewashed, and surrounded by other walls of the same material. There is an air of cleanliness and tidiness about the yards and houses which contrasts favorably with many other sections of China. The people are not by any means immaculately clean, nor their homes paragons of order, yet there is a decided improvement in these respects over some portions of Eastern China.

The hotels along the main roads in this province are somewhat noted for their elegance and comfort. Our first night's experience was not altogether encouraging; the house was pretentious in appearance, and the room of honor, in which officials and wealthy men have feasted and slept for many years, was delegated to us. The unpretentious rooms on either side of the narrow but very long court, leading straight up from the street past kitchen and dining courts to our room, were filled at an early hour by poorer travellers. The court itself was crowded with chairs and baggage, while half-naked coolies were running hither and thither before settling to a bath and the opium-pipe. Unclean water was dashed right and left from the walks along the fronts of the rooms into the centre of the stone-paved court. Everything was in commotion as we arrived, and a few minutes later the regular disorder grew into a mob, which continued until our faint tallow dip expired. Travellers were hustling each other to get the best rooms; coolies threw down their burdens anywhere for the moment, sat down at the tables, drew forth their old palm-fans, and sipped wretched tea until they recovered sufficient strength to take their packs inside. Then followed ablutions from tubs all along the stone court between the guest-rooms. Hot water was in demand along the whole line, and half-naked waiters rushed in and around the naked phalanx bearing pails of steaming water. Other waiters were running to guests with tea-cups and large teakettles with long noses. One traveller after another settled to his board bed in the windowless rooms, the stenches of which are unbearable to a foreigner. The coolies, ten or more crowded into rooms barely large enough to give them space for their mats, smoked opium and chatted until midnight, while the crowd from the street pressed into every available corner to watch the queer motions of their illustrious guests. We rode up to the end of the court, and stepped from the chairs into our room, and a screen was drawn in front of it a few feet from the door, to hide us from the eyes of the crowd, which followed us from the street. It requires a good guard to beat back the boys and girls who press around the sides of the screen. The teacher and " boys " were busy for a time in persuading the curious to fall back so as to give the tired foreign gentlemen fresh air and quiet. Our room, although the best, is stiflingly close, windowless, damp, and covered with mould, with a thick crust of wet dirt upon the old, half-rotten floor.

Some happy guests had scribbled verses and wise sayings thickly over the once whitewashed walls. Their effusions were evidently written in the autumn, when a friendlier air and more wholesome odors circulated in the open court from whence came all our air and light. Mosquitoes and fleas, the bane of summer travel, hunted us up at an early hour, and abode with us till the morning. It was late at night before sleep visited my eyelids, and then but for a troubled moment, the only recollection of which was a tormenting dream. Fancy led me to a great gathering of some sort in the far-away land, where old and familiar faces greeted me as I wandered from point to point. Making a call upon some old-time friends, I suddenly found myself swarming with insects having horns and stings, some creeping, others flying, but all intent on tormenting me. In despair I tore my hair and clutched the enemies from my body and dashed them upon the floor and stamped upon them, vowing that I had spent my last night at a temperance hotel. I awoke to find it all a dream. A story told me the day before about a missionary travelling through these parts may have had something to do with my nervous sensitiveness. He arose at midnight to wage war upon the creeping hosts, and actually caught forty-two, — the vanguard, I surmise, of an irresistible army.

Mr. Hosie, British consular agent, gives his experience at another inn somewhere in this province : —

"Now that I am on the subject of Chinese inns I cannot do better than give a Chinaman's own ideas on the point. It is the custom of those who can write to scribble verses on the walls of their rooms. These verses are often amusing, and they frequently contain plays on characters. Others,

again, are written in praise of the inn ; but I found one to-day
in the room in which I breakfasted so much in accordance
with my own experience that I cannot refrain from repro-
ducing it in English garb. It should be mentioned, too, that
the inn was decidedly superior to the average. The verse
runs thus : —

‘ Within this room you ’ll find the rats,
　At least a goodly score ;
Three catties each they ’re bound to weigh,
　Or e’en a little more.
At night you ’ll feel a myriad bugs,
　That stink and crawl and bite ;
If doubtful of the truth of this,
　Get up and strike a light.’

“ There may be a little exaggeration of weights and numbers, but the lines are a faithful attempt to portray a part of
the truth. Had the author given us eight more lines on mosquitoes and odors, the picture would have been tolerably
complete.”

The similarity of the Sz-Chuanese to the Cantonese
has been frequently noticed by other travellers. Just
how vivid the likeness may be to the rural populations
of western Kwangtung is unknown to me, but it is certain that many men here do resemble in feature and
expression the Cantonese seen in the eastern province.
There is no doubt, if the records of the seventeenth century are to be relied upon, that after the immense destruction of life at the close of the last dynasty there
was a great influx from that and other provinces, so
that the present population is to a great extent of semi-
foreign extraction.

The customs of the people differ largely from those
of other provinces, and in a measure from district to
district within this province. I judge there is more
independence on the part of the women and a better

division of labor. Very few women are seen in the fields, but many upon the highways, with children, tramping to and from fairs at the market-towns. I was greatly pleased, however, to see them, dressed in bright colors, heads neatly adorned, and with more grace of carriage than is usually seen in the Chinese woman, pacing along singly or in companies, with their husbands or sons bearing the babies and little ones strapped securely to their backs. I seemed to detect in their cheerful faces and their condescending behavior to their lords that they were well pleased to show off their importance in public as well as in private. I hope the fashion of this locality will become epidemic, and woman receive her just deserts all over the old empire. The country ladies and small children wear head-dresses and trousers of white home-made cotton cloth, beautifully ornamented with black braid or silk thread, while little boys and girls have frocks ingeniously embroidered upon the shoulders, bosoms, and sleeves. There is a great deal of this kind of ornamental work throughout the province; men wear girdles and large money-purses or tobacco-pouches similarly ornamented. Between Yung-Chang and Lung-Chang districts I saw in the little country shops a variety of small trinkets, such as money-purses, ties, and girdles of silk in the natural color.

At Yung-Chang, ninety miles from Chungking, we crossed the first stream of any note; it is a broad, swift river, and empties into the Yang-tsze, or Golden Sands, at Lu-cheu. It is navigable for small boats, but in low water rocks and rapids make the navigation difficult. There is a very fine stone bridge in the immediate vicinity of the city, one hundred paces long. Coal-fields are of frequent occurrence all the way from Chungking to Lung-Changhsien, a distance of four hundred li.

The coal is transported largely by land, and upon the backs of oxen and cows or coolies; cumbersome frames, to which are attached two strong hampers, are lashed to the backs of the cattle; each animal bears about three hundred pounds of bright bituminous coal. The roads are very uneven and now very wet, but the animals were unshod; they wear, however, as a usual thing, tight straw sandals which come up over their hoofs.

The country continues prosperous; is, if anything, in a more flourishing condition than farther back, and shows no signs of former rebellions, such as we see in Central and Eastern China. There are large market-towns every thirty li, with many villages between, and hamlets scattered everywhere over the face of the country. The last two nights we have been lodged in very comfortable *kungkwans*, quarters attached to hotels for official travellers. Our last night's kungkwan is said to be the best in the province, and I can easily believe it, for in the dim past it was once richly carved and lacquered and well floored. Although gilded and garnished, it proved a veritable paradise for rats, which, after eating up the remnants of a chicken, betook themselves to Dr. Morley's bed, squealing and rooting about in the straw during the night; but his sleep was too sound to be disturbed, even by such uncanny companions.

Leaving the main road to Chenteu at Lung-Chang we turned to the southwest, toward the great natural brine-wells called *Tsz-liu-tsin*, two days' journey distant. We rode through the city and suburbs in the early dawn, before there was much activity apparent; but from the width of the streets and the size of the buildings I judge the city to be in a thriving condition. We skirted a small river awhile, but soon left it, striking off among the luxuriant paddy-fields. We could trace the main road for some distance as it stretched over the hills to the northwest, its course being indicated by large stone arches.

Our present road was considered somewhat unsafe; and the magistrate thoughtfully added 'to our escort, and evidently enjoined upon the men the necessity of extra precaution. The valley soon gave way to hills, and the scenery became wilder and prettier; groves of pine covered the white sand-hills, which afforded us some relief from the fierce rays of the sun. The farm-houses also partook of the wilder aspect of the country, and unwhitewashed, hid themselves in leafy bowers. The hill-fields were covered with hemp, sugar-cane, and *kaoliang*, a sort of broom-corn. In the lower land, where water is plentiful, there were rice-fields, but the plants were badly blighted and eaten by a peculiar worm.

Thirty li from the city we came to the busy market-town of Hwangkiachang. It happened to be the market day, and there was a plethora of humanity struggling in every available quarter. The country roads were all alive with men and women, rushing into the town bearing their little gleanings from the fields and the products of their clumsy handicrafts. Old men and women, side by side, carried eggs, chickens, ducks, pigs, ginger-root, pease, plums, apples, and balls of very fine hemp thread. This region, I find, is a sort of rival to the province of Kiangsi in the production of grass-cloth; it is, if anything, of better quality, and far more reasonable in price. This is also a centre for the manufacturing of cane sugar of a very good quality. It is exported in large quantities, and sells for four and five cents a pound. Orange-groves became frequent as we neared a town called Niu-foo-teu. Another article of some interest I saw carried to town with a string tied around its neck; namely, smoked dog. It was impossible to determine the breed, which was rather small, thoroughly dried, and smoked black. I found by inquiry that it brought from six to seven cents a pound in the market, and was considered a great delicacy for the sick and a wonderfully strengthening tonic. We lunched in a long straggling town called Lung-shih-pu, but our quarters were so wretched we were glad to hurry back to the street and the broiling sun. The highway from this point becomes decidedly interesting and thronged with salt-carriers. A portion of the salt manufactured at Tsz-liu-tsin is distributed to the inland towns by these carriers. It is borne in mat bags covered with oil paper, the sides being often protected with large thick leaves; each carrier bears from one hundred and twenty to one hundred and fifty pounds.

It was four P. M. as we descended through plantations of orange and other fruit-bearing trees, to the not too hospitable town of Niu-foo-teu. We took up our quarters at a dilapidated tea-shop near the centre of the place, said to be the best in the city; but it was a doubtful story, for in a roundabout way I heard that an official was occupying the larger establishment. The weather was hot, and our room small, dark, and saturated with irremediable odors. It is bad enough to have the front of a room border upon the drains and the coolies' restaurant, while the sides open into opium dens filled with naked smokers; but to have a huge pigsty on the back, and be separated from a score of pigs merely by a gaping board-partition a half-inch in thickness, and then have one's bed snug against said partition, is enough to make a strong-minded man quail at the nocturnal prospect. It seems scarcely reasonable to expect the gentle goddess of art to receive much patronage from so slovenly a proprietor as ours, or that her bewitching grace should be invited to such a den; yet in the dim light of evening we saw two or three passable pictures, and one of conspicuous merit, reaching almost from ceiling to floor. At right angles to it, strange to say, was a religious picture, — a scene from the New Testament: "A sower went forth to sow," etc. The shopman had purchased it from some Christian colporteur; perhaps from the Russian, Mr. Molliman, who sold books here some years ago, and who I was told came near losing his life by an infuriated mob. I was glad to find the picture and the Scripture account in a place where so many travellers will see and read it.

No doubt many of the books sold by missionaries and Bible agents are destroyed by fire or put one side and never read. I traversed a city not long since, and made a large sale of Scriptures and tracts, and was much encouraged at the thought of so many eager buyers perusing these books. But my zeal was somewhat damped on my return to see a bright bonfire in a public place, and men busily feeding it with the very books I had sold. Pictures fare much better; the women and children are greatly pleased with them, and have them mounted and hung upon their walls. The fumes from opium-pipes, and from certain other quarters, are demoralizing; and the short red taper, which gives but a feeble light at best, flutters on the brink of annihilation, and I now betake myself to the couch of honor by the pigsty.

CHAPTER VII.

China lays claim to few works of antiquity; and these are useful, rude, and simple, rather than artistic or scientific in character. The building of the Great Wall required little or no engineering skill, and the same may be said of the Grand Canal. Civil engineering is unknown, as the roads and water-ways prove; and as there has ever been a want of trained artisans, no industry has made any considerable advance beyond its first rude conception.

Every branch of ancient industry is known, however, in a clumsy way, but nothing is perfected. Perhaps of all the ancient or modern works, the boring and working of the great salt-wells, called Tsz-liu-tsin, "self-flowing wells," have made the greatest demands on Chinese ingenuity and perseverance. No one can visit this remarkable section of Sz-Chuan, and see the operation of this ancient industry, without feeling more respect for the people who designed and executed an undertaking on so prodigious a scale sixteen centuries ago.

These great brine and fire wells are five hundred and eighty li, or one hundred and seventy-five miles, from Chungking. The most convenient way to reach them is to leave the provincial road at Lung-chang, four hundred li from Chungking, and travel southwest one hundred and eighty li. They are upon the left bank of an affluent of the Yang-tsze, two hundred and forty li from the point of junction. The little river is navigable, and a large fleet of small boats ply incessantly up and down, bringing bamboo for piping, and transporting a large portion of the salt to Lu-cheu, a large city at the mouth of the river.

The day was intensely hot as we skirted along a little river flowing between gently undulating hills. We dreaded leaving a shady nook, where we halted for a few moments by the side of a rock on which the monks had chiselled a house for the gods, now overgrown with trees, brambles, and flowering shrubs; but at last plucking up courage we started, and after winding through rich valleys, came to a high hill from which, ten miles away, upon a smooth, table-like ridge, a great number of wooden frames or towers loomed up against the sky. It was the most un-Chinese view imaginable; nothing of the sort had been seen elsewhere in the empire. The *chaitsz*, or city of refuge, occupied the brow of the hill, and by the afternoon light was magnified to undue proportions. Passing to the left of this, we wound around the foot of the hills, crossing a number of deep crevasses, the waters of which emitted strong gaseous odors. We rode through village after village, and picked our way through squads of salt-carriers and their burdens in tunnelled tea-shops. At last, after some two hours' hard work, we emerged from these successive hills, tunnels, and windings, and reached a point where the shipping and lower part of the straggling town could be seen. It was still early when we entered the city, which is exceptionally hilly, the streets seeming almost perpendicular. They are narrow and crowded, and blocked in some places with thousands of large bamboo poles, in process

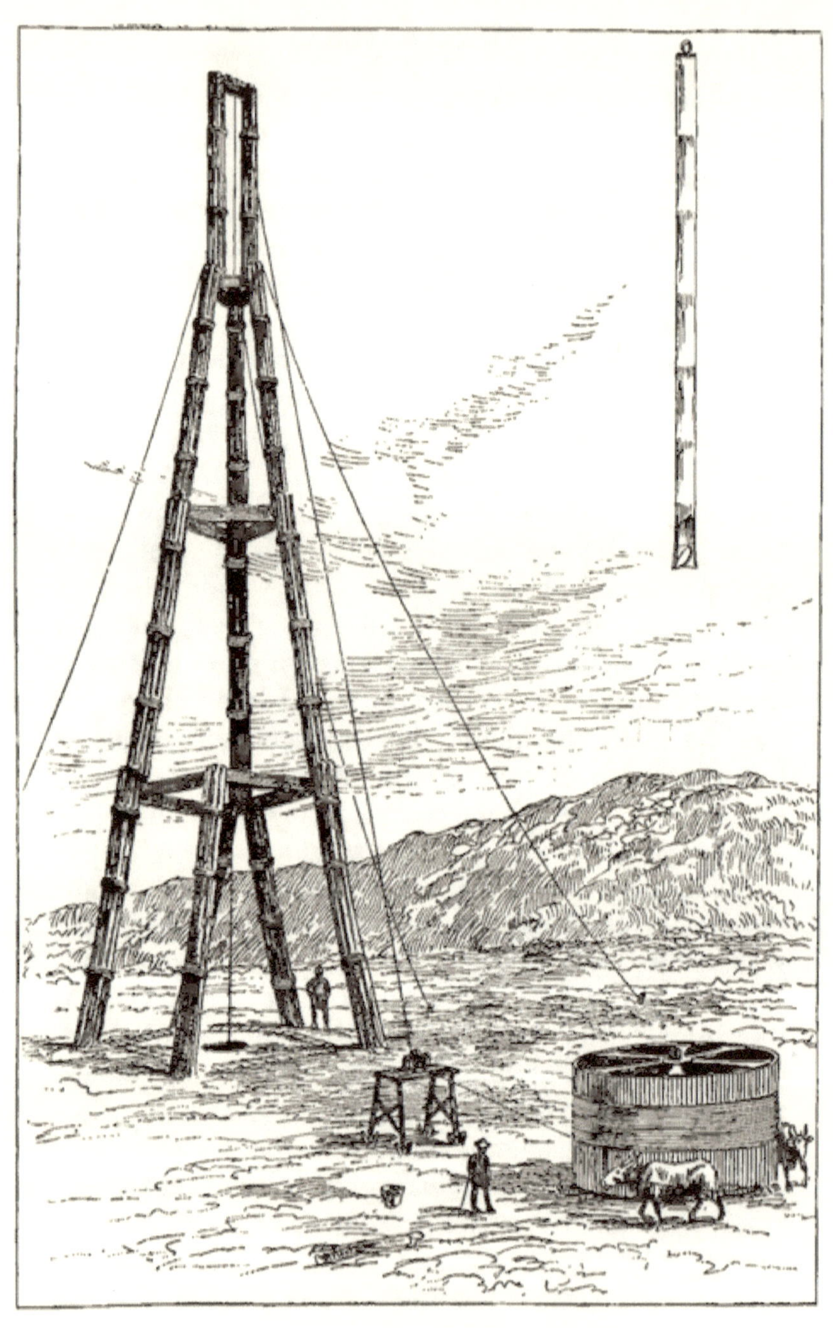

A BRINE-WELL IN OPERATION.

of preparation for brine and gas conductors. I noticed limestone for the first time in two hundred miles, and this a mere ledge between red, gray, and greenish sandstone deposits. There is an appearance of wealth and business prosperity not seen in other towns: the people are better dressed and very orderly; the shops are larger, and a number of them are well stocked with a great variety of foreign articles. The bustle and push seen on every hand bespeak a wide-awake and money-making people. I had sent my teacher ahead to secure lodgings for the night, and as we reached the centre of the town he made his appearance much excited because the hotels had refused to receive foreigners, fearing that the rush of people who would come to inspect the strange animals would injure their business.

A halt was made in the square, where several streets converge, and a council held; while we debated the measures to be adopted, the crowd momentarily increased, and became somewhat excited. Just then the bright idea of marching our exhausted coolies half a mile up a steep hill, to the branch magisterial office, flashed through the head of our Honan teacher. The order was given; and with many groans and no little cursing our jaded men lifted their heavy burdens to their shoulders, and with the aid of our escort a path was made through the dense crowd. The street was closely packed with sight-seers all the way to the yamen, and when the outer court was reached an unruly mob took full possession of it, leaving little space for our chairs.

This abrupt and unceremonious advent was no fault of our own, as an official messenger had preceded us to notify the magistrate of our coming; the fault lay between the messenger and the secretary of the yamen. We sent our cards to the magistrate, and when a proper time had elapsed and we received no answer, our teacher and our escort threw open the great doors to the guest-hall, and conducting us in with much ceremony, bolted the doors behind us in the faces of the mob. The menials about the yamen were no less surprised than the roaring crowd by this sudden and successful manœuvre.

As usual on such occasions, the official was "not in town," though probably not twenty paces from us. Meantime we occupied the seats in the cool guest-hall as composedly as if in a wayside tea-shop, laughing inwardly at the turn affairs had taken through the stubbornness of the hotel-keepers and the unnecessary fright of our writer and escort; the din of many voices resounded from the outer court, while the secretary and underlings rushed in and out receiving instructions from the *absent* official. Tea was brought, and we sipped it leisurely, keeping up a running conversation with the secretary and our writer. The latter was determined to carry things with a high hand, and insisted that the guest-hall should be turned into a bed and dining room for the honored guests. The secretary pleaded that it was impossible, and that they were alarmed for our safety, of course. As the officials had volunteered to give us protection on the journey, and were rather jealous of the prerogative, my mind was very easy, knowing full well that having possession of the yamen, a hotel would be secured in due time. A messenger was despatched by the secretary to the largest tea-shop to have the best room put at our disposal. He also sent secret messengers to the camp, and made a sudden parade of soldiers through the streets, and ordered five to act as guards to our lodging. Increasing our escort with his own men, he gave each one a rawhide whip consisting of several thongs, and paraded them at the great door, ready to make a sudden plunge into the crowd when we were seated in our chairs.

We exchanged the proper compliments with the trembling secretary, took possession of our chairs, and at a word the doors were opened and the charge was made in fine style. The whips played right and left into the ranks of timid men and women, who would give the last cash in the sleeve to have one square gaze at us. I bent forward and wreathed my face with all the smiles in my possession, but found it tiresome business during the last half-mile. I felt rewarded, however, it gave such delight to the closely packed mass of bent heads and fixed eyes ; it is easy to be a martyr if by it thousands are made happy. Leaving the busy street in the middle of the town we turned into a long, wide corridor, which led to the square in front of our rooms ; guards stood at the gate, and the obstinate proprietor, now in his right mind, met us with all his blandishments of manner. Several merchants, some being from distant provinces, stood at the entrances of their side-rooms as we came to the front, and the escort assisted the " great men " from their chairs to their room.

There is no doubt about the importance of this town ; the presence of a thousand bankers from Shansi (nearly all the bankers of Sz-Chuan are from that province), and many hundreds of merchants from Kiangsi, and thousands of business men from other parts of China show the magnitude of the trade centred here. A strong military force is maintained to guard the government interest in the salt trade. The young official was very considerate of our welfare, sending in great haste cushions and hangings for the straight-backed chairs.

The lofty wooden frames previously mentioned as seen ten miles away are but a few of the innumerable ones scattered throughout the city and for many miles into the country. These frames are usually constructed of rough trees tightly withed and wedged together. The first story has five sections, the second four, the third three, the last being made of two perpendicular timbers, with a strong cross-beam, surmounted by a large hardwood wheel or pulley-block, over which the long rope is drawn up and lowered in the process of raising the water. They are from sixty to one hundred and sixty feet in height, varying according to the depth of the wells or the bamboo tubing which brings up the brine to the surface. Each frame is the product of many scores of small trees, spliced and tightly withed, tapering in size from bottom to top, as the rough sketch indicates.

Single and double lines of pipe, made from very large bamboos, — nicely jointed and covered with hemp and pitch, — run from the brine vats near by the wells, either upon the ground or upon high trestles, through the suburbs to the country wells to conduct the brine to the boiling factories. There are also similar pipes to convey the gas from point to point as needed. The huge frames, the myriads of ropes stretching from them in every direction, the numerous aqueducts leading from a thousand wells, the broad low buildings above the wells, and the factories are the outward expression of a vast industry, second perhaps to none in China. A hasty glance at one of the medium-sized wells, the process by which it is worked, and certain facts relating to the industry in general, I am sure will be of more than common interest to the reader.

It may be well to say that wells of great depth have been operated for at least sixteen centuries and possibly twenty. It is recorded in the biographies of the Taoist popes of Lunghu-san, in the province of Kiangsi, that the first pope, in the first century of our era, was called to make a journey to Sz-Chuan to cast out evil spirits from the salt-wells. We are not positive that these particular wells are the ones referred to, but from the fact that inflammable gas issues from some of the borings, it is quite probable that these are the identical wells. These are all artesian fountains, found at different depths. It would be impossible to find out the number of wells which have been in operation at different times : no doubt many thousands, but not above one thousand are in active operation at the present time. A well that flows to-day may be dry to-morrow, and continue so for days or even years, when it will be renewed ; or one that yielded twenty thousand pounds of water per day twenty years ago may not give one fourth this amount now ; the quantity varies, and the length of time for the flowing is very erratic.

It may seem incredible that seventeen hundred years ago the Chinese of Sz-Chuan possessed sufficient mechanical skill and enterprise to bore through the solid rock to the depth of from two to five thousand feet. A few hundred feet would not seem so remarkable, even when we take into account the primitive methods of their mining, and how easily they are discouraged by small disasters in obtaining coal, iron, copper, and other minerals ; but they have surely made a remarkable exhibition of genius, patience, and pluck in what they have done in these brine-wells.

These wells, but six inches in diameter, worked piecemeal through rocks to such depths, and by comparatively clumsy appliances, present a stronger argument to my own mind in favor of the latent power of this race than do their walls and canals. I was told by a number of intelligent aged men that the wells varied from

a few tens of feet to four hundred chang, of twelve
Chinese feet, deep, or that the deepest were 5,900 English feet.

To convince myself of the accuracy of their statements, I visited a medium-sized well within the town.
Mr. Wang, the proprietor, is a very intelligent and
wealthy gentleman, and has charge of forty such wells.
The bamboo tube was in process of lifting as we entered
the establishment and took our places near the swiftly
running rope. After a few minutes the tube came to
view, and was lifted to the top of the frame, and the
contents, about two hundred catties of strong gaseous
fluid, discharged into a receptacle, and carried by an
aqueduct to the great vat. The gas from the mouth of
the well was so strong when the tube was lifted that we
had to move away. The water-buffaloes, three in number, were now unhitched, and the tube replaced. The
great horizontal wheel unwound the rope very slowly at
first, but after a few seconds the celerity was so great
that we had to stand at some distance from the wheel
and hold our hats on. The manager said the well was
two hundred and forty chang deep, and that there was
two and a half li of rope attached to the bamboo tube
or pump. We now stood by the wheel, — a horizontal
one, — about twenty-two feet in diameter. The fresh
buffaloes were urged to their best speed ; and in about
twenty minutes, or perhaps a little less, all the rope was
upon the wheel, — fifty-one complete turns of, say, sixty-
six feet each = 3,366 feet, — a little less than the
amount stated by the manager. As the layers were one
above the other, the deficiency, if any, was thereby made
good. It has been stated by some one that the buffaloes
are soon used up by the severe work, and consequently
a very heavy item of expense. It may be so, but being

changed, as they are, every half-hour, I see no reason for any unusual mortality among them.

No doubt the methods and machinery used to-day are the same as centuries ago. If rude and clumsy, compared with those employed in Western lands, entailing much loss of time, and in the end more expensive than modern machinery, it cannot be denied that the Chinese have, in their own fashion, reached quite as remarkable results as have those of the West.

The accompanying diagram, although rough, will help to illustrate the process. A piece of wrought iron some fourteen feet long, with a sharp steel flange at the bottom, is the first section of the instrument for breaking the rock, being lifted and worked as seen in the drawing, by four or eight men, as needed. As the boring becomes deeper, other rods are securely attached, as seen in the right of the diagram, and bound tightly together by elastic bamboo splints, which allow the ends of the iron rods to strike gently together. A heavy weight is attached to the lever and increased as the boring proceeds.

Time is of little consequence to the ordinary Chinaman in the usual pursuits of life; and an enterprise, if brought to a successful issue within a generation or two, is considered satisfactory. But here his patience and faith have been cruelly taxed. The time and expense have been great drawbacks in sinking the deeper wells. It is no unusual thing to be thirty and forty years boring one well; and a change of owners often takes place, the originators using up all their capital, and turning over their interests contingent upon success.

I hinted to the manager that foreign machinery would be less expensive and more effective. After our departure he sent and brought the owner from his country villa to visit us; he had with him his son and several neighbors. When I asked him how long he had been in the salt business, he laughed heartily, and said with dignity, " Ever since the first Emperor of the Min dynasty ; for twenty generations, sir." I could scarcely suppress a feeling of admiration for the aged aristocrat as he stroked his long gray beard, and showed in his face evident signs of family pride and self-complacency over the remarkable success which had crowned their efforts. Not all the kings and princes sit upon thrones of state. Some one has said: " There is, however, among all nations, savage as well as civilized, another nobility, — the divine nobility of goodness and genius, — which often places one man many centuries in advance of the common crowd."

This tall form and benignant face impressed me as many ages in advance of the common herd around us. His good-looking son, dressed in rich silk, wore upon his breast a silver watch, — the envy of many and a treasure never dreamed of by his forefathers. He was anxious to journey at once to Shanghai and take immediate steps to import foreign machinery and bore a number of wells, but the elder men thought that such a course would bring upon them a great deal of opposition from the other companies.

The following facts given by the gentlemen connected with the " Well of Abundance," which we visited, and corroborated from various other sources, will give a fair idea of the working of this well and the other processes gone through, the extent and the monetary interests connected with the business in general, etc.

This well was thirty years in boring, and is two hundred and forty chang, of twelve feet to the chang = 3,360 English feet, deep. The frame over the well, by which the water is raised, is one hundred and seventy-two English feet high; the bamboo tubing (pump) is one hundred and thirty-three feet long, the pieces of bamboo being one foot or more in length, and securely fastened with iron clasps; the bamboo rope, about two inches in diameter, two and a half li long, is renewed every ten days; sixty water-buffaloes are used at this well, changed after each two hauls; the buffaloes cost sixty dollars each; thirty men are employed at fifteen hundred cash ($1.40) and board per moon, — four meals each day, as usual in Sz-Chuan; the lifting and replacing the tube occupies about twenty minutes; about ten thousand catties of water is lifted each day; a load consists of two hundred catties, and sells for forty tael cents.

This well at its best yielded over forty thousand catties of water each day. The iron pans used in the great evaporating factories are manufactured at Kiangtsin-hsien, and are about six feet in diameter, weighing one thousand pounds each, and costing forty dollars. I was taken through one of these factories where there were quite one hundred kettles or pans. After the boiling the salt is dipped out into bamboo baskets and washed. It is sold at wholesale for from fifteen to seventeen cash per catty, or one and a quarter cents per pound.

There is no official salt station, but there is a government tax of one hundred and fifty taels upon each *tsai* sold to merchants. The tsai is an indefinite quantity, but reckoned here at 100,800 catties. The present total production is about three hundred tsai, or 30,240,000 catties, of which the government purchases six and five tenths per cent. The duty collected on what is sold to merchants amounts to near 460,000 taels per annum ($686,500). The salt is of two kinds, — very coarse white crystals, and a fine-grained, dark-greenish kind, which is exported in large, hard cubes or squares. I was told that this market sent salt to seven tenths of the province, to all parts of the province of Kwei-cheu, to two prefectures in the province of Yun-nan, three prefectures in the province of Hu-peh, namely, Ichang, Kincheu, Shinan. The amount in tons would be near 190,000, which at twenty-six dollars per ton would realize $4,940,000. This amount, I presume, is over and above that taken by the government. It is impossible to be exact as to the amount of any industry in China, in default of published statistics. This province has always had an abundance of salt, and the products from the thousands of brine-wells which are found in over forty different districts is enormous.

.The "fire-wells," as the natives call them, are of great antiquity, and have been utilized since the time of the great Chu-ko-liang, A. D. 250. These wells are of about the same depth as the others, and are side by side with them. The gas is confined in great reservoirs by means of very rude appliances, and is distributed to the different factories as needed. A fire-well is quite as productive, if not more so, than a brine-well; it will furnish sufficient gas for a great number of factories, and each jet, — or sufficient amount to keep such a kettle as above mentioned boiling, for a year, — sells for one hundred and eighty dollars. It is used most prodigally, not only in the boiling of the salt, but for torches throughout the great establishments during the daytime. The gas burns with a yellowish-white flame, and with very little odor. Baron Richthofen visited Sz-Chuan many years ago, but did not see those wells. Being a truly scientific man, and possessing every advantage money and influence could bring, he acquired a very accurate idea of the great industry, and I am inclined to quote what he says in reference to it : —

" Tsz-liu-tsing is situated about seventy miles east of Kia-ting-fu, and almost equidistant from Su-chau fu and Lu-chau. The place with its surroundings is said to be the most populous and lively region of Sz-Chuan. As in all great manufacturing places in China, the people have the reputation of being very rude. I did not see the locality, because a visit to it from either the Min River or the Yang-tsze can scarcely be performed in less than a week. The salt-wells are distributed over an area of twenty-seven li diameter. To make a well, the Chinese use a long and elastic bamboo pole supported in the middle by a cross-piece, a rope made by coupling the ends of long (not twisted) slices of bamboo, and an iron instrument which weighs one hundred and twenty catties. The rope is fastened on the thin end of the pole, and the iron on the end of the rope. A slight up-and-down motion of the thick end of the pole makes the iron hop and bore a vertical hole with its broad sharpened edge. . . .

" When a portion of the rock is mashed, clear water is poured into the hole, a long bamboo tube with a valve in the bottom lowered, and the turbid water raised to the top. For the protection of the sides of the bore hole, pipes of cypress-wood are rammed in ; and to prevent the water contained in the surrounding ground from getting access to the well, the pipes are attached to each other at the ends with nails, hemp, and tung oil. The inner width of the pipes is about five inches. As the work proceeds, the pipes are rammed deeper, and a new one attached on the top. The rope, too, is made longer by coupling to its end another length of bamboo strips.

" Besides these wells, there are others which are bored to the depth of from eighteen hundred to two thousand feet.[1] At that distance below the surface petroleum is struck. Immediately on reaching it, an inflammatory gas escapes with great violence. Work is now stopped, and a wooden cap fastened over the mouth of the pit, perforated by several

---

[1] Three to five thousand. — V. C. H.

rows of round holes. In each of them a bamboo pipe is inserted, and through these the gas is led under the evaporating pans. The pipes ramify, and on each end a tapering mouth-piece terminating in a small aperture is attached. The gas is thus used for evaporating the brine. The enterprising spirit which induced the Chinese to examine the ground to so great a depth is said to have had its origin in the drying up of a brine-pit. The proprietor was in hopes of meeting salt at a greater depth, but found in its stead the gas. Ten years ago, when the country was infested with rebels, they removed the cap from one of the gas-pits, and put fire to it.

" The gas-pits and the brine-pits are owned separately by corporations. The owners are subjected to control from the government, which is, however, not vigorous enough to prevent very large frauds. The management of the government monopoly is in the hands of a taotai who resides at the place ; but I did not succeed in ascertaining the intricate and yet somewhat loose ways in which the profits are divided. The salt-works of Tsz-lui-tsing yield, however, a considerable revenue to the government, besides having enriched numerous proprietors, giving occupation to a resident population said to amount to several hundred thousands, and furnishing one of the chief articles of traffic and commerce."

The number of " fire-pits " is twenty-four; the salt-pits are " innumerable."

It will pay all travellers to Chenteu to make the détour from the main road to visit these wonders of antiquity. Where in all the world do we find an enterprise of such age and on so grand a scale ?

BORING THE BRINE-WELLS.

CHAPTER VIII.

July 7, Tsz-cheu. From the brine-wells to the main road, and onward to Chenteu, we are constantly reminded of the fertility of the soil and natural beauties on every side. One is rather surprised at the endless succession of beautiful views and luxuriant fields. Look where you may, bright green hills and verdant vales waving with heavy crops meet the vision.

The towns and cities are thriving, and well governed for China; the roads are in good condition, and ornamented with massive and richly carved archways.

We must remember that the rural scenes are always changing; from generation to generation there has been an endless circle of rotating crops. From each farm two to three crops are taken annually, and often three to four different products from the same ground at once. Here I find corn, beans, and sweet potatoes growing together; there millet, cotton, and peanuts. Corn is in all stages of growth, — sere and hard, silking, tasselling, breast-high, knee-high, and again just out of the ground. The springs are early, summers moderate, autumns late and warm, and winters very mild; consequently no month in the year finds the country shorn of green growing crops.

I judge that the Romanists are numerous in this part of the province, and the converts are well cared for. In some of the villages children came about us with red and white crosses sewed on their coats and dresses either in front or behind. It was stated at Chenteu that they were not children of Catholics, but of heathen people, who by putting these crosses upon their children would save them from being kidnapped by the priests, — a rather improbable story. There is a French priest at the brine-wells, and a church said to consist of a hundred families.

The bridges through this section are gems of the best Chinese art, and reflect great credit upon the people. A tablet is placed at one end of a bridge recording date of construction and the donors' names.

As we neared Kien-cheu the beautiful river Lu came into view, winding through a country of surpassing beauty and fertility. A few miles from the city three ancient and very striking towers are seen at one glance upon elevated points: one on the opposite bank of the river; the second square and of nine stories, just before us by the roadside; the third thirteen stories, four-sided, and slightly concave; the last is of somewhat remarkable workmanship and some of its decorative figures are fine. Mr. Baber has given a very full description of this pagoda, and I quote from him, as I did not take the time to visit the interior: —

" Five minutes before reaching its gate we espied a temple of unusual appearance, and strolled into its court, sure of finding something new or curious; but it turned out to be, not a temple, but a very ancient pagoda surrounded by low buildings. The pagodas with which Europeans are familiar are polygonal in plan and generally built of stone;[1] but in this province the older examples are square, and, what is singular in a country where stone is so extensively used, are of brick, coated with a durable white plaster, the well-known *chunam*. As one journeys across China the gradual change in style of

---

[1] Very few are built of stone in Central China. — V. C. H.

these picturesque towers is very striking. In the typical pagoda of the southeastern provinces the successive stages decrease both in height and diameter; but as the Sz-Chuan border is passed cases begin to occur in which the fifth or sixth stories are of the same breadth, or, as it seems, of even a greater breadth than the base, so that the outline of a side of the building — that is to say, its profile — resembles the arc of a bent bow when held with the string vertical. Still farther west, as in the country we have reached, the old pagodas are square, and their upper stages are generally of very little height. In this Kien-chen pagoda each of the four faces are slightly concave; it is built of chunamed brick; the stories have imitation doors and round windows, and the cornices which divide story from story are not prominent; so that were it not for the suddenly pointed summit it might almost be taken for an English church tower. It is very unlike the common idea of a pagoda, and yet it is a most authentic pagoda and a very old one, for high up on its eastern face, above a bas-relief of Buddha, is the inscription ' Shih-kia-mu-ni Shê-li pao-ta' (Buddha Shê-li Pagoda). What is Shê-li? I appealed to the attendant priest, who is attached to the place, for information. ' A Shê-li,' he replied, ' is a particle of the essence of Buddha, having no special shape, color, or substance, but in general it is a minute speck resembling a morsel of crystal, and giving off intense light. Its size may, however, change infinitely, and it is impossible to set limits to it. An iron chest cannot confine it in the custody of unbelievers, and its radiance on occasion pierces everything, so that there is no concealing it.' Much more of such definition was offered me, which might have been credible if one could have understood it; but I have a reminiscence which almost amounts to a sure recollection that Shê-li is a transliteration of some Sanscrit word meaning *relic;* in which case the inscription indicates that the pagoda contains a relic of Buddha,[1] doubtless a par-

[1] Not necessarily Shih-kia-mu-ni, but any Buddha or Pusa. Any priest having entered the Paradise, or state of perfection, can subdivide his essence infinitely and dwell in pagodas or holy places, and thus help mortals to salvation. — V. C. H.

ticle of his ashes brought from India by a pilgrim. The extant journals of Fa-hsien, Heüan-chuang, and others show that one purpose of their visits to India was to obtain relics (probably the term they employ is Shê-li, but I have no opportunity of examining any of their accounts) ; and here is a fairly authentic instance of the way in which they dispose of their collections. Eight of the thirteen stories of this pagoda are ascended by an interior staircase, the walls of which are painted throughout with pictures of Buddhist saints and worthies, much in the style of the ruined Burmese temples at Pagán. The priests had no knowledge of the date of the building, and affirmed there was no means of knowing it. I inquired somewhat deeply into this question, even sending to the prefect of the city to ask his opinion, but he replied that the date could not be ascertained."

A large temple of unusual interest stood near by, and a large grove spreads its green canopy over temple and pagoda. From this point to the city gate the smooth wide road is securely walled with cobble-stones. Here horsemen lounged by the side of their tired and half-famished beasts, as they ate bran or coarse rice from long hempen bags thrust over their heads.

The main street of the city is filled with apothecary shops and banks. The kungkwan was placed at our disposal, and we halted long enough to change our escort and rest our jaded coolies. Leaving the city we crossed a wide and well-covered bridge ; it was filled to overflowing with all kinds of small articles such as travellers would be likely to require or country visitors might fancy. At the end of this most interesting bridge we turned abruptly to the right, and again turned to the river, which we skirted for nearly two miles.

In no part of the world have I seen a greater display of agricultural products. Over the rustic roadside walls crept and twined many beautiful vines, some sparkling

with the morning's new-blown flowers, others full of
buds or laden with half-matured seed-pods. Gourds
hanging from trellises and masses of bloom graced the
door-yards. There was a rich display of pole-beans and
others creeping along the walls; some were full of
bloom, others drooping under the weight of scores of
tender pods a foot or more in length, ready for the
market basket. Here we came upon dark orange-groves,
with fruit the size of walnuts and cherries; there we
passed apple-orchards, the fruit not much larger than the
Siberian crab-apple, but remarkably bright-tinted and of
good flavor; the trees were vigorous, and the limbs bent
to the ground with the weight of the apples. Large,
far-spreading walnut-trees graced the roadside, filled with
nuts; they afforded a most grateful shade. The low-
bent pumalo branches and the dark orange-trees across
the road seem scarcely in keeping with the hardy apple-
trees near the house; yet such is the perfection of the
climate and richness of the soil that walnuts, oranges,
apples, peaches, pears, plums, cherries, grapes, corn,
cotton, millet, wheat, opium, groundnuts, hemp, sweet
potatoes, leguminous plants, melons, peppers, etc., grow
within an area of one mile. There is, however, a great
dearth of cultivated flowers; beyond a few hollyhocks,
china-asters, canna, and tuberoses, few flowers are to
be seen at this season. Almost all varieties of plants
flourish with little attention, and the great number of
wild-flowers show the wealth of the Chinese flora.
When the Chinaman is an expert gardener, his attention
naturally turns to shrubs and to the creation of fanciful
forms rather than to color and fragrance.

The housewife or female domestic seldom or never
cultivates a taste for flowers or beautiful plants; consequently the door-yards are untidy and littered with all

manner of waste, and their apartments are cheerless as prisons, — devoid of light and beauty.

In the distance, across the even-flowing stream, slowly revolved an immense water-wheel, quite fifty feet in diameter; while in the centre of the river, in front of the prosperous town of Shikiaotsing, was an island covered with such a mass of bright-green wild grass that it seemed like a floating garden. There were reminders of foreign habits in some of the rural scenes, and I could but recall the " touch of Nature " which makes for our world wide kinship, when I saw an old woman sitting under a tree by the roadside, with a little table upon which apples and greengages were tastefully arranged, while a number of the third generation played around her; or when a red-faced farmer came down the road with an ear of boiled green corn in each hand, nibbling as he came. Such sights are not only homelike but exceedingly cheerful to the weary traveller, who finds in the customs and manners of this people so few resemblances to those of his native land.

We left this paradise all too soon, and entered the long, disconnected town which we had seen in the distance, which is a centre for several important industries. Tanneries could not be far away, as there was a fair display of tanned hides, especially those of sheep and goats; these skins were well cured and colored. Glue was seen in many shops, and quantities of white and yellow wax. One street was given up to the packing of sugar, manufactured near by from sorghum, and exported from the province. There was also an abundance of cake-salt of dark hue piled up before the shops, block upon block. This salt comes from the four hundred wells in the immediate vicinity; they are mostly of small size, varying from one hundred to one thousand feet in depth. I visited one, and found nine hundred feet of bamboo rope on the wheel. One ox is sufficient to draw the water from wells of this depth. We went into one factory and found half-a-dozen evaporating pans. The place was very dirty and smoky, owing to the use of coal instead of gas.

We lodged half-way to the top of the Lung-chien-yi Mountains, — a beautiful range which skirts the Chenteu valley on the east. A heavy rain came on soon after we entered our close and dismal quarters, and the air was soon cool. We could have enjoyed our mountain lodgings if we could have cleared the place of half a hundred filthy coolies, and subdued an indefinite number of smells. It is no pleasant experience to lie through the long night near an open door, which not only admits the damp air, noxious vapors, and fumes of opium, but also the gabble of sleepless Chinamen, who seem to delight in turning night into day.

By nine o'clock the following morning we reached the highest pass, and looked down upon one of the most celebrated valleys of the world, — the most important centre of Western China, around which cluster stories of ancient and modern exploits, such as few localities in China can boast. The highest point on the road was nine hundred and fifty feet above the plain. Mr. Baber makes the mountains fifteen hundred feet above Chenteu; possibly the higher peaks may reach that altitude. The rain left the roads in bad condition, and the fleeting mists danced above us all the morning; but the air was sufficiently cool to make our tramp over the sandy rocks delightful, although they were rather wet; the road is wide, and being largely cut from the solid sandstone, is kept in excellent repair. At intervals we met relays of carriers with light and precious merchandise, which is

thus moved in order to avoid the dangerous navigation
of the river.   We also saw many mounted travellers and
fine gentlemen in sedans.   The mountains lacked wild
ruggedness, and had more the appearance of a cultivated park where natural forests blended gracefully with
groves of orange, pear, tallow, and apple trees; rice
grew in the level hollows, terrace upon terrace being
watered by small rivulets directed hither and thither
without pumps, while on the higher slopes corn and
millet cheered the hearts of wine-bibbers.

Here and there along the rivulets and nestled in
sunny nooks were thatched cottages, a group of which
occasionally attained to the dignity of a village, with its
forge and smith, where a variety of rough implements
were made for the not too fastidious husbandmen.

The houses of Sz-Chuan are mostly of one story, and
except in the larger cities are flimsy affairs; the walls
are of pounded earth, and the roofs thatched with straw.
The walls are whitewashed as a rule, and frequently
some attempt is made at rude decoration.   There are
few fine temples except in high mountains, or in and
near the great cities.   Few priests are seen on the
highways.

There is some evidence that Buddhism and Taoism
have flourished in these rural districts as they have in
Kiangsu and Kiangsi.   There are many private sign-
boards in towns and villages, as in some other parts of
China, notifying the public that such and such a Tao-sz,
or Men-cheu, resides here.   He is ready to select lucky
sites or determine the character of those selected, to
exorcise demons, monsters, and evil influences from
homes and other places, to perform incantations over
the sick, and even say mass for the dead.   He is one of
hundreds in every populous district, holding appointment

under the Heavenly teacher, or Taoist pope, of Lung-hu Mountains, of Kiangsi, and recognized by the Government as guardian of public and private spiritual interests. The members of this order are scattered all over China, and are not distinguishable from ordinary subjects except when robed for religious duties. They draw certain fixed rates for all their services, and must go here and there as required. This peculiar order, not unlike the men who stood before Moses in the presence of Pharaoh, has doubtless as great an influence in China as the Nile sorcerers had in Egypt. They are little known by foreigners, and their arts, although wonderful, do not come prominently before the Western student.

There is an absence here of fine ancestral halls, such as exist in many parts of China; I have not seen one with any pretensions to elegance or solidity. In the absence of great temples we naturally look for more than the usual display upon these venerated halls, but this is not the case. Along some of the highways of Nganhui and Kiangsi, these edifices embody the best designs known to Chinese artists, and are prominent landmarks in every village, being of stone and brick and two stories high; but here the weak character of these structures and the freshness of the filial arches show that the present inhabitants have not been here very long.

A half-hour's ride, winding around pleasant slopes and down green glades, past many inviting copses besprinkled with small wild-flowers, brought us to the border of a large quarry, where several masons were busy cutting stone for the city. We are now on the edge of the valley, and after a moment's halt are off at a rapid pace, and within twenty minutes enter the first town of note, — the only one of much importance in the vicinity of Chenteu, forty-six li distant. Baskets and bags of rice, wheat, and barley were seen all along each side the street, while crowds of dull peasants stood in the centre of the broad space, inspecting the grains and chattering like magpies. Our small escort, poor and ragged, with the aid of my saucy head bearers, mowed a swath through the blue humanity, occasionally punching some unfortunate ones in the ribs with the sharp end of the poles. I counted five who were thus punched and almost tumbled head-foremost into the baskets of grain, and not one had sufficient spirit to resent the outrage. The more I called out and expostulated with the scamps, the faster they went, and the more reckless their bearing toward any one in their way. They seemed to take demoniacal delight in swaying right and left and gouging some lout who was bent over, testing the qualities of the new rice or wheat.

A furious storm of rain and wind came on, and our journey was slow and dreary, pelted as we were by the pitiless tempest. The broken rice-fields had lost half their beauty, and a shadow of gloom rested everywhere. The plain is thickly dotted with evergreen groves, — really parks, and securely walled; each one has a temple hidden in the dark recesses; the extent of the plain is less than I anticipated, nor is it as thickly inhabited as I had supposed. The foot-hills are discernible on every side, and the towns are not more numerous or populous than upon the Grand Canal in the province of Kiangsu. A few thrifty market-towns along our course, owing to the storm, were very uninviting. One half the people were asleep, while the rest languidly lounged about or did some necessary work in the laziest possible manner.

CHAPTER IX.

The low city wall could be discerned peering above
the trees and buildings a mile or more away. The
eastern suburb, through which we straggled, was a sea
of mud and dirty water, owing to recent rains and bad
paving. The street is unimportant, though of good
width, and no such crowds of people are seen as congregate at the principal gateways of Nanking and many
other large cities.

The shops and wayside stalls are well stocked with a
great variety of odds and ends. Being in covered sedans
we attracted very little attention until we had passed the
narrow gate and were upon the Cheapside of Chenteu.
Here we saw more life, better shops, an open and pleasant street, wider than in most provincial capitals, but
not so broad or neatly kept as I had anticipated. The
shops, although attractive and having a large assortment
of articles, are still small and scantily furnished as compared with those of Hankow, Nanchang, and Suchau.
Leaving this deservedly famous thoroughfare we filed
into a much narrower street on the right, which was
devoted to tailors and outfitters; a few sharp turns
brought us to Cotton Street, — a very busy and important place, but destitute of the glitter and color of East
Street. A messenger who had preceded us by an hour

or two had secured the best rooms in a first-class hotel,
— the best to be found; but while they were large and
pretentious, they were really dark, damp, sickening cess-
pools. Ancient carvings, worm-eaten veneering, huge
gateways, and lofty walls decorated with blood-and-
thunder pictures are well enough in their way, and
strike the native traveller as the perfection of harmony;
but they are poor comforters for the weary foreigner,
who longs for privacy, clean rooms, and pure air, rather
than for tawdry decorations.

The landlord did not blush to ask us a dollar and a
quarter a day for what he would not presume to charge
a native official fifty cents. While debating the advisa-
bility of occupying these disagreeable quarters, on account of the noxious vapors rising from air-holes near
the mud floors, a bright idea flashed into my mind
which I immediately acted upon. The proprietor was
sent for with haste; he came, bowed, and placed himself
in the attitude to receive our commands, which in outward form expressed true humility. You may imagine
his consternation when requested to bring a load of mud
and plaster up the beautiful star-shaped apertures all
around the palatial reception hall, and a load of lime to
sprinkle over the floors and central court-yard.

He received the commands as coolly as would a porter
to strap a trunk, or lift it into an express-wagon; he
hastened out upon the new commission as though an
every-day affair, and not the most unique occurrence of a
lifetime. Any other than a Chinaman would have debated or laughed at the command, viewing it either as
too serious or too comic to be obeyed. But no muscle
moved on his face, no unusual twinkle came to his eye;
he apparently said : "I am a machine, sir, and always
obey the stronger force, and that without dissent." This

inherent element in the character of the ordinary Chinaman would be explained perhaps by the great M. Pierre
Laffitte in such language as this : " From the moral
point of view, the persistence of Fetichism in China has
developed the sentiment of fatality and of order, con-
currently with a disposition to submission, — not, indeed,
absolute submission, but relative ; of a kind closely ap-
proximate to the spirit of scientific subordination." It
was of little moment to me whether " scientific subordination " or "absolute submission " controlled the mind
of the man on this occasion ; he acted as if the sentiment
of fatality was preponderant.

A young man came and filled up the holes, the ornamental stars in the stones ; the lime was brought, and
we made it the serious business of an hour to see every
inch of the court sprinkled ; the great official guest-hall
was next whitened, as well as the two back rooms, the
alley, and various other places, even to the side bed-
rooms. The mud floor of the guest-hall was so damp
that it readily absorbed several siftings. The great divan itself was sprinkled, and the remainder of the lime
poured out under it. No Chinese house ever received
such a cleansing. We now called our reception room the
" white room," being no longer the black room it was
when the last official vacated it. The guest-hall was still
so damp after we had used all the lime we dared, that
the teacher was sent to ask the manager for mats to be
spread over the damper places. We were told that the
mats upon the guest-beds were at our disposal. Every
bed was pillaged ; new and old mats, inhabited with
colonies of living and dead fleas and unmentionable
vermin, were brought forth and spread over the floor,
and feeling somewhat uncertain about their sanitary condition, we saturated them with lime.

We now congratulated ourselves upon the improvements as much as if an epidemic of yellow-fever had been stamped out, and fell to arranging our apartments for work and pleasure. My journal must be written up, letters sent off, the history of the city studied, our wet clothing and bedding dried, and an appetizing dinner despatched.

With an indefinite picture of the old city in my mind, I saw a confused vision of broad streets, marble bridges, palatial temples, crumbling monuments, wide and swift-flowing rivers, stately barges, gentlemen in silks and satins, — waving silk fans, written over with characters of gold,—and crowds of merchants and scholars, politely standing aside as the honored foreign guests walked down Cheapside; to these were added æsthetically arranged shops, and many other pleasing features, which have been portrayed from the days of Marco Polo to the time of " the latest traveller." There would intrude upon the canvas the massacres of Kublai-Khan ; the hecatomb of hundreds of thousands of innocent persons ; the fearful slaughter of later days, with smoking streets and broken walls. Behind all, covered with smoke and carnage, rose several giant forms who figured largely in the pomp of war and the tinsel of a barbaric court nearly two thousand years ago: shoulder to shoulder stood Liupei, Changfei, and Kwanyü, a triumvir of China's bravest heroes and most talented statesmen. Such a reverie could not last ; the brain mist rolled away, and the sunlight danced again upon a whitened court-yard. The lines were stretched from door to wall, and the wet garments hung up to dry. Our neighbors were not inactive ; a Fookien official, with a large family and no end of trumpery, had completed his long and trying journey, and tumbled into the court upon our left, with noise enough for a regiment of cavalry or a travelling circus. The children began to investigate the division doors and other openings into our apartments. An official from the distant city of Hauchow was upon our right, who was thoughtful enough to send out and bring one or two singing girls into his apartments; with them came the banjo and some stringed instrument, and a screeching and thrumming were kept up till late at night. We could scarcely interfere with the regulations of a great hotel, and must patiently endure the bacchanalian songs. Officials and wealthy travellers send out for players and singing girls, and turn their private apartments into playhouses instead of visiting public theatres and low houses when resting at cities on their route. Such occasions are well spiced with wine and gaming, and usually end with a debauch. The anchorages around cities and towns are made gay and lively at night by gondolas plying to and fro, and stopping at the junks for the gaudily dressed girls to play and sing their amorous ditties.

It is not often that the traveller can visit in the same hour the grave of an emperor of the third century of the Christian era, and the birthplace of a philosopher and founder of a religion of the time of Pythagoras.

We had the pleasing prospect of such an experience, and made preparations before retiring for an early start the following morning. Our sedans were in readiness at the appointed hour, and we were borne swiftly through half-a-dozen short, badly paved streets to the south gate, which is narrow and low. Immediately after leaving the city wall we entered a richly cultivated country, divided by rivers and canals, and level as the hand. The streets through which we had come did not average above fourteen feet in width, very neatly paved, for the most part, with broad slabs of red sandstone, and kept unusually clean.

Leaving the gate, we came at once upon a dirt road, now very muddy from continuous showers. The bearers plunged right and left into the thick pasty soil, stumbling and reeling along the low dike, brushed and hustled by all sorts of merchandise. It seems strange that a great thoroughfare leading to populous towns and celebrated historical centres should be so neglected by a large and wealthy city; especially when the mountains ten miles distant are full of sandstone. Such, however, is the appreciation the Chinese show of convenience and of historical monuments. Long processions of peasants came splashing through the water and mud, bearing huge bundles of rice-straw and other bulky commodities.

The wheelbarrow, the most useful carriage in China, reappears, and has the same squeak as in the East. Horsemen came dashing along upon exceedingly fine ponies, gray and bay, and two or three beautiful pie-balds; one does not wonder that the people of this province take great pains to groom their ponies, they are so remarkably handsome.

A mile or two to the west of the gate we came to the famous temple dedicated to military heroes, called Wu-heu-tsz. Here is the tomb of Liupei, warrior and Emperor of the Shu-Han, who reigned from 220 A. D. to 222. It is supposed that it was not earlier than 300 B. C. when the Mongols first took possession of the central districts of China in sufficient numbers to form vigorous settlements.

They must have increased enormously before the time of the usurper Liupei, who extended the civilized area into Yun-nan and Kwei-cheu; he had already borne the title of Han-chung-wang, — middle King of Han, —

for a number of years, and as early as 185 A. D. he successfully fought the Yellow Turbans. He was grandly supported by his ardent friends and admirers, Changfei and Kwanyü, who with him, side by side, have since lived in the affections of the Sz-Chuanese.

The plain, as I have already remarked, is broken or diversified by beautiful evergreen groves. Into one of these dark and silent retreats our bearers took us after half an hour's ride. It was quite three quarters of a mile in circumference, and filled with the wide-spreading nan-mu and cypress. Some of the larger trees are said to be fully a thousand years old. In this fairy retreat, more like the famous groves of Japan than are those usually seen in China, stands an ancient temple, now in process of renovation. The central figures, as would be expected, are the triumvir, with Chu-ko-liang, Counsellor of State, and the son of Liupei. Kwanyü occupies a separate niche suitable to his dignity, as he has been for many centuries the Chinese Mars. Although in life an associate-general of Liupei, in these later centuries his fame has quite eclipsed that of his friend and master, and he is, in fact, the only rival to Confucius in the empire. The same lofty titles, sacrifices, and honors are bestowed upon him as are given to the universal statesman and philosopher. Changfei's image confronts us in a conspicuous place; he is greatly respected for his bravery, and his divided body is worshipped in two distant prefectures. The only antiquities of note are found near the great altar, and consist of three drum-shaped pieces of bronze, placed before the statues, the larger one in the centre. Stars or suns are wrought upon the face of each, and it may be that the three stars of the kingdom symbolize this trinity of heroes.

A friendly priest led the way from the great temple

to a smoothly paved avenue, high-walled, and completely arched by rows of mammoth bamboos, which interlocked their feathery plumes forty feet above our heads, and so dense was their foliage that they excluded the rays of the noonday sun. At the end of this grassy walk we came to a large, conical mound, some thirty feet high and one hundred in diameter, upon which were tall and thrifty nan-mu and cypress trees. Strong palings and walls encircle the sacred mound, and a simple stone slab is fitted into the front wall, while on either side are strong wooden gates, never opened except to repair the grounds and at the time of the spring and autumn sacrifices. The tablet is severely simple, having the emperor's title only inscribed upon it. Would it not be well to add the name of this emperor to the Positivist's Calendar? It might follow that of Alexander, and a pilgrimage could be made to this spot by some apostle of that school. It ought to fall in the sweet month of May, and not in broiling July; and no doubt Chinese annals would be flexible enough to fix his birthday at the most convenient season. His lofty title was, and now is, Han-chau-li-ti.

Retracing our steps to the front temple, we took a final survey of the beautiful and costly images, and hastened to another grove of greater extent and equal antiquity. It were vain to attempt a full description of the numerous objects of interest along the way. I seemed to be in a land not unlike China, yet possessing many foreign features peculiar to this garden-plain. It was as if a portion of the tropics had been put down between deep, fast-flowing rivers. We crossed the rivers on solid bridges, or kept along the banks as occasion required; we passed in quick succession from grove to grove, where thrifty gardeners cared for legions of fruits and vegetables. Here was a mill grinding out snow-white flour, the great overshot wheel groaning under wide-spreading banyans. The village life was as interesting as the scenery, and I could but feel that for once I realized my ideal of thrifty, happy Cathay.

We turned aside for an hour into the celebrated monastery of Tsao-tang. The grove is a very fine one, and was once the retreat of an eminent scholar, but through misfortune or gift the property has passed into the insatiable maw of the Buddhist Church. It is not remarkable for any great display of costly buildings or images, but for the classic atmosphere which surrounds the enclosure; for its beautiful walks, its extensive tea-saloons, and the quaint designs in the arrangement of the buildings, gardens, bridges, and walks; for its lake, well stocked with fat fish of many hues, and lazy turtle which float from side to side and lift their sparkling eyes to the crowds of merry children, who toss cakes and sweetmeats to them from the rustic bridge. The upper classes — mostly men and small boys and girls — saunter about in the cool shades, stopping to lounge in the pavilions or covered bridges to sip tea and nibble at confectionery. Here is happily blended the scholarly aroma of antiquity and the esoteric teachings of higher Buddhism. Gross idolatry seems out of harmony with the classic surroundings, and by common consent has been relegated to the background. A smart young priest recognized an old acquaintance in me, and showed his delight by taking us to every place of interest and pressing us repeatedly to drink tea and regale ourselves with sweetmeats. Although a place where one could profitably spend a full day, the prospect of something better lured us on; for we journeyed toward the reputed birthplace of Li-lao-chwen, the founder of Taoist philosophy.

A theatre was in full blast at the outer gate of the Tsing-Yang temple as we approached. Our presence was more attractive than the contortions and screeches of red and yellow robed men and boys. The leaping and dancing harlequins, with all their pheasant feathers and horse-tail whiskers, long boots and flowing sleeves, spears and swinging fans, could not hold the attention after we came upon the scene. A crowd of unruly urchins haunted our steps as we examined the many wonders within the enclosure.

Passing from the first temple, which was not unlike those in other places, we entered a magnificent court, in the centre of which is a marvellous two-storied octagonal tower made of wood, and raised upon a high foundation of carved stone. Each corner of the building is supported by a large wooden pillar, richly carved with dragons and phœnixes, beautifully lacquered, and heavily gilded. The whole tower, except the roof, which is covered with yellow glazed tiles, is lacquered and ornamented with gold figures. It is needless to say that the effect is wonderful; I have not seen anything in China to equal it for richness, symmetry, and beauty. It is pierced by three arches and ascended by the same number of broad stone steps. Within may be seen a life-sized image of Lao-tsz seated upon the famous crane which is supposed to bear him through the heavenly spheres. The image is most striking, — that of a very old man, complacent, of a heavenly countenance, and perfectly unconcerned with sublunary affairs. It is enclosed within a fine glass baldacchino to keep it from dust and the undue familiarity of the crowds of visitors who swarm around it. Over the main archway is written "Lao-er-puh-lao," "Old, yet not old." The elegantly carved central stairway leading to the tower, as well as

PICTURE IN THE TEMPLE AT MOUNT OMEI.

See page 215.

that to the temple in the rear, is securely guarded, and visitors are never allowed to ascend directly in front of the philosopher nor of the Taoist Trinity.

The main temple, a hundred feet in the rear, is an immense structure, similarly lacquered and gilded, and no less beautiful than unique. The Taoist Trinity occupy three great thrones, and present an awe-inspiring vision to the ignorant crowds who press about the doors. They do not, however, receive as much admiration as is bestowed upon the pair of fabulous bronze animals at either end of the hall. These ancient casts would attract attention in any museum, and would do honor to any country or period of art. One of them seems to be a fabulous water monster, about the size of a large goat, with a sharp horn in the centre of the head; it is seated upon its haunches, and faces the front doors. The other is the perfect image of a fair-sized goat, and occupies the same position as the first. They are of yellowish-green color, and polished as smooth as glass by the patting and rubbing which they constantly receive from adoring pilgrims.

The priests could give little information as to their age or purpose, but said they had been there since the erection of the temple, more than a thousand years ago, and were in the old temples for many centuries before. The present temple is said to have been planned and erected under the direction of Li-yuen, founder of the Tang dynasty, and descendant of Lao-tsz, who is now worshipped in a separate temple near by.

Not far away are two artificial hills surmounted by towers consecrated to the birthplace of the philosopher and the academy where he taught his disciples. We were guided up the steep walk to the former mound, passing under trees of dense shade laden with small round nuts. The image of a beautiful woman, said to be that of the philosopher's mother, sits enthroned in the centre of the building; she holds in her right hand a half-open peach which discloses the face of an aged man. The image of a babe stands directly before the goddess; it has a long white beard, is naked to the loins, and with two fingers points toward heaven. I was twice told by the officiating priest that Lao-tsz was born where the mound stands.

It has been claimed that Lao-tsz was born in the kingdom of Tsu (now the provinces of Hupeh and Hunan), near the Blue River. He is said to have been born 604 B. C., fifty-four years earlier than Confucius. Is it possible that my feet press the soil once trodden by the greatest recluse and scholar of antiquity? Did the man who left his impress so deeply upon his age that all future generations have felt his influence look out upon this plain as I now do? Are these sleepy-headed, opium-smoking attendants who wait at his altar and caress the bronze animals the best representatives of his school?

Have I, at last, seen the place of his birth, and that in which he taught, and probably the richest and most beautiful Taoist structure in the world? Is it possible that one who has pored over his immortal work, the "Tao-teh-king," and dug like a miner for nuggets of gold among the fresh, pure thoughts of antiquity, should now turn aside, — not to weep, nor to recall some appropriate thought-gem to lay afresh upon his neglected altar, — but to seek a refuge from the yells of half-dressed boys, and the nuts with which they pelt me at every convenient turn?

Alas! has it come to this, that a fond student of the mystic philosopher cannot linger one short hour over the place of his nativity without being hooted at and mobbed at every corner? Farewell, shades of Lao-tsz, I leave thee for my sedan, which will afford a partial shield from all this degradation.

It was proposed and seconded that the following day be partially devoted to a visit to the ancient palaces occupied by the Emperor Liupei 220 A. D., and to the examination halls, which are in the old palace grounds. The site being within the city walls, we preferred to go on foot, and thus satisfy the curious-minded, and also make a sale of books.

I have as yet said little about the streets, houses, and merchandise of this celebrated capital. A city so highly extolled by Marco Polo and other writers of later date ought to present some remarkable features. It is spoken of as of great size and population, the people civil and exceptionally polite, dressed in silk, and enjoying far more luxuries than in other capitals. While I have no mean opinion of the city, it does not now present these conditions. The fact is, there are few broad streets, the widest not being more than eighteen feet; a few of these are well paved with blocks of sandstone, but most of them are in bad condition, and some are not paved at all. The houses are of wood, with but one story; the shops are narrow and not very deep, but many of them are lacquered and prettily gilded with considerable artistic taste.

The articles exhibited are of numerous varieties, embracing all the provincial manufactures and some from every other province, as well as from foreign lands. Upon one street there is a grand display of wearing apparel, especially for ladies, and an infinite variety of small silk ornaments. There are few wholesale houses, and little heavy merchandise is seen moving about the streets. The people are no finer-looking than in other parts of China, and wear no more silk than in Suchau or

Nanking.   The masses have stolid, uninteresting faces ; many are of low stature, and great numbers are afflicted with skin diseases.

I saw more dwarfs in two days than I have seen elsewhere within two years.   It is a great centre for sedan-bearers ; they come from all parts of the province with mandarins and merchants, and are dismissed upon arrival, the sedans sold, and they thrown at once out of employment ; the greater portion must find their way back to their homes empty-handed.   The result is that thousands of them crawl into tea and opium shops, use up all their hard-earned money, pawn their clothes, and eventually get a poor coffin and a bad grave.   They have been seen to congregate in great numbers at the East Gate, and auction off one garment after another, until the last rag is reached, and even that taken off and held up to the populace.

There is the same interest here at the sight of a foreigner as we have noted elsewhere.   The city exports very little ; my next-door neighbor, an official from Hanchow, pointedly said : " There are but two articles of export, slave-girls and satin coverlets ; you can buy a good girl for three dollars, and a beautiful brocaded quilt for eight."   His eight-year-old slave-girl now trotted off for his towel and hot water, then brought his pipe and paper light, replaced each article after its use, and then stood coyly in his bedroom door as he exhibited the good qualities of his pet monkey in the court-yard.   This traffic in girls is not secret, but is openly practised with full official sanction.

There are three methods of slavery in this province, more generally practised perhaps in the great and populous valley of Kien-chang.   First, officials and wealthy merchants residing here for a time purchase young girls for a mere pittance, use them as slaves, take them east on their return home, and sell them again at large profits. Second, there are persons who make it a business to purchase the fairer ones, take them down the river to Hankow, Nanking, Suchau, Shanghai, and other places, and sell them for immoral purposes. Third, there are great numbers kidnapped and taken out of the province by stealth, and disposed of in various places. Whenever it suits the natives they charge the missionaries who have girls' schools with similar crimes. Two weeks before our arrival in Chenteu great excitement prevailed on account of reports spread over the city accusing the missionaries of heinous acts.

The markets bear witness to the wonderful fertility of the plain, and as we wended our way along the busy streets I could but observe the great variety of vegetables and fruits: cabbages, both native and foreign, in great abundance, a round vegetable like the khol rabi, radishes, turnips, bamboo sprouts, garlic, onions, spinach, sweet potatoes; of fruits there were apples, peaches, plums, oranges, pears, grapes in several varieties, líchí, lénêng, lemons, all clean and tastefully arranged; there was also an attempt at floral decoration. Instead of stalls and baskets filled with dead fish and tubs of wriggling eels, as seen in most Chinese cities, we have long, clean sandstone troughs by the sides of the streets filled with pure fresh water and green tussel-weed in the bottom. The fish, mostly of small size, are all alive and swimming about as in crystal fountains. It was one of the most cheerful sights, — a perfect contrast to the usual Chinese fish-market, which is a place to escape from with all haste.

Arriving at the gate of the palace, we were detained upon the great platform at the head of the steps while the porter hunted up the keys. A noisy crowd collected about us; and to interest and profit them we commenced the sale of some illustrated Testaments and histories of Moses and Daniel.

Admitted at last, after more crowding than was pleasant, we were rewarded by a sight of the broad old walk which leads to the emperor's palace. The present high building is entirely new, except perhaps the sandstone columns thirty feet in height and twenty inches in diameter. Some of the stone foundations remain, but are badly patched by successive additions; yet for eight feet in height much of the original material is still there, and some of the ornamental work may be seen in less exposed places. This is remarkable, for the red sandstone upon which the carvings were executed is soft, and if exposed is likely to crumble. Near the building is a very peculiar tower fourteen feet high. It must have been a bell-tower. The top, which is fast crumbling, is in the form of a temple, and most chastely carved; below this is a square six feet high, and pierced on all sides. Five or six steps lead up to this tower from the temple, or palace front.

The monument is attractive and really beautiful,—the best work of its kind I have hitherto seen. It is a pity that the Government, while attempting to preserve the ruder works and their locality, should allow this genuine work of art to remain unprotected.

The only other finely executed work here is at the extreme end of the grounds, before the shrine to the God of Literature. Here is a raised platform, upon which is a well-executed dragon in a block of red sandstone five feet square. Above it is a peculiar horizontal shaft of stone twelve feet long and fourteen inches in diameter, richly carved in relief. Its intended use was more than we could divine, unless, as we surmised, it was for a protection bar to the dragon stone, to be removed on state occasions. The examination halls are scattered about over the open space, and are capable of seating 17,100 students. On our return we visited the San-Yi temple, dedicated to the triumviri. It is really beautiful, — spacious and cool even at midday. The great tea-saloon, in the centre of a broad square, is adorned with a score of elegant hanging tablets, the sides being decorated with stone tablets, all containing historical inscriptions. The city gentry find this a quiet and attractive retreat. A funeral cortége came through the long corridor as we made our way to the street.

There are other famous places in and about the city which would well repay investigation; but July is a terrible month in which to roam through Chinese streets, and I felt obliged to be prudent.

I am told the Catholic establishment is interesting; that the bishop lives in the style of a high mandarin, having the two flag-poles before his palace, and that he puts on all the outward show of a great civil official. The Catholics are numerous here, as at Chungking, but a former statement, that they number twenty thousand in this city, is no doubt wide of the mark. I have learned that records made some years since are very untrustworthy.

The size and population of Chenteu have been discussed by other writers with a great diversity of opinions, and I may not be able to add much of interest for the general reader; yet I feel constrained to say a word, giving my own impressions from the information gathered on the spot.

Mr. Baber, who on all subjects he touches generally

gives us solid information, did not see fit to give more than a passing notice to the capital and its environs. No doubt he considered the statements of previous travellers to be accurate and sufficient for present purposes. But in view of the future possibilities of this centre, standing as it does in one of the rich plains of the world, and extending its influence not only to every part of the great province, but to Thibet, and as in the near future it will inevitably play a remarkable part in a re-adjusted empire, I feel impelled to add my mite of information. Politically it has always been a centre of very great influence, dealing directly with all the numerous half-civilized tribes on the wide fringes of the province, and even with Thibet itself. Religiously it controls greater interests than any other provincial city, and under the new régime is sure to become a great manufacturing and commercial centre. Its present arsenal and foundries will soon rank with the best in the empire. It has been noted during many centuries for its great and beautiful bronze castings, which may be found by thousands to the southwest. Mr. Baber speaks of it as one of the largest Chinese cities, having a circuit of about twelve English miles. Mr. A. Wylie gives it as thirteen miles, including the lesser city, which is attached to the west side. Marco Polo makes it twenty miles in circuit; if it were of such extent, and packed as it seems to be, the population would be far more than three hundred and thirty thousand, as put down by Mr. Baber.

After walking over the city I concluded that its extent had been overestimated, and I consulted the provincial records with this result : —

" In the twenty-seventh year of King Hwei of the Tsing dynasty, Chang Yi, Minister of State, made the great wall, twelve li, or three and a half miles, in extent. During the Sui dynasty Yangsui added to the west and south angles, making a small wall three miles in extent. During the reign of Hsitsung of the Tang dynasty, about one thousand years ago, Kaoping made an outer wall twenty-five li, or seven miles, in extent, and eighteen English feet high, with surrounding dikes, eight miles in length. Probably the walls had been of dirt before this time.

" Later Cheng-cheu, Lu-fa-yuen, Wen-kang-chang, and Fa-chen-ta successively renewed it. Chao-Tsing of the Ming dynasty made a wall of brick and stone. Ching-hwai dug the channels without the city, and the canals within. At the end of the Ming dynasty the wall was destroyed. The first year of the Kang-hsi, A. D. 1662, of the present dynasty, it was rebuilt thirty Chinese feet high, eighteen thick, twenty-two li and three fen long, or 4,114 chang, with 5,538 embrasures. . . . The distance from the East to the West Gate is nine li three fen ; from the South to the North Gate seven li seven fen, with four gates and defences, and eleven armories. In the fifth year of Yung Cheu, 1728 A. D., the governor of Sien-teh repaired it anew. In the forty-eighth year of Kien lung, 1784, the Viceroy petitioned for six hundred thousand taels to renew it from its foundations. The Manchu city is in the western section, and was built in the fifty-seventh year of Kang-hsi, 1718 A. D., — four or five li in extent."

The Min Sheu myths say : —

" When Chang Yi and Chang Yoh were building the city wall of Chenteu, it kept falling down. Finally there came out of the river a great tortoise, and made a circuit. A diviner told them to follow his track, and the wall would stand. They did so, and the tortoise went into the excavated moat ; therefore it is called the city of the tortoise. The original wall of earth was seventy feet high and twelve li in length."

By these records we find that the wall was rebuilt frequently, dating from very early times to 1784. It was repeatedly destroyed by incursions or floods, and it was not until the Min dynasty that a brick and stone wall was made, probably of the same extent as at present, — twenty-two li and three fen, or about six and one half English miles, in circuit.

This gives ample space for three hundred thousand inhabitants, together with the suburbs three hundred and fifty thousand, and no doubt these figures are quite large enough. Yet the census of 1877 returned the number of families at about seventy thousand, and the total population at three hundred and thirty thousand. There has been without doubt an increase within ten years. This would not include the transient population, which is considerable.

The weather was becoming intolerable; and confined as we were within lofty walls, not an atom of breeze could penetrate our rooms. We concluded therefore to beat a hasty retreat, and hired two empty coal-boats to take us to Kia-ting-foo, one hundred and twenty miles. Although possessing little comfort they answered our purpose well enough, and cost the mere pittance of two dollars and a half.

We went on board below the East Gate bridge on the morning of the 12th of July. It was with considerable difficulty the boats were brought to the shore, as the bank was thickly lined with freight and passenger junks, no one of which would give way an inch, fearing the strong current would sweep them down the rapid stream. We scrambled on at last with our baggage as best we could, and forced a passage-way between the boats. The street we had just traversed exhibited an unusual number of finely lacquered coffins, of which I do not remember seeing as many or as fine elsewhere. When once out in the stream we shot down past the suburbs and the shipping in a few moments, and entered the larger channel which flows past the west of the city. We joined it a few paces below the famous bridge described by Marco Polo six centuries since : —

" The city is watered by many considerable streams which descend from the distant mountains, surround, and pass through it in a variety of directions. Some of these rivers are half a mile in width; others are two hundred paces and very deep, over which are built several large and handsome stone bridges, eight paces in breadth, their length being greater or less according to the size of the stream. From one extremity to the other there is a row of marble pillars on each side, which support the roof; for here the bridges have very handsome roofs, constructed of wood, ornamented with paintings of a red color, and covered with tiles. Throughout the whole length also there are neat apartments and shops, where all sorts of trades are carried on. . . . These rivers, uniting their streams below the city, contribute to form the mighty river called Kiang, whose course before it discharges itself into the ocean is equal to a hundred days' journey."

No doubt the Venetian writer got most of his information second-hand, and very greatly exaggerated. Where are the marble pillars, and the stream half a mile wide ? The bridge cannot be above three hundred feet long; it has nine piers, and is out of repair. It has the appearance of great age, and the wooden covering is in a tumble-down condition. Below the junction of the streams a large number of down-river passenger boats were seen near the banks, and we came to a very fine stone bridge in full view of the An Sheu, or Marco Polo bridge. We noted the suburban shops, which are rather small; their business seems confined mostly to coke, wood, coal, and coffins; of wood there were piles in every direction along the bank. Our course for fifteen miles was generally southward, and through an almost tropical country. The luxuriance of vegetation of all descriptions was a subject of frequent remark. Stolid indeed must be the traveller who can glide down the swift-flowing river without going into rhapsodies over the ever-changing and always beautiful scenes in every direction.

Marco Polo calls this the Kiang Shui, or " Yang-tsze waterway." The Chinese consider this, strange as it may seem, the main upper stream of the Yang-tsze. Hundreds of small boats are working up the current along the bank, one or two men from each boat in the water up to their waists, pushing and pulling, and one or two on shore tracking.

All along the river are huge water-wheels, singly or in pairs, and sometimes as many as ten of these squeaking monsters were slowly revolving in concert at one race. On the outer rim of the wheel are tied diagonally a great number of bamboo tubes, three or more feet in length, which catch the water and bring it to the top, being so arranged as to discharge their contents into a trough which carries it away to the fields. The stream is narrow and shallow, and evidently directed to suit the purpose of the peasants. In places its banks are faced with red sandstone, again with numerous bamboo bags, filled with cobble-stones. At some places the navigable portion of the river is greatly reduced by the building of dams obliquely half-way across, that the water may be diverted to the wheels.

Before we made twenty miles, several unusually fine stone bridges were passed, and one in particular was worthy of note. The arches were of perfect form, and on either side of each arch were projecting buttresses, not more than five feet above the surface of the water. Upon each buttress stands or reclines a figure of some animal of life-size. On the upper side there are seven or nine different water monsters, while on the lower side are the same number of land animals. The figures were so perfectly executed that there was no debate as to which was the water-buffalo, and which the wild boar, as might be the case in some localities.

Early in the afternoon we took our farewell view of the rich and interesting plain, and floated quietly into the midst of low green hills, well wooded, and decorated with an occasional pagoda of striking form, having only three or five stories ; rather slender for beauty, and with too striking a contrast between the different segments. Kiang-kao and Peng-san-hsien, near the river, are pleasant and attractive places, but we did not stop.

The hills rise from four to six hundred feet, and in places come close to the water's edge, their subdued and quiet aspect tending to dreamy reveries. The fierce afternoon rays were shut out by wooded peaks, under whose shadows we floated, and the tired boatman laid aside his oars, and took a quiet smoke. We drifted along, turning with the murmuring eddies, and catching at every turn some new and interesting feature.

Mr. Baber tells us that he caught his first and last view of the celebrated Mount Omei from the hills far above Kia-ting. He describes the mountain as appearing unnaturally lofty, through some atmospheric influence. We had strained our eyes all the morning and far into the afternoon, to get a glimpse of the majestic pile. Every dark cloud was thought to be the mountain, provided it was high enough. As the fleecy clouds rolled away and packed themselves around the region where the giant ought to be, our interest became intense. It was not, however, until we had entered the rich alluvial plain of Kia-ting, that the day-dream passed, and we saw the wondrous "Eyebrows" peering out of dark clouds. Toward the evening of the second day's floating upon the beautiful Min we came to anchor under lofty trees near to the city wall of Kia-ting-foo. We had made three hundred and fifty li, or one hundred and ten miles, in the space of twenty-three working hours.

CHAPTER X.

Mount Omei is a centre of natural and artificial wonders, the like of which may not be found elsewhere upon the globe. I speak advisedly. The world is large, and in regions like Switzerland and Alaska, Nature seemingly has been taxed to the uttermost to produce a combination of natural objects of surpassing beauty and grandeur. Here, however, near the borders of Chinese civilization, we find a region of unequalled sublimity, — a combination of lofty mountains, of swift rivers, of valleys of wondrous fertility. Then also of the works of man there are many, — such as thousands of brine-wells, a great silk culture, of which it is the centre, a white-wax industry, mountains chiselled into the forms of idols, colossal bronze statues, pagodas, and one temple wholly of rich bronze. Great Omei mountain is hundreds of li in circumference, rising 11,100 feet, its highest point enveloped in the everlasting clouds. All these wonders are within a radius of forty miles from our anchorage, and within this prefecture of Kia-ting. A mile or two below, upon the opposite bank, abrupt red sandstone bluffs were in full view from our boat. White pagodas and fine temples grace the tops, which are wreathed with beautiful evergreens. Upon the face of the highest cliff, which descends straight to the water,

is the famous carved Mi-lêh Buddha in a sitting posture,
and over three hundred feet in height.   Small trees
grow from the head of the colossus, and he is said to
have an artificial nose.   The guards, on either side, are
of immense size and finely chiselled : —

"The violence with which the waters of the Yang-kiang dash
against the opposite cliff produces a rapid of very formidable
character, known as the 'Buddha's head rapid.'   The adjoining hill is named the 'Ice-clond hill' and also the 'Nine-
summit hill,' being indicative of its configuration.   In the
early part of the eighth century a Buddhist priest named
Hai-tung conceived the idea of a huge figure of Buddha, to
avert dangers incident to the spot, — a design which was
brought to completion after nineteen years' labor ; and there
the figure now stands in a recess of the rock, — an image of
Mi-lêh Buddha, the most gigantic piece of sculpture in China,
and perhaps in the world.   Fan Ching-ta, who visited the
place in A. D. 1177, gives the height of the figure as three
hundred and sixty feet, circumference of the head one hundred feet, and breadth of the eyes twenty feet.   The ears, he
says, were made of wood, and the whole was screened by a
thirteen-story pavilion. . . . .

"Whether it be a freak of Nature, or the work of some wag-
gish priest, I know not, but suspect the latter ; for the vegetation on the crown appears so trimmed as to form a perfect head
of hair ; while creeping plants are pendent from the upper
lip, muth resembling a moustache.

"Both in this and the adjoining cliffs the caves of the Mantsz are very numerous, and some are found also on the right
bank."

One would suppose Buddhist ambition to be satisfied
with an undertaking of this magnitude, but we are told
by a Russian traveller that it is a mere infant beside one
a few days' journey distant.   There he found a mountain
— a small one of course — fashioned by the hand of
man into the form of Buddha.

We were ready at an early hour the next morning, the 15th of July, to start on our two days' tramp to the Sacred Mountain. The chair coolies and baggagemen are not more angelic in this paradise than in less religious quarters; and we had the same bickerings and delays over opium, tea, tying up of tails, buying sandals at the last moment, arranging burdens, changing chair poles, getting new ropes — and the head man, Teu foo, only knows what besides. We lingered in the little boat awhile watching a variety of manœuvres on shore and on boats and rafts. A small raft floated by with two men fishing with an otter; the animal seemed quite as earnest and conscientious in the discharge of his duties as the men. Long narrow rafts covered with all sorts of merchandise worked swiftly past us up the stream. While standing at the entrance of the street directing the details of equipment, and at the same time driving a fairly good sale of books, I observed a proclamation near by, and curiosity led me to examine it. It informed the public that there had been much fighting and stabbing with knives and use of the sword. Arms of all kinds were prohibited. In case there should be any use of such weapons resulting in death in drunken brawls, the parties to the fight would be dealt with as murderers.

Kia-ting is the natural centre of the silk trade for the prefecture, and until recent times controlled to a large extent both manufacture and export; but on account of excessive imports much of the trade has been driven away, and is now centred at Suchi, a thriving town ten miles distant. The streets of the city are wide and smoothly paved with broad blocks of red sandstone. The shops are large and well stocked with native and foreign goods, many fancy articles from distant sections of the empire, and a more than usual amount of light textile fabrics from Europe. Upon one street was seen a fine display of cutlery of every conceivable form and quality, also some excellent work done in brass. Chenteu-foo excels in the manufacture of implements of steel and copper, as well as bronze, and that city has branch houses here.

Reaching the opposite end of the city, near to the gate, we came upon a row of restaurants near the city wall. The bearers could not resist the temptation of certain fragrant dishes, and as usual dropped everything and made a general rush for the tables. I got out and walked to and fro upon the wall, and amused myself tracing the outlines of the Tung and Min Rivers, and examining the stone Buddha, which appeared to much better advantage here than from the other part of the town. Numbers of well-dressed ladies and children sauntered along as if out for a holiday, and I was much struck with their good forms and intelligent faces. The people were very civil, and disposed to give any information we desired. Before leaving we climbed upon a little hill above the gate which commanded a fine view of the beautiful city. Outside the wall we came at once into shady nooks by the swift-running Ya, which were more than usually grateful, for the morning was very sultry. After a few li of delightful progress amid low hills and grassy vales, we struck straight for the river's bank, and were packed into two small boats for a two hours' pull against the fiercest current yet met with.

Navigation on the Tung and Ya Rivers is full of difficulties. The floods of water which sweep down these streams in summer is amazing. They are each nearly half a mile wide, the banks full to overflowing, as they rush on, rolling and thundering. Boats are almost carried up the current hugging the gravelly banks; a small boat requires a dozen men to pull and pole. The crossing is both difficult and dangerous at this season. None but very light-draft boats and bamboo rafts are used; of the latter there are great numbers. The small river coming from Omei, and passing through the centre of Suchi, is navigable to that place for fair-sized ferryboats. After crossing it some fifteen li below Suchi, our road took us through an unusually fertile and interesting district.

We halted at Suchi for lunch. The public house we entered was full of pilgrims, male and female. Seven ladies sat at one table drinking tea and finishing a dessert, as we entered, and a Buddhist priest, a sort of cicisbeo, lay on the divan near by. He was smoking opium, and was waited upon by two or three servants. The table was given to us, but the priest held on to the divan until the impatient lady pilgrims roused him from his stupor by continual calls. One of the fair pilgrims accosted my teacher, who is disposed to be somewhat of a wag. His laconic reply was, "Burn your own incense, and I will mine." He purchased a yellow incense bag at the city, and carried it like the pilgrims; but I almost blush to say he made no secret of its use, having crammed it with tobacco and his foreign pipe.

After lunch we priced silk, and hastened up the steep hill at the west end of the town, which commands a superb view of the widely scattered city and the beautiful valley, sweeping away to the distant west, an unbroken sea of green. Oh, what a sight! Nothing could be prettier; the lovely little river, like a silver thread, could be traced in its windings amid groves and verdant fields. Away in the distance a pagoda, almost snowwhite, rose from out the green, but there was no trace of a city. The town lies on both sides of the river, embowered in evergreen trees, and is very populous. This is one of the great centres of silk culture in China, and the valley one of extraordinary fertility, containing millions of mulberry and white-wax trees.

There is no prettier journey than from Suchi to Omei-hsien, a distance of fifteen miles. The rice-fields are now laden with a rich harvest, which will be gathered a month hence. Over all these smiling fields are rows and rows of valuable trees. It was nearly evening as we approached the walls, and I was beginning to doubt the veracity of my bearers, when suddenly the head of our escort called out: "The white-wax trees!" They are snow-white, from lowest branch to seven-leaved twigs. One is almost inclined to doubt the reality at first. Surely it has not been snowing in this almost tropical clime. Let us halt and have a good look at this singular phenomenon. This pure, white, cotton-looking stuff is only on the under and outer sides of the branches, and is about a quarter of an inch thick. A few main branches of the tree have been preserved, and these, trimmed of all laterals and twigs, have grown out almost horizontally, with a tuft of green leaves at the end. There are a few dried-up bags of the tung-oil tree leaves hanging to the boughs; otherwise the trees are clean and smooth, with ten or twelve branches well laden with snow-white wax. Lovely, wonderful sight! As far as one can see are rows of this tree. What is it, and why different from the same or similar species at Ningpo or Kiangsi? This species is, I think, as yet un-determined, being quite different from the *Ligustrum* met with below Kia-ting-foo. It has unequal pinnated leaves, from three to seven, and a wing-shaped seed. Mr. Faber thinks it one sort of the *Fraxinus* genus, but cannot determine which. It may possibly be a species of the Tung-tsin. It grows wild on Mount Omei, but destitute of wax. The following items in reference to its culture and the wax were gathered from the farmers near our monastery upon the mountain.

The tree, like the willow, grows readily from cuttings, which are put out in the second month (March). Within three to five years the tree is of suitable size for use. It furnishes a rich sap, which of itself is of no value, but the keen agriculturists of this valley have learned how to utilize it. The wax itself is the product of a small insect brought from the distant valley of Kien-chang, — nearly four hundred miles from Omei, — from five different places among the aboriginal tribes south of Kia-ting-foo. The little insect lays its eggs in those distant mountains upon the paokêh-tree, but produces little or no wax there. These egg-cocoons are brought in great haste from their native places in eleven-ounce packages, and sold to Kia-ting merchants ; they are then distributed without delay, tied into green tung-oil tree leaves, and hung upon the trees, where they hatch almost immediately. It requires thirteen days of day and night work to make the journey and get the eggs here before hatching, for which a man carrying sixty-six packages receives the fine sum of nine dollars. Each package in ordinary times sells for about one dollar and ten cents, but under extraordinary circumstances for seven dollars. Within fifty or sixty days from the time the eggs are hatched the wax appears upon the tree, and gradually increases to the eighth month. The insect, which when first hatched is white, and scarcely visible, thickens and grows darker as the season advances. It lives upon this oily sap, and deposits a perfectly opaque wax. Great care is necessary that the period of work is not pro-

longed beyond a certain time, lest the maggot should
develop wings and fly away, thereby causing much loss
to the owners. In the eighth month the branches are
cut off and scraped; both wax and Coccus are boiled
together, then strained and moulded into requisite forms.
The wax sells for about sixty cents per pound at Kia-
ting-foo. At Hankow, Nanking, and other large cities
in the East, the price, owing to imposts and freight, is
more than double that sum. A tax is levied before it
leaves the district. The whole amount of production
for this district might be 1,400,000 pounds. Each
tree in its prime produces from two to four pounds
biennially.

Although the insect does its best work on this particular tree, for some unexplained cause it does not propa-
gate well outside its own mountain home and upon the
paokêh-tree. Being a subject of much commercial importance, I am inclined to quote the remarks of Baron
Richthofen, which have come before me since the above
was written. He did not see this particular region, but
his remarks will be read with great pleasure by those
interested in the productions of China. Baron Richthofen says respecting the white-wax culture : —

"This is a valuable and very interesting product of
Sz-Chuan. It is largely consumed in the country, and much
of it is exported to other provinces. The white wax of commerce is made exclusively in the department of Kia-ting-fu,
near the western border of the Red Basin. Sz-Chuan people
know that it is also made in Shantung, Chekiang, and Fukien,
but speak with contempt of the inferiority of the wax of those
provinces. According to my information, none is made in
Kwei-cheu and Yunnan, or in any of the northern provinces.

" The department of Kia-ting-fu is a region where much
level ground spreads between gentle hills, and bears therefore an exceptional character in a country so uniformly hilly

as Sz-Chuan. Its climate is warmer than that of the plain of Ching-tu-fu, but not so warm as that of the valley of Ning-yuen-fu, which is better known as the region of Kien-chang, and highly reputed for its beauty of scenery. With admirable sagacity the Chinese have found out that the breeding of the wax-insect and the production of wax through it are two distinct processes, which cannot be combined profitably in one and the same locality, but if judiciously separated may lead to unexpected perfection. The regions of Kien-chang and of Kia-ting-fu divide the labors and the profits. In Kien-chang, near the cities of Ning-yuen-fu and Hwui-li-chau, the insect-tree is planted. It is an evergreen with large and pointed ovate leaves. It is so valuable that it constitutes a separate article of property distinct from the soil on which it grows. On this tree the wax-insect lives and breeds, but secretes little wax. It is evidently under conditions best fitted for its healthy development. The wax which is made at Kien-chang is just sufficient for the small local consumption and the supply of Yunnan. At the end of April the Kien-chang people leave their country in great numbers, each with a load of the precious eggs upon his back, and travel on a very mountainous road to Kia-ting-fu, which they reach after a fortnight's arduous walking. The road is said to present then during several weeks an exceedingly lively aspect, chiefly at night-time, when they go with lanterns. The heat of the day must be avoided, because the sun would quickly hatch the eggs. These are described as a substance resembling flour, and contained in a bag of the shape and size of a pea. Three hundred of the little bags weigh one tael.

"The insect produces no eggs in Kia-ting-fu. The natives believe the climate is not warm enough. It appears, however, that the plentiful secretion of wax indicates a sort of diseased state, owing perhaps to a too luxurious food. The wax-trees are planted on fields, either on level ground or on the lowest portions of the slopes of hills. They are very plentiful in the districts of Omei, Kia-kiang, Hung-ya, and Lŏ-shan, all of Kia-ting-fu. Every attempt to produce good wax in other regions has failed."

It is an error to say that no eggs are produced in Kia-ting-fu; but those produced here do not yield as good wax as those that are brought from Kieu-chang.

The night of the 15th was spent in the beautiful city of Omei. All the public houses were crowded at an early hour with pilgrims. We managed, however, after much persuasion, to get sufficient room to spread our beds. A Buddhist priest of stately mien, with a stride like a Highlander, walked in company with me for a few moments before entering the city. He was from Peking, had been two months upon the journey, and carried all his earthly treasures nicely packed in two bundles, at the ends of a " carrying pole." He was very sociable for a time, as we swept along the smooth path, which wound through the rice-fields. Twilight was approaching, and he dashed ahead to secure a bed. We rode through the greater part of the strange city before we came to our lodgings, and only got a shelter by plucky pushing. We sat in the crowded street while unnumbered parties of boys and girls came and inspected us. How thoughtfully, silent as ghosts, they eyed me, giving knowing glances and nudges to their companions, as they moved away for others to take their places!

Suffocation would hardly express the feeling, when windows were filled with heads, chair-poles covered with half-naked urchins, and the broad, hot street crowded with unbathed, sweating humanity. My teacher was in a towering rage, as usual, when matters went wrong. An escort had been sent forward to secure lodgings, and finding every place full, they quietly sat down to tea and to smoke, instead of looking farther, or inducing the proprietor to empty a room containing twenty pilgrims for us two poor foreigners. Not relishing making a nocturnal show of ourselves in a crowded street, in which.

the prospect was fair for a rush to see the red-headed
and gray-headed monsters, we plunged into the long hotel, which was actually swarming with men and women,
and in ten minutes had secured an eligible front room, —
all door and window in front, without a bed, but having
a corner in which to spread one. A pig-sty to the left,
twenty pilgrims to the right, and a court full of people
in front, gabbling like geese. The air was stiflingly hot,
and the stenches almost unbearable, until a heavy thun-
der-storm swept over us. Rooms on either side of the
long narrow court were crowded with men and women ;
and the following morning, although rain still fell, they
brought forth their staves and umbrellas, and started for
the sacred heights. What lifting up of expectation to
those approaching for the first time, and for those sore-
footed brethren hailing from Peking and Yang-Chao! We
joined the exodus, and in the gray mists of the morning
tramped along the wet streets and out of the south gate,
striking at once into groves of the wax-tree, and up hill-
sides garnished with a luxuriance of summer products.

The grand heights just before me, now clothed in
white mists, are really the beginning of Kún-lún of fable
and story. Have I at last reached the verge of the
Taoist and Buddhist Paradise, near the home of the
" Western Mother," — the heaven of fancy woven into a
hundred religious tales ? Did kings and warriors of old
travel thus far, and from the mount gaze upon the snow
range rising between this and Thibet, and imagine themselves on the confines of the spirit world, and believe that
in some of those glittering heights far beyond, " jewelled
heaven " took its rise ? These very peaks, the gorges,
the deep gurgling streamlets, the pillared rocks, and
dark chasms have been fruitful sources of numberless
myths, legends, and miraculous stories, which from re-

motest antiquity have circulated among millions of the aboriginal tribes as well as among the Chinese. It was near the end of earth to the ancient traveller, and the peak but "one step from heaven."

Let us, then, ere we ascend higher toward this wonder-land, listen for a moment to a far-famed wanderer, as in a Wu-chang tea-saloon, in the good old days, he portrays to a new-made friend the wonders he had seen. He tells him of the white tiger (an image of which may be still seen in a wayside shrine half-way to the top), which "attracts other beasts to its side by its mildness. Its kindness to other animals is such that it will not even tread on living grass, and eats only what died of itself." He draws a picture of the Yao-Ko, a divine steed of such fleetness that fable tells us he could go ten thousand li in one day. There is the Pisieh, which guards the mountain fastnesses, and drives away the vicious beasts who would harm the innocent. He had seen the Tien luh, "beavenly deer," which has power to bestow official blessings, and the Wenpao, "spotted leopard," which can hide himself in the fog; also the Yuen, "white gibbon," brilliant as a gem; the Yung, an ape with hair like golden threads; the snow-white deer; and the Kwei, weighing a thousand catties, which was a one-legged monster resembling a dragon, or an ox and man combined. Still other won-ders were the flame-devouring flying-squirrel, called Wu-chu; the musk-deer which may be found high among the rocks and bamboos; and the moh, a kind of tapir which devours iron as if it were sugar cakes. He next de-scribes the marvellous birds which he had seen, and the wonderful trees.

Beggars, small and large, were out in force at this early hour, and, posted at their accustomed places, told their piteous tales. Banyans of thirty and forty feet in

girth stretch their giant arms across the road in front of
temples, and above curious shrines. A delightful hour's
walk brought us to the Shen-chi monastery, where on
this side of the city begin a series of wonders which
extend in ever-increasing interest to the highest crag of
Omei, which is one hundred and twenty li away and
11,100 feet above the sea. Without warning we found
ourselves standing within the precincts of an unpre-
tending temple court, surrounded by a number of very
large and unusually well-executed works in bronze.
The first to attract my attention was a fifteen-storied
tower or pagoda about thirty feet high. Each segment
or story displayed a vast number of images and intricate designs, each differing in form and design from
bottom to top. The priest said the tower was of
great age, and of no later date than the Han dynasty.
After researches, however, showed it to be of the
Min.

Upon its surface were 4,700 images of Buddha, besides many other queer figures, eminently worthy of
careful study. The symmetry and fine workmanship
are manifest at first sight, but a closer inspection proves
that all the figures of ornamentation and lettering are
most exquisitely wrought. Vandals have broken off
many of the heads of the smaller images, and done
some other slight damage to the monument, but on
the whole it is wonderfully preserved, possessing as
it does so many delicate figures. After an hour or
two of careful study from every possible quarter, I
am confident in saying that China has few monuments
equal to this, and none excelling it in symmetry of
design and excellence of execution. Some of the lower
projections have suffered much from the hands of pilgrims, who consider a copper cash brightened upon the

sacred metal as possessing very great merit, and to be worn as an amulet. This, as well as all the better works of art, is covered with a wooden structure, which serves two diverse purposes, — protection from the weather and from destruction by fire. I noticed subsequently that many of the larger and more valuable monuments have thus greatly suffered during the past hundred years. Only a few yards distant I saw a mammoth bronze image of the god Pu-hsien, thirty feet high, standing upon a reclining bronze elephant. Pu-hsien is called the eldest son of Buddha, whose marvellous glory is exhibited above the " diamond pillars " east of Mount Omei. This statue is of early date, going back nearly a thousand years. It is in good condition, and is a rare work of. art ; the trunk has been polished almost as bright as a mirror by constant patting and rubbing.

Over the gateway-tower hangs an immense pure bronze bell weighing twenty thousand pounds, and covered with finely engraved characters, detailing doubtless many incidents connected with the early history of the place, but my limited time did not permit an attempt at translation. These old Min bronze bells and colossal idols scattered over the empire indicate the religious condition of China at that date, as well as the great wealth of the empire. I claim to have discovered in this quiet retreat some of the richest and most interesting monuments to be found anywhere in the province, and I sincerely hope future travellers will turn aside, and at least look upon the wonderfully wrought tower. These unexpected discoveries under the very walls of the city whetted our appetites for the richer works of man and God, which we were confident must be revealed to us in our upward journey.

The silvery tones of the grand old bell had died away

GREAT BRONZE PAGODA AT OMEI.

in the echoing hills as we resumed the line of march.
The broad valley, rich in all material wealth, narrowed
by degrees until the checkered and fitful outlines of the
enclosing slopes gathered their bright-green robes around
us.   The valley sent purling brooks toward the city,
which by the hand of man, in occasional seasons of
drought, are conducted from terrace to terrace, thus
watering myriads of rice-fields.   The orchards of the
wax-tree now cover the narrow valleys, and rise, tier
above tier, upon the hill-sides, becoming thinner as they
reach the mountain forests.   We passed under the grateful shade of giant banyans, the intense heat rendering
the cover all the more delightful.

A large monastery, enriched by many acres of fertile
ground, surrounded by a dark canopy of moss-and-fern-
grown trees, and cooled by a broad, foaming stream,
which roars past its gateway, greeted us as we toiled
over sand and smooth-washed cobble-stones.

The evanescent clouds disclosed anon to our upturned
eyes the distant peaks towering in sublime grandeur
above the placid valleys humbly veiled in purple mists.
Along the broad slopes and up the deep cañons were
forests of fir and nan-mu, concealing all rough and
unsightly objects from our eyes.

Ten miles from the city we entered a wild ravine, where
a mad torrent wrestles with a limestone ledge, cutting
deeper and deeper, now wider, now narrower, into the
solid stratifications, bending and winding upon itself
through one of the most romantic gorges imaginable.
A hundred secret fountains play from the overhanging
cliffs, sending their pure greenish floods down the perpendicular rocks into the little river.   Now some stream-
let dashes from a towering crag far above the rocky
path, and the breezes from some higher pass, dancing

through fern beds, gently lift the falling spray, and sprinkle the flushed faces of the pilgrims.

We sat in a wayside inn, drank white tea, and coaxed the embarrassed waiter to pluck a few ears of green corn and roast them in the ashes; we exhibited to the ever-increasing crowd the aneroid, compass, and thermometer, and told the wiser ones their use, the height above the sea, etc. We lingered in a deep-shaded tea-shop, which was perched upon a mountain ledge, and from which we had grander views; here were great piles of coffin planks and logs scattered about waiting to be sawed. The trees grown upon the mountain are considered more sacred than elsewhere; and I noticed afterward in my rambles among the forests, that it was no unusual thing to find trees marked as having been selected by gentlemen for their own coffins.

The stone-paved path becomes more difficult of ascent as it winds around high ragged rocks, and a step only lies between the perpendicular towers and the fearful chasms below. In places are tons of earth, rock, trees, grass, ferns, and flowers helplessly massed, and filling the road and narrow pass even to the edge of the cliff; over these we must scramble as best we can. It is no uncommon thing during one of the terrible storms which visit the mountain at this season of the year, for mighty rocks and tall trees to come crashing down from impending heights, carrying destruction to homes and fields.

While plodding upward under the torturing flames of the noonday sun a restful combe was reached, and a sharp turn in the road brought us in full view of a suspension bridge made entirely of iron. It was unexpected, — not that the Chinese are ignorant or incompetent in such matters, for such works are common in some districts, — but I was unprepared for the sight in this secluded spot. It is stretched across a cascade some fifty feet above the water, and in plan is very similar to American suspension bridges : the iron bars are attached to a double set of pillars, twenty feet apart at each end. It is a foot-bridge, and not used for heavy traffic, and consequently the pillars and fastenings are flimsy affairs compared with our bridges. From outer posts to inner or bridge posts it is twenty feet, and the span of the bridge is one hundred and forty feet; the top bars of wrought iron, running from outer pillars one hundred and eighty feet, the iron bars or rods being one and one half inches in diameter. The lower frame of the bridge consists of six equal rods, attached to the upper rods by iron posts. It is five feet wide and planked. I found it swayed considerably as the centre was reached, but no more than would be expected from such material.

A little way beyond, if the longer road is taken, you come upon one of the quaintest and most interesting retreats found in the mountain. The name given to the locality is " a pair of flying bridges." Why it should take such a name is more than I can tell. The Chinese have wonderful legends about flying bells and scissors, and even huge stone vessels ; of such there are many in Nanking and other great historical centres. The visitor may see a bronze bell in the northern part of Nanking, fifteen feet long and seven feet diameter, which is supposed to have winged its flight from heaven ; also, two great shear-shaped bronze instruments, — use unknown, — which are said to have fallen from heaven. I notice that a Chinese poet alludes to a certain wonderful temple which fell from above. These objects remind the student of Greek legends; the Palladium at Troy was believed to have fallen from the sky. The ancient gods were of rude stones, and were believed to have flown or fallen from heaven, and many similar examples could be given; this is, however, the first time I have seen " flying bridges." Be it as it may, you suddenly find yourself in the centre of a fairy dell, standing upon a narrow neck of land not above fifty feet wide, while two little rivers, coming from distant mountains, having sung through enchanted vales, now rush in white foam on either side; they are completely hidden from view, and their presence is divined from two stone moss-covered bridges, and the terrific roar from the cascades a little way above. The little frenzied streams have worn their channels seventy-five feet deep, while they are not more than eight feet wide. The old moss-and-fern-grown bridges which span them are sacred treasures of a distant past; and as one peers into their deep yet sparkling depths, he has photographed in his memory an ineffaceable picture of exquisite loveliness. A tea-shop fills the empty space between the bridges, and a succession of famous temples rise and widen with the broader space between the streams to the south. While my companions went up one of these rivers for a bath, I examined the temples, and studied the half-defaced monuments in hopes of finding some historical incidents of importance; but the inscriptions pointed to nothing earlier than the Sung dynasty, so I betook myself to a flirtation with ferns, flowers, and birds, and had the unusual luck of finding some wild spearmint. I felt with the poet who long ago sung:

> " I love the brooks which down their channels fret,
> Even more than when I tripped lightly as they;
> The innocent brightness of a new-born day
> Is lovely yet."

We tramped through several dense groves, alive with birds and numerous cicada, who nearly deafened us with their constant buzzing. As we ascended, the air became cooler and clearer, and on every side appeared an unsurpassed wealth of vegetation and color. We could overlook our path, winding by streams and over mountain spurs, tracing its general course to the city of Omei. After a smart climb of half an hour through woods and past large temples, which would be interesting in a less celebrated mountain, with eager steps we hastened through an ancient arched temple which spans the road, climbed over three hundred broad stone steps, and with panting breath stood before the object of our search. An ancient tablet informed us that this was the "First of Mountains;" another tablet, over the great gate, told us that we had reached Shen Wan-Nien-Sz, the "Holy monastery of a myriad years." We ascended its courts, and found ourselves more than three thousand feet above the sea, and seventeen hundred feet above our last night's lodging. At this height, all around us are wax-trees fruit-trees, tea plantations, and thousands of acres of maize and millet.

In the absence of the abbot two or three young priests gave us a hearty welcome, supplied us at once with boiling tea, and threw open the doors of our allotted apartments, which were the best the monastery afforded. Half an hour later, Mr. Faber, who had parted from us six weeks before, and had reached the temple seven days since, came in from a botanical excursion. A scar upon his forehead and a halting step were the evidences he brought of hard usage; but we were glad to learn that they were not received in mortal combat. He had fallen into the hold of his boat coming up the river, and injured his knee; and, while botanizing, had slipped from a cliff, and plunged his head into a mossy hollow between rough rocks.

CHAPTER XI.

Long before daylight there were sounds of sonorous bells and the beating of drums, together with the plaintive yells of a half-grown boy. While the older and more worldly priests clung to their couches, this lad and an octogenarian said prayers and dusted the halls. If I had been nearer, and my ear trained to Buddhistic chanting, the following petition would have edified my tortured mind : —

" O magic bell! the first in harmony,
    Loudly diffuse this priceless chant.
    May it penetrate even the heavenly courts above,
    And reach to Sheol's halls below,
    That all of heaven and earth may be controlled.
    We pray that the princes of the realms below
    May be advanced in dignity and wealth;
    That those in the *three worlds* and *four divisions of life*
      May all escape the *wheel* of *revolutions ;*
    That the ten orders of spirits in the *nine prisons*
    May fortunately escape from the *bitter Ocean.*
    May every fifth day windy be and tenth a rainy one,
    Lest we fall upon years of drought and famine,
  That the south may be a boundless sea and the east a forest,
    Just as in the adorable days of Yao and Shun.
    May shields and spears forever rest,
    And no more may be the warrior and the battle horse,
    And that the battalions of the wounded dead
      May all be born into the Pure Land.
       That birds and animals
    May not be caught within the nets,

That spendthrifts, shopmen, and merchants
May early return to their homes.
That there may be the *five locations* and *ten worlds*,
And that earth may endure and heaven be eternal,
That altars near and far may be increased,
That blessings be multiplied and age lengthened,
And that monasteries may be undefiled,
And the Buddhist laws forever prevail,
That the gods of the land and *dragon spirits*
May with single-mindedness protect the law,
That fathers, mothers, teachers, brothers, may peace enjoy,
And that every generation of those already dead
May together ascend upon *that shore*."

The last line refers to Paradise or the Western Land.

" Hail! undefiled person of the Law, Pi-lu-che-na-Buddha;
Hail! complete person of the Law, Lu-ha-na-Buddha;
Hail! millions of ages of transformation, first teacher, Shi-kia-mu-ni;
Hail! the one to be born, Mi-lêh, precious Buddha;
Hail! the one of the Western Happy Land, Omito Buddha;

" Hail! one of the golden boundary of the five lights, great of wisdom, wonderful teacher, Wen-Shü-Pu-Sa;
Hail! the one of Omei mountain silvery boundary, great of energy, Pu-hsien, King of vows, Pu-Sa ;
Hail! the one of Puto mountain porcelain boundary, great in mercy and compassion, sovereign hearer of sounds — Pu-Sa;
Hail! the one of nine-flowered mountain, sovereign lord of the spirit world, king of earth's secret abode, Pu-Sa, Nan-wu-ta-fang-kwang-fuh-hwa-lien-kin-nan-wu-hwa-lien-hai-hui-fuh-Pu-Sa!"

Later on, as the echoes of worshipping bells died away, there was a dress parade of the *male cicada* band ; there were trumpets, saws, files, and jews-harps, — a mixture of such screeching as never before greeted my waking hours. There was an occasional note which seemed familiar and brought back memories of other days. It was a prolonged sad and beseeching note, which sounded like " see, see, see! me, me, me!" I never had less desire to " see me " than then, and if they had bad the least conception of propriety they would have practised in the tops of the trees and not before my windows.

Still later there visited my leafy bower a choral of sweet songsters. Their time was well chosen, and their notes the sweetest of the sweet.

Before sunrise several bronze bells were beaten, and their harmonious notes resounded from cloister to cloister, filling the air with a music such as I have not before heard in China. The priests had exhorted me to close my window, as thieves and wild beasts prowled about the temples; but I left it half-open, thinking best to trust my riches, as everywhere on my journey, to the discretion of the night watchmen. To-day the warning was renewed, and the story of several men killed by a tiger repeated for my benefit; other wild beasts are here, and no one knows when they may pounce upon the innocent pilgrim, and of course a foreign visitor would be a rare treat. My teacher, wiser than his pupil, has armed himself with a strong club, and exhibits it whenever he leaves his room for a stroll. I may be led to do something desperate if many more such stories are told me. There is a large stone pillar-support, two feet high, just under my window, and by its help a thief, or even a tiger, could climb in with great ease; I shall roll it away and relieve my troubled mind. A path runs along under my bedroom windows, and upon the other side of it, not ten feet from where I sit, is a dense forest of high nan-mu and firs covering the side of the cliff, which makes a very abrupt slope to a corn-field several hundred feet below; beyond this towers a pine-clad peak fifteen hundred feet, and seems in the clear morning atmosphere to hover directly over us; but I am assured that it takes two hours to reach its top. The mists are sifting through the firs as I write, and the temperature is 74° at eleven A. M., at this, the hottest period of the year.

I have already discovered at least four beautiful walks, which take me to fairy retreats, all of which are so intrinsically lovely that it would seem invidious to make any distinction; so I take them by turns, and hold my mental reservations a secret, lest the fairies who bathe in the rich-colored ether above the sparkling pools should be offended. If I wander past my window eastward there are great trees, long creeping vines, shrubs of a dozen kinds, some full of flowers, others of berries. The birds sing from a hundred boughs, and great maltese-colored squirrels, with long bushy tails, leap from branch to branch, seeking the denser thicket below. Butterflies of all hues, beautiful moths, and multifarious insects flit across my path. With care I pick my way down the shelving rocks, clinging to twigs and dry roots, then circle around beyond the temple, leaving the priests' gardens and aqueducts to my right, and the corn-fields and graves to the left. I pluck sweet berries as I advance, until a well-trodden path is reached, which leads by easy stages to a bower where trickles from a limestone ravine a beautiful fountain. Here, if the hour be well chosen, are seen blithe damsels and athletic boys gathering grass and twigs from the corn-fields and rocky ledges, their baskets tightly strapped to their backs and short sickles in their hands. They scamper away like fawns when my helmet comes into view, and from some secure retreat, far from danger, watch my course. The limbs of the plum-trees bend low with luscious purple fruit, and coarse, large pears hang from slender limbs by the roadside. There are houses in the vale below, but enclosed in thick groves, so that but an occasional glimpse is had of their brown roofs. The roaring stream comes into view as I proceed, and long lines of pilgrims are seen, as ants, winding slowly up, cooled by the mountain's afternoon shadow. Beyond the stream rises a cone-like mountain of much celebrity as the home of many large snakes, and long lines of temples are perched upon its crown, hedged by great trees.

If fancy takes me northward I cross the road by which the ascent was made to the temple, and a smooth path beguiles me along the edge of a cliff which is covered with tea-gardens, while here and there are ancient Buddhist graves, long since emptied of their holy treasures. Verdant fields and groves stretch away to a large stream five miles to the west, where a score of happy hamlets nestle, and beyond which tower a lovely range of green mountains, fully three thousand feet above the smiling vale. Around me everywhere are trees and flowering shrubs and shallow caverns filled with ferns and lichens. At last a point is reached from which, in the evening hour, it was my fortune to see, mirrored as in the very heavens, the temples upon " Eyebrows," eight thousand feet above me and fifteen miles away. For once not a cloud flitted about the sacred height, and the setting sun shed an amber hue over all the peak, " with tints that brightened and were multiplied," which gradually changed to purple and gray as the evening advanced.

To the west I may roam through cultivated fields, past old temples, down to an iron bridge, all hedged in from the farm-houses by the well-grown corn and thickets of larch and wax trees. To the south I may wander under giant trees which rise high above the temples, some filled with clusters of white blossoms and sparkling beneath the rays of the late afternoon sun.

The shady banks are masses of bloom, and conspicuous among the flowers are the tender pink and white begonias. The bamboo troughs are overflowing with pure cold water coming from a distant spring. I pass the temples dedicated to the Goddess of Mercy, where an old man sells four kinds of tea and crystals with drops of water in the centre, and skirt along beautiful parks till I come to an opening in a forest where the short, fine grass is so inviting that I throw myself down at the foot of a tall, straight pine. " Open patches where the sun gets in and goes to sleep, and the winds come so finely sifted that they are as soft as swan's-down." Above me towers a mountain eighteen hundred feet high; below me is a deep ravine; all around me crimson, blue, and white flowers; while richly colored birds soar aloft, and with one strong note swoop down into the hospitable tree-tops. Such is this incomparable retreat.

This celebrated monastery, the glory of Western China, dates as far back as the Tsin dynasty, A. D. 265, and was founded in honor of Pu-hsien, who is generally believed to have come from the spirit mountains of India upon a white elephant. Historical characters of that age do not bear very close scrutiny, and Pu-hsien is no exception to this general rule. He is called the " wide-spreading sage," and one of the four great Pu-sa universally worshipped in China. The other three are Wen-shu of Mount Tai in Ho-nan, Kwanyin of Nanhai (Puto), and Titsang of Kiuhwa. These four Pu-sa — Bôdhüattva — are beings who have attained to perfect intelligence, are in the third class of saintship, and have to pass through the world only once more before becoming Buddhas. Next to Shih-kia-mu-ni and Omito Buddha, they are the most celebrated gods in China, and draw millions of pilgrims from all parts of the empire to their sacred retreats. These popular saints, as they may be called, have attracted the rank and file, and receive from the ignorant more honors than the real Buddhas.

The monastery, which was called " Clear Water " eight hundred years ago, is situated upon a narrow cliff, along which the ascent is made to the top of the mountain, from whence is seen the manifested glory of the " wide-spreading sage." It consists of a series of wooden buildings of great size, enclosing wide courts, and one brick building — the only one I saw on the mountain — of very peculiar construction, and surmounted with a perfect dome.

To this holy place, made sacred by centuries of worship, and rendered famous by the visits and princely gifts of emperors, empresses, kings, and feudal princes, it is my delightful privilege to invite my readers, to visit in imagination these scenes which have left an enduring impress upon my mind.

It would seem that the Creator could have added nothing more to bring all the surroundings into harmonious beauty. The towering mountains, the gently sloping spurs, the ledges and palisades in the distance, the cool streams, the winding vales and forest-trees, the purple-tinted air and silver clouds, and the myriads of songsters bewilder the imagination ; and, like the Queen of Sheba, we feel that there is no more spirit in us. " It was a true report that I heard in mine own land of thy acts and of thy wisdom. Howbeit I believed not the words until I came, and mine eyes had seen it : and, behold, the half was not told me."

I shall give the result of my own investigations, which were made under the most favorable circumstances, for many days together, at the height of the midsummer pilgrimages.

We will begin at the hostelry just above the stone archway, and in full view of the forest-crowned hill, where the pilgrims' staves are fashioned into strange forms. Here weary pilgrims, group after group, sit at square tables and drink tea; some, already overcome with fatigue, have fallen asleep, with their burdens still upon their backs or spread upon the tables. A dozen lounge about the door, waiting for the more favored ones within; they are footsore, and many of them are readjusting their sandals, and tightening their ankle-bands, in preparation for a further march. Their rough staves lie by their sides, and their oil-paper umbrellas are tightly strapped to their backs. Every person carries an umbrella, for the weather in July and August is most fickle. Of the pilgrims fully one half were women, and they, as a rule, were above forty years of age; some were quite young and in care of chaperones. I also observed a curious custom they have of travelling in companies of seven. Golden numbers run through the religious folklore of China, as in other lands.

The rich and the poor walk together, and kneel in the same circles around the altars of their honored gods. But how differently they dress! Here comes a queenly dowager, with staff and a retinue of servants, her head adorned with gold and pearls, and heavy gold rings in her ears. An ornamented head-dress of satin folds tightly about her glossy black hair; gold bracelets of enormous size are upon her wrists; her dress, which descends nearly to her lily-flowered shoes, is of brocaded silk or satin, with a thin jacket of rich material. She has her fur and wadded garments well packed and borne by a servant, ready for use when the elevation is reached. Of this class of ladies there are as many types as there are counties or towns represented. It is folly to suppose that the Chinese people dress always and everywhere the same, for their apparel is as diverse as that of any nationality. The poor are clad in homespun blue, green, or red cotton stuff; their dresses are shorter and more convenient for climbing. All kinds of head-dresses are represented, and all devices in jewelry; for even the very poor wear jewelry, and are as proud of their silver and pewter ornaments as the rich are of their jewels. Nearly all have small feet, and to make the journey over rough stones at all comfortable, they tie corn husks around the small shoes, and then attach sandals to these. The ascending pilgrims have bundles of incense and many pounds of copper cash, but those on the descent are not burdened with either.

Groups of tired women sat chatting and drinking tea at tables in the great, dimly lighted hall. As I pass them their voices are hushed as if by magic, their uplifted teacups are held suspended; consternation is depicted upon their faces as they gaze upon the strange apparition. I sit down at one of the square tables beyond them, lay aside my staff like a veritable pilgrim, take off my helmet (the same one I wore four years ago when leaving Toronto), wipe the drops from my brow, and survey my surroundings. An old priest, who has made more offerings of tea than prayers, quietly pours from the great crock an amber-colored fluid which he calls "sweet tea," and places it before me. But wait! What gigantic form is that which towers up among the rafters of the two-storied building not twenty feet from me? The fading afternoon light is not strong enough to give me more than the outlines of the co-lossus, but a nearer inspection discloses the fact that I am in the presence of a bronze image, once covered with gold, now washed with a reddish composition like copper. It is an image of Omito Buddha, and dates back to the Sungs, — perhaps to the tenth or twelfth centuries. It is about twenty-five feet high, fairly well proportioned, and artistically is not devoid of merit. The pedestal, differing from many such monuments, is of bronze instead of stone. It is strange that a casting of such antiquity should occupy such humble quarters. The only satisfactory explanation is that formerly it had a separate temple and pagoda either here or higher up, and that the temple and wooden pagoda were destroyed by fire, and this, with other smaller images saved from the wreck, was removed by the Mins to this place. There are four huge pillars of the masan-tree near the image, — remnants of a former temple, and held sacred by the priests. This tree is doubtless exhausted, as now it will not grow higher than an ordinary shrub. This Omito, or Amita, Buddha is, by all odds, the most popular of Buddhas with the Chinese, and his origin is more obscure than that of any other. He has several titles, such as " Eternal," " Boundless Light," " Sovereign Teacher of the Western Heaven," " The All-Merciful," " The All-Sympathizing," " Guide to the West." Many theories have been propounded to explain his presence and popularity. It is quite probable, as Dr. Eitel suggests, that the doctrine of this Buddha " may have risen from Persian or Gnostic ideas influencing the Buddhism of Cashmere and Nepaul." He was little known in China before the fifth century ; his name is now upon the lips of every devotee, whether performing at his or other shrines. I have seen worshippers go the round of all the gods in a temple and repeat without intermission " Omito-foo." His name is used everywhere and under all circumstances. If a man is particularly good and kind to others, he is sometimes spoken of as an "Omito-foo man." This god is believed to take great delight in helping mortals in their troubles, and his name is almost as dear to the devout Buddhist as that of Jesus is to the Christian. He is also the central attraction to the Western Heaven, and is alone able to save humanity from the endless cycles of transmigration, and give a safe transit across the high-billowed, bitter ocean into the happy land.

Returning to the monastery and its quiet court, where the birds sang in the japonica-trees, and a pet red crab of knowing mien watched me from a crevice in the bricks, I decided to visit a mat shed near by in which are half-a-dozen bronze idols with broken noses, twisted hands, and contorted faces, — remnants rescued from the fire and waiting sorrowfully for new habitations. On a little tray on long legs before one of the scarred, veteran images, a red rag, not two feet square, hides some marvellous thing from view. My guide throws aside the rag, and lo! Buddha's tooth is there, which, by request, is handed to me. It measures fourteen inches in length, eleven inches in the widest part, and is about three inches thick. It is of beautiful yellow ivory, as smooth as glass from handling, has about twenty veins of transparent enamel, and weighs eighteen pounds. It is, of course, a very large elephant's molar. When I said to the devout guardian of this part of Buddha that the god must have had a rather large head to accommodate four such teeth, his reply was, " Yes; but it is a matter I don't fully comprehend." While rolling it over (I did not whittle it like ——) and commenting upon its origin, whether of whale or elephant, the guardian struck the old bell to arouse the maimed idol, upon which several faithful pilgrims bowed to the tooth as it lay in my hands. The Buddhist worshippers do not kiss the relics or gods as Romanists do the bronze statue in St. Peter's, and the rusty chains which are said to have bound the apostle in prison. Their affection is displayed in rubbing the hand or foot of an idol, or scouring a copper cash upon the metal. I was told that this was the only tooth Buddha had; but an old priest who could not tell a lie followed me into a shady nook not far away, to point out the tree he called *masan*. He told me there, in confidence, that it was not his only tooth; that he had four in China, — one on Mount Kiu-hwa, one at Puto, and another at Tsin-liang, in the city of Nanking. This tooth was brought to China, it is said, about a thousand years ago, and taken to the capital for the emperor's inspection. It is admitted that he was somewhat sceptical as to its genuineness. It has been kept in a separate temple, called Fuh-ya-tien, for many centuries.

We finally climbed the last flight of steps and walked through the lofty portal, which is securely locked at dark. I observed upon my left a statue of Ta-mo, the last of the Indian patriarchs who came to China. He is gotten up quite gingerly, with hair, goatee, mustache, eyebrows, all of blue. Opposite is the mountain king, also in blue, and with two frightful tusks protruding from his mouth. Above the massive gateway is a small temple-shrine where the Taoist god, Yu-hwang, sits as doorkeeper to his majesty, Pu-hsien. A come-down, indeed, for the Pearly Emperor of high Heaven! But the attributes of the gods are interpreted so strangely that this degradation does not seem incongruous to the Chinaman. Inside this gate is a large, airy court, surrounded by lofty buildings; upon the left are well-furnished rooms for officials, and now occupied by our party. Before us rose a temple one hundred and forty feet long, and deep and lofty. Within are a few fine pieces of bronze; but the images are mostly of clay, and badly executed. Pu-hsien, the central god, sits in a monstrous lotus-flower upon the back of a white elephant. The shrine, frame, and canopy are beautifully carved and colored, and must be fifty feet high. To the right and left are the eighteen *lo-han*,[1] and to the right of the canopy is the Goddess of Mercy, life-size, robed in yellow, holding a small child upon her knee, while an infant rests gently within her flowing sleeve. Here barren women come and pour out their griefs. Near the door of exit in the rear is a finely executed statue of Wei-to, who upholds the majesty of Buddhist law. We pass into another and larger court filled with blooming hollyhocks and flowering shrubs, from which high, towering peaks are seen beyond the temples. To my left is the great dining-hall, and opposite are sleeping apartments. Across this deep court rises the famous wooden temple erected by the Emperor Yungchen about A. D. 1703, and retouched by Kien-Lung, 1736. An octagonal iron incense-holder of ancient manufacture, twelve feet high, and of three stories, stands upon the platform before the great doors. This temple front is made up largely of carved and latticed doors and windows, which were richly gilded by the last-mentioned emperor; but a hundred and fifty years have borne hardly upon the decorations, which are now dingy and somewhat shabby. I was bewildered on entering by the vast number and great size of the images on thrones and platforms.

The floor is a hard chunam of vermilion color, and in places polished smooth as a mirror. The most prominent figure is a half-nude Mi-lêh Buddha seated in a richly carved throne, which rests upon a high platform.

---

[1] Immediate disciples of Buddha; found in all temples.

Before him are two ancient bronze incense-holders and an antique blue porcelain vase filled with freshly gathered hollyhocks. Mi-lêh is no small person in the Buddhist pantheon; he was considered the principal saint in S'âkymuni's retinue, but not as one of his ordinary disciples. His antecedents are not known. "He was appointed by S'âkymuni as his successor, to appear as Buddha after five thousand years. He is, therefore, the expected Messiah of the Buddhists, — residing at present in Fuchita, but already controlling the propagation of the Buddhist faith." Lobscheid calls him "the past Buddha." He is the personification of charity, and from the broad grin upon his face, is often called the "Laughing Buddha."

Behind this finely gilded statue, upon a high dais eighty feet or more in length, are three colossal bronze gods eight hundred years old, sixteen feet high, and eight feet broad at the base. The central image represents S'âkymuni; to his right is Lôchanâ, second person of the Trinity, as taught by the Yôga school; and on the left is Vâirôtchana, as the third person. The process of regilding these superb busts was going on, and thus afforded every opportunity for close examination.

In this temple, out of the host, there is another idol worth mentioning, as none of us had seen it elsewhere in China, — a Thibetan or Indian god called the "Holy Ancestor of high Heaven;" he holds a white rabbit. I afterward learned from a picture discovered in a more obscure temple that this deity belongs to some of the aboriginal tribes on the western borders of Sz-Chuan, who make repeated pilgrimages to this mountain. The one hundred and eight medallions frescoed upon the lofty ceiling, which portray as many different historical events, were once extremely bright and beautiful; but not having been retouched since 1736 they are in rather bad condition; still, some of them are very beautiful and well worthy of attention.

The temple I have endeavored to describe had more than ordinary attraction for me, and even a fascination which I found it difficult to throw off. Often after the tramp of pilgrims had died away, between the evening meal and late mass, I walked noiselessly from court to court, standing awhile in the cool shrubbery to cast furtive glances at the dark-blue vault studded with unnaturally large flashing orbs, reflecting bright rays upon the solemn and mystic retreat.

> " The day is done, and the darkness
> Falls from the wings of night,
> As a feather is wafted downward
> From an eagle in its flight."

My friend the faithful priest, an octogenarian, already fifty-eight years in this temple, is usually found seated by the bell near the feet of his beloved Mi-lêh Buddha, or bending over the precious incense-holder and patting gently the overflowing incense with his little trowel, or gathering the unburnt stubs of incense, and arranging the tapers. His pipe stands against the sacred dais with a cigar in the bowl, and when he has put the curling incense in order, he sits down, and in solemn silence solaces his tired nerves.

I enter unobserved and stand watching him till his task is done, and then advance to the centre of the temple. " Take a seat here," is his salutation. I sit down by his side, and in the dim flickering light look at my aged friend, whose face, though thin and wrinkled, is bright and sunny as a boy's. His eyes twinkle as he takes his pipe from his mouth, looks up, and propounds some simple question.

We chat till, one after another, the wave tapers go out; one only of the original eight remains. He now rises and knocks off the charred bamboo wicks, and again takes up his pipe. A translucent horn-lamp hangs high up before the first person of the Trinity, but the light is too dim to see his face. A few sticks of incense smoulder in the urns before the eighteen lo-han, but practically all is darkness. I now pace up and down the wide temple, guided by incense sparks, as the last taper is gone.

It is dark in courts and corridors, the bells are silent, and every voice hushed, as I glide lightly through the wide, open space and through a dark alley by the Goddess of Mercy to the first-described temple, where, seated in a large chair, with his head upon the little table before the idol, slumbers a diminutive novice ten years old. His little bell-rapper lies by his head, and a dying taper sheds a yellowish light upon his untroubled face. The elder priests are gathered in a side hall, holding high carnival with a few pilgrim friends, and a select few are seated around a large square table playing chess and telling great stories. I gaze at the lad for a moment, then gently lift the rapper and give the bell a smart stroke, and step back into the darkness. In an instant he is upon his feet, and in another he grasps my leg for a frolic right in the presence of the great Pu-hsien.

In the early morn all is activity; the halls have been swept and dusted ere I enter. The old man, with trembling fingers, arranges fresh flowers around the mouth of the vase, and places a cup of clear cold water before Mi-lêh Buddha, and says, in heart, " Drink of the fresh water which my own trembling hand has brought you, and look favorably upon the beauties of my garden." He turns from his loving task as half-a-dozen matrons enter the temple and prostrate themselves in turn before the sev-

eral gods, and stick a few chips of fresh sandal-wood into
the smouldering ashes of the great urn,— the first offerings of the day. One of the dames after worship searches
her money-bag, extracts one cash from its contents, and
chinks it upon the alms-tray. The other women stand
gazing at the mighty gods after their devotions, quite
forgetful of further duty. The old man seizes the club
upon the table, and gives the bell several smart raps, and
says : "Buddha wants money as well as incense." Another woman fumbles long in the depleted money-purse,
brings forth a cash, and tosses it upon the tray. These
go, and another squad enter and do likewise; thus the
devotions continue until dark. While I stood in the
temple twelve women came and worshipped, and paid
into the treasury five cash,— less than half a cent; small
mites indeed, yet ere the year closes several hundreds of
dollars will be collected.

I must now take you to the central objects of attraction
in the monastery,— namely, the bronze elephant, and
what the Chinese, for want of a better term, called the
" revolving spire," constructed of brick. The elephant,
cast in several sections, is of the purest and most costly
bronze known to the Chinese, and is of uncommonly
good workmanship. It was made at Chenteu (the provincial capital), by imperial order, in the tenth century.
It occupies the exact centre of the " revolving spire,"
which from traditional authority was built over it about
A. D. 1580. The elephant stands upon four bronze lotus-
flowers nearly one metre in diameter, and twenty centimetres high. The height of the statue, including the
lotus pedestal, is two metres and ninety-five centimetres,
—about nine English feet. Its length, exclusive of tusks,
is four metres and ninety centimetres ; its width, two
metres and ten centimetres. It is adorned with various

THE CELEBRATED BRICK SPIRAL TEMPLE AT WAN-NIEN-SZ, MOUNT OMEI.

trappings, and surmounted by a magnificent pure bronze image of the god Pu-hsien. The two statues have the aggregate height of eight metres and ten centimetres. This wonderful work of art has suffered in three conflagrations, and has also received minor injuries which have been repaired at a recent date. The tusks were melted in one conflagration, and those added are in three pieces each, and not well executed. The legs and trunk have been injured by devotees rubbing cash upon them. Both images are hollow, of course, but the casts are from six to eight inches thick. As a monument dating back to the tenth century, perhaps, it has few or no equals in China. The form is perfect, and the execution is in the best taste.

The " revolving spire " is composed entirely of brick and stone, with not a stick of timber within or without. Tradition and the united testimony of the priests give it the date I have mentioned, and add that it was built as a thank-offering by the mother of the Emperor Wanli, who visited this mountain in her pilgrimages, and was so much interested in the long-famous elephant that she devised and ordered built this unique and truly wonderful edifice. The walls form a perfect square, with pendentives, and a circular dome of the following dimensions and internal arrangements. Length between the inner walls, nine metres and sixty centimetres; thickness of east and west walls, three metres and twenty centimetres, — total length or breadth, sixteen metres. Height of walls to base of dome, seven metres and sixty centimetres; height of walls to lower angle of corner pendentives, four metres and fifty-seven centimetres; height of walls to lowest shelf for idols, three metres and fifty-five centimetres; total height to top of dome (within), about twelve metres and sixty centimetres. These measurements were made with great care by Dr. Morley and myself. I have little doubt it was designed to exhibit in brick the process of creation, as understood by the ancient Chinese, with some deviations to meet Buddhist theological ideas.

The square, or lower part, symbolizes the earth; the round dome, heaven. From heaven, or *Taiki*, come the. sun and moon, which we have in the two small orifices in the eastern and western sections of the dome. From the sun and moon, or, in other words, the *yang* and *yin*, we have produced the Four Forms, called in the Yiking "young sun" and "young moon," "old moon" and "old sun," which are represented by the pendentive corners. From the Four Forms come the Eight Diagrams; we have them in the eight small pendentives above the Four Forms. Then we have seven shelves on the four sides filled with small bronze gods, — at one time as many as three thousand; they represent the seven stories of heaven as held by the Buddhists. The building faces exactly east, and the sun's rays strike the jewel in the god's forehead twice each year through the small orifice in the dome, and, similarly, the back of his head from the west. Below, on the inside, we have twenty-four recesses for different deities, each one metre sixty centimetres high, and of oval form, seventy-six centimetres wide, and eighty-seven centimetres deep. These represent the twenty-four terms of the year, — the half-moon feasts. There are twelve outer doors, ten of which are closed, which represent the diurnal divisions of time. There is a lofty wooden structure enclosing the building, covered with clay tiles to protect it from snow and rain and the consequent growth of shrubs and grass from the interstices upon the dome. The dome was once covered with different-colored porcelain tiles, and above the cornices profusely decorated with costly statues of men and animals. This beautiful covering, which must have cost myriads of dollars, was destroyed in a great fire more than a hundred years since. The roof was left an unsightly mass of débris; and thus remains for lack of funds and enterprise, and must be so until some gracious sovereign or empress shall look with favor upon Wanniensz.

Mr. Baber, no mean authority, thinks the structure un-Chinese, and probably built by Indian Buddhists, and consequently older than the time of Wanli. His quotation from the " Topography of Sz-Chuan " does seem to show that the present building is a restoration by the empress, and not a creation. I judge that the original building must have been erected when the elephant was cast, in the tenth century. While it is a unique structure in very many respects, and would seem to claim greater antiquity and foreign builders, I am doubtful about assigning it greater age than 1530 A. D., and am confident that in design and workmanship it is purely Chinese. The character used to indicate renovation has also the meaning of to "build," or "found," as a temple or other structure. Tradition has much weight, as it points to a later period and makes the empress its foundress. The age of the Mins was one of masonry, and nearly all the great monuments in stone and brick do not antedate that dynasty. There are many similar structures found scattered over the empire, — similar so far as oblong brick domes can represent such art. There are several very large rafterless temples in the prefecture of Nanking, built from bottom to top entirely of brick and stone. Some are nearly square, with an approach to a circular covering. I am informed on fair authority that there are just such buildings as this at Lo Yang, in the province of Honan, but much smaller. The internal designs, as I have shown, are purely Chinese, and the exterior decorations are Chinese-like, and much resemble those found upon the brick monuments of the Min dynasty. In the second story of a large building in front of this temple, and level with the god Pu-hsien, the visitor will find a life-sized statue of the mother of the Emperor Wanli. She is richly robed in yellow satin, and is worshipped as the patroness and guardian of the "revolving spire." This hall is also hung with fifty-seven ancient paintings upon cloth, said to be gifts from border tribes, or from Thibet. I judge them to be Thibetan from the inscriptions found under each picture. Altogether, the buildings and monuments here found are remarkable, and are deserving careful study.

In some respects, the building, the worship, and the pilgrimages made by the Chinese and other races to this sacred shrine remind one of the Caaba of Mecca in the Middle Ages. The temple is larger and more solidly built, and is of different form from that structure. The last month of each year that city and temple were crowded with long trains of pilgrims, who presented their vows and offerings in the house of God. Seven times, with hasty steps, they encircled the Caaba and kissed the black stone; seven times they visited and adored the adjacent mountains, etc. Here, at certain seasons, trains of pilgrims come with music, banners, and chants; they circle around, they bow, they pray, and make their sacrifices. They encircle the sacred elephant, which is not less sacred to them than the black stone of the Caaba. Each tribe either found or introduced into the Caaba their domestic worship. In like manner, we find Chinese from all quarters, Thibetans, and border tribes coming at different seasons. They have their own peculiar methods of worship and deities, but all equally reverence the bronze elephant.

The Thibetans make regular pilgrimages to this building during the winter months, and many aboriginal tribes come with offerings. I had the good fortune to find underneath the thick coating caused by burning incense, some fragments of Thibetan classics. Further investigation revealed several layers of writings, extending from the small recesses to the base of the dome. These leaves of classics were covered with one or two layers of papers, upon which had been portrayed in black ink, upon a red ground, a great many strange figures representing their gods. I was permitted to bring away several of these old parchments, which after careful cleaning were decipherable. I was told that they were pasted here more than fifty years ago, and a priest said they would be renewed by the same people on the occasion of some great vow. I do not feel sure that the images are Thibetan; they may belong to some aboriginal border tribe. Another very curious custom prevails: a bronze god is cast, with the donor's name upon the back, and set up in the "seven heavens" of the building, and after some generations the family take it back to their home. There had thus accumulated at one time some three thousand such images, but not half that number now remain.

It has been found necessary, for the preservation of the elephant, to build a high stone palisade or fence around him and to tip it with iron spikes; it is the work of the present year, and replaces a wooden one which was an ineffectual guard against relic-hunters. Within this stone cage, high above the reach of pilgrims, are some very ancient porcelain vases and valuable incense-burners.

In front of this temple I again had the good fortune
to discover a very curious metal machine, spoken of by
the priests as the Lah-ma-king-tai, " Lama praying
tower." It consists of a three-story cap and a square
base. The cap or tower is hollow, and the lower story
octagonal, and covered with Chinese characters, some
of which were so much defaced they could not be read.
The second and third stories are circular, and seven
quite distinct circles surround them. The base has a
roundish knob or pyramid in the centre, and on the
diagonal corners two sunken eyes. The characters upon
the cap as it covers the base are inverted. Its measurements are as follows : thickness of square base, eleven
centimetres ; side of the square, fifty centimetres ; height
of cap, fifty-two centimetres ; height of top story, nineteen centimetres ; lower, sixteen centimetres ; height of
octagon, sixteen centimetres ; circumference of octagon,
one metre sixteen centimetres.

The oldest of the priests could not give us any particular information about its use. They said it had not
been used for a hundred years, and that it had been
here, they supposed, from the casting of the elephant,
and was once in use. They further said that it was not
now complete, that some of the internal machinery was
wanting. There is little doubt that if the characters upon
the octagon portion of the cap were complete they would
determine its age. The characters upon the fifth square,
in connection with the cyclical inscriptions upon the
second and first squares, while they do not absolutely
settle the date of its manufacture, surely point to the
Sung dynasty, and to the reign of Chi-ho, A. D. 1054, as
the year of its casting. Unfortunately, the first square
has but one character remaining, but that is an important one ; and putting it in connection with the four

characters of the second square, the reign is almost determined; and adding the fifth square, which gives us the ancient name of the monastery, we have pretty good evidence that the weather-battered machine was cast in or about A. D. 1054, and for the ancient monastery of "Clear Water." The question is, Did the Buddhists of that age use an instrument of this kind in their temple worship, and if so, how extensively was it used? Or was this a gift from Thibet, and if so, why were Chinese characters engraved upon the squares, where we should naturally expect Thibetan? If we were sufficiently familiar with the religious customs of Thibet and the border tribes of China, much light might possibly be thrown upon the ceremonies connected with the use of this strange machine.

While rummaging in out-of-the-way corners one day, as was my habit during the first half-month, I came upon a finely carved stone with an impress of Pu-hsien upon his white elephant, evidently playing some musical instrument. Afterward I came upon some very good stone rubbings, which I secured. The text at the top is written in an unknown language, not Lolo in form, being, I judged, nearer to the language of the Sifans. The people from Sitsang and other outlying countries are great scribblers; for the temples, within and without, wherever a smooth place is found, are covered with their writings.

Near to the brick "spiral," under the same temple covering, is Wo-fuh, the "Sleeping Buddha." He lies upon a high couch covered with two cotton coverlets; his head rests easily upon a clay pillow, but some sympathizing sister or brother has embroidered a very fine one of satin, and placed it at the back of his head, ready for his waking. This Buddha is supposed to be

S'âkymuni in a five or ten century sleep. Behind the sleeping god are three statues of Lao-tsz, S'âkymuni, and the God of Mercy. A strip of red cloth stretches across their heads, thus symbolizing their perfect unity. A stone tablet near by with Chinese and Mantsz characters tells us that this was the gift of a Teu-sz, — a semi-independent prince. This chieftain had vowed that upon making a fortune he would honor these deities. I was somewhat surprised to hear that the Western pilgrims brought great quantities of silver coins and disposed of them to the priests, who marketed them at Omei-hsien, where they are made into ornaments, etc. My teacher secured me two, which turned out to be rupees of dates 1840 and 1876. " Our gracious Queen " looks as happy on Mount Omei as in England.

Who was Pu-hsien? This is a question which, if truly answered, would throw a flood of light upon the dim horizon of early Buddhism in Western China. It is, I fear, a question which will never receive a satisfactory answer.

The only accessible records tell us that he came from India upon a white elephant in the third century (some writers say second century) B. C. The name itself is purely Chinese, and literally interpreted means the "Universal Sage." The first character in his name is made up of the radical for " sun " or " day " and the phonetic equal. There may be the meaning of " equal in brightness to the sun," or " illumination as from the sun," or " light personified." The cosmopolitan character of the worship in this mountain, and the ardor with which the aborigines worship Pu-hsien lead me to query if this mountain, especially the glorious peak, which is incomparably grander than any other in China, was not once the centre of an elaborate system of nature, and particularly of sun, worship ; and that Pu-hsien is a pure creation by the Buddhists to satisfy the native religious instincts of the people, who gave up the direct worship of the sun, accepting Pu-hsien as his incarnation. Max Müller says: " It is generally, if not always, the sun or the sky which forms the bridge from the visible to the invisible, from Nature to Nature's God. But besides the sun, the moon also was worshipped by the negroes as the ruler of months and seasons, and the ordainer of time and life." Buddhism, no doubt, found its way to this region at an early date, — say second or third century, — and by degrees it won over, in part, a large number of aborigines ; and finding their foothold for pure Indian Buddhism precarious, they compromised with the people by incarnating their sun deity in the form of a man bestriding a white elephant, riding along the clouds. They may have induced the natives to believe that the natural phenomena manifested daily in the valley below the cliff was none else than the presence of this god. The tradition that still lingers among the people that Pu-hsien converted the tribes around the mountain by the magic use of his yu-yuh mace is also interesting. He wandered among them preaching, and whenever a person scoffed he threw his yu-yuh at him, and his head dropped from his shoulders ; but when the man repented the head was replaced.

The building too seems a compromise between Buddhism and nature worship, especially the ancient sun and moon worship.

The windows in the dome to admit the rays of the sun and moon, the orientation of the building, the elephant and god, and the various symbols, all point to a period anterior to any settled faith among the natives. If an appeal is made to the nomenclature used by the people for the caves, grottos, rocks, we find nearly all such as would be given by nature worshippers or Taoist recluses. It is a matter of history that many hundreds of years before Buddhism entered China, Taoist recluses, or Alchemists, lived here in caves and. practised their arts. One Chinese poet speaks of Lao-tsz having lived here.

Max Müller tells us : —

" This presentiment or incipient perception of the infinite passes through endless phases and assumes endless names.

" I might have traced it in the wonderment with which the Polynesian sailor dwells on the endless expanse of the sea, in the jubilant outburst with which the Aryan shepherd greets the effulgence of the dawn, or in the breathless silence of the solitary traveller in the desert when the last ray of the sun departs, fascinating his weary eyes, and drawing his dreamy thoughts to another world. Through all these sentiments and presentiments there vibrates the same chord in a thousand tensions, and if we will but listen attentively we can still perceive its old familiar ring even in such high harmonies as Wordsworth's.

<blockquote>
" 'Obstinate questionings
Of sense and outward things,
Fallings from us, vanishings;
Blank misgivings of a creature
Moving about in words not realized.' "
</blockquote>

Is this where Indian Buddhism and Taoism first met face to face, and where the conflict of battle commenced ? Step by step did the new encroach upon the old, until a lasting peace was made upon the basis of a fair compromise ? Like the structure of this mountain, with its granite rocks deep down in the sunken gorge, nearly hidden by red and gray sandstone, and overtopped here and there by limestone, so Buddhism has covered but has not obliterated an ancient faith; the superstitions and long-exercised customs show through its flowing folds.

July 26. There have been great doings to-day, but a faint show of the display which will be seen a few days hence, so my old friend of the elephant house informs me. Beside the regular run of pilgrims, which is large this month, there came a concourse of men and women, with boys enough to make things lively about the old barracks. They were from the opposite side of the mountains, dressed in fantastic-colored raiment, bearing idols, pagodas, umbrellas, and every conceivable banner and flag, together with music and fire-crackers. At a distance the banners and flags and the gayly attired throng were not unlike the marching of several Sunday-schools out for a picnic. They turn into the first temple, and march quickly to all the great gods and pay their respects, with repeated prostrations and by tossing upon the incense-urns bundles of incense. The music and chanting continue without interruption during the marches from temple to temple. They make the rounds of every structure in the monastery with superstitious strictness. They lodge here to-night, and while I write they are making a great disturbance in the " revolving spiral." Their banners were written over with religious sayings, and from them I learned that the delegation was composed of both Buddhists and Taoists.

I had the good fortune to-day to purchase a passport to the Western heaven for the moderate sum of two cents, with an official letter to Titsang, guardian of Hades, who will pass the spirit of the individual whose name is written upon the document through his realms, across all the ferries, and finally by the help of Pu-hsien over the great bitter sea, which is said to have waves a thousand feet high. Both Titsang and Pu-hsien are working hard in the spirit world and on earth to carry out their numerous vows for the salvation of men and women, and at the same time doing something to work out their own salvation from Pu-sa saintship to Buddha saintship, which means the bliss of Nirvana, or the kingdom of perfect happiness.

The custom of giving or selling the passport dates from the Emperor Chitêh, A. D. 757. The passport and letter are taken by the pilgrims to their homes, and worshipped. When some member of the family dies, the documents are carried to the grave and burnt, after the name of the person and the date of his birth and death are filled in. It is gotten up in good style, has a picture of Omito-foo, a pagoda, the bitter sea, and a boat in readiness for the departed spirit. On the other shore a person advances with a pagoda in his or her hand, and the great defender of the Law, Weito, stands there with his sceptre in hand, to take possession of the wanderer.

An old sore-eyed monk climbed the three hundred steps with me for the money, and as we toiled up he pressed my shoulder and said in a confidential tone, " You have a valuable thing there."

A crowd of pilgrims stood around my teacher's window as we passed, looking at our religious books. He was explaining to them the pictorial life of Moses. There is scarcely any bigotry in the monastery, and the priests care little how much we teach while they receive a good rent. The head priest broke one of the great prohibitions to-day by sending me a large piece of pork.

A THIBETAN TRIBE DEITY FOUND ON MOUNT OMEI.

See page 215.

CHAPTER XII.

Mr. Faber and Dr. Morley had already made the great ascent, had looked upon the " glory of Buddha," the snowy range in the west, and had brought back a glowing account of the wonders to be seen, while I lingered amid smoking incense eight thousand feet below.

The 28th of July dawned gloriously over the heights. Preparations were matured in half an hour, and Dr. Morley and I, by turning some sharp angles around the monastic halls, secured a path where we had more shade than by the regular road.

The following paragraph, taken from the "Topography of Sz-Chuan," is descriptive of the peaks which tower up beyond the mountains which we started to scale before twilight : —

" Upon the top of Omei is the ' Cliff of Glory,' back of the bronze-tiled temple, by the side of the bridge called ' Heavenly Genii.' On the top of the mountain, before the tower to the Goddess of Mercy, is a terrace for beholding Buddha's glory. Below the diamond rocks there are seven-jewelled terraces, which are also called seven precious cliffs. Below the cliff are stone terraces upon which are engraved " *Yü-yi-*yin-yë-tsing-*kih-lin-*chen-yüch-shen-teh-tao-chü." " The place where Yü-yi and Kih-lin possessed themselves of the Tao-yü-yi becoming a sun wraith, and Kih-lin a moon spirit."

The sentence is of very peculiar idiomatic construction, and I have not tried to give a literal translation, but the idea involved. The characters still remain, but the terraces cut into the cliff by which they were reached are gone. Here we have the very centre, as I have before intimated, of sun and moon worship.

The air of sanctity which gathers around a legendary retreat like this is scarcely conceivable to a Western student. The mammoth characters carved upon the smooth face of the crag, now inaccessible to man, do not carry us back possibly above twelve centuries; but tradition, which was then hoary with age, points back to the early days of religion in China, when sun, moon, and stars were being peopled with the spirits of heroes, and of men like ourselves transformed and transported to the worlds of light.

Imagine my delight in discovering the slowly obliterating characters, lighted up by the gleams of the morning sun. I stood in the tall shrubs and tangled grass growing upon the edge of the awful precipice, and scrutinized as intently as any pilgrim could those significant inscriptions, — significant to the scholar, who would fain link the present with the past of four thousand years. None but a true religionist, born in the atmosphere of Confucian reverence for Chinese written characters, can appreciate fully those sacred writings clinging to the rock and hung in space.

The Brahmans tell us " that the author of a Sûtra rejoices more in having saved one single letter than in the birth of a son; and remember that without a son to perform the funeral rites, a Brahman believed that he could not enter into heaven."

The hand of time alone dares to desecrate those holy inscriptions.

On the left of the terrace for beholding Buddha there is an isolated peak called the " diamond," as if cast from molten metal, and each one gazing at it receives its reflected rays of light. Below this are a myriad of serrated rocks brought together into one cluster of pinnacles, and called the " seven-jewelled terrace." Below this terrace is a rock house of numerous chambers. Farther on, to the left of " Thunder Mountain " there are two rocks like eyebrows called the " face of the genii ; " there are also stains, or marks of hands, called " palms of the genii." All of these are upon the mountain-top, and separated from the world of mortals, no one being able to reach them. Farther on are the " elysium rock islands," straight down from which is the " seamless pagoda." ·

Fan chen-ta, of the Sung dynasty, about 1050 A. D., visited the mountain and recorded what he saw in the following language : —

" I ascended to the bridge of the ' Heavenly genii,' to the ' cliff of glory,' where I offered incense. The small temple above is covered with the bark of trees. The uncle of Wan-chan, a councillor in the court of appeals, once changed the bark for tiles ; but a year of snow and frost sufficed to ruin them, and a change was again made to bark, which lasts two or three years. The men said mid-day was the time to see Buddha's manifestation ; being too late I found it best to retire to my lodging, and returned the next day. As the clouds rolled up from below the cliff by the side of the valley, between the mountains of ' thunder caverns,' I shrank back with fear, for they rushed on like ranks of soldiers to battle, until within a short distance from the cliff, when they rested. From the top of the cloud there appeared an aureola of mixed colors and several layers. Out of the midst was a clearly defined image, like a genius, or god, astride an elephant. In the time of taking a cup of tea the aureola vanished. Again at

one side, as before, the glory reappeared, but in an instant
was gone. In the centre of the cloud there then appeared
two bands of golden light, which darted athwart the middle
of the cliff; the men called this the 'lesser glory.' At sun-
set the clouds vanished, and perfect calm prevailed throughout the mountains. At night a million lights issued from
below the cliff, reaching to the utmost limit of vision. The
night became intensely cold, and I could not stay.

"On the Pin-shen cycle, A. D. 1056, I went again to gaze
upon the cliff. Back of the cliff are the myriad overlaid peaks
of the Min range, and a little to the north the Wa-wu [tiled
house] Mountains in Ya-cheu. A little to the south side is
the great Wa-wu, near the Nan-cheu — Laos peopled (proclaimed so A. D. 850). They are in a manner really concealed
in the Wa-wu. The Wa-wu also has a 'glory' called the
'dividing branch' of Buddha's glory. Back of these are the
snow mountains of Si-yuh [western countries], high, rocky
summits, reckoned in a general way to be one thousand
peaks. When the sun first rises and shines upon them the
snow in the gorges is bright as polished silver, and the morning dazzles one with its brightness. This snow has remained unmelted from ancient times. The mountains extend
into India and other foreign countries, and beyond I know
not how far, but they are seen as distinctly as though upon
the table before me, — a marvellous and incomparable sight;
a diadem for a whole lifetime. I again repaired to the cliff for
devotions; suddenly a mist rose from every direction, perfectly
white, and sweeping on in great confusion. The priests said
the silver color was the world's boundary. In a moment it
rained and soon poured in torrents; the mists divided and
vanished. The priests said the rain is for the baptizing of
the cliff, and that there would be a great manifestation of
Buddha. The morion-like gauze cloud spread out below the
cliff, rose brilliant and beautiful, came within a few chang of the
cliff, and stood there. It was unbroken and shone like polished gems. At the time minute drops of rain were falling,
as at the finishing of a shower. I leaned forward and gazed
upon the centre of the cliff; there was a great aureola resting

upon the level cloud; outside this was a triple halo, having the colors of ultra-marine, yellow, red, and green. The glory was in the centre, like bright space, serenely clear. Each person looking saw the image of himself in the empty place exactly as in a mirror, and there was not an infinitesimal part obscure. If I lifted my hand or moved my foot the image followed the motion, but I could not see the person standing by my side. The priest said this was body-shooting light [photographic light].

"When this glory was exhausted there arose a wind in front of the mountain, and the cloud was borne along by it into the snowy range. There again appeared an aureola similar to the other, and spread athwart several mountains; it was a marvel of colors, massed into the perfection of beauty; and there appeared a series of peaks covered with trees and plants, fresh and elegant, of many rich colors, so brilliant that I could not look directly at it. The clouds and mists now rolled away, and this halo alone was bright. Whenever there is a manifestation of 'Buddha's glory' this cloud is first spread; therefore it is called the *Teu-lo-min*. In the time of eating the 'glory' gradually moved over the mountains to the west. Upon 'Thunder cave' mountain there issued another 'glory' as before. In a very short time it also sped away over the mountains into the level wilds. It now revolved about to the cliff, and came directly in front of it, but with color and form entirely changed, like unto a bridge of gold or an inverted rainbow of Wu kiang (Soochow), both ends embosomed in purple clouds."

Fan-yü-tsz of the Min dynasty thus gives us his impressions : —

"At the very highest pinnacle is the Kwang-Siang Monastery; in front of this is the Buddha Observatory. The sun had already set, and I could not see afar off, so I ordered the priests to commence service. When I and the Councillor Advocate had finished our homage to Buddha, we went to the Lång Ying tower to lodge. At break of day I went up first.   The sovereign of day ascended on his chariot; not yet had a particle of cloud arisen.   All the peaks for a thousand li, with all their angles, could be counted.   They rose tier upon tier, perfect as a picture.   In an instant there issued out of the centre of the cliff a thread of white cloud, which gradually opened and spread out, more and more, extending farther and farther, now floating over the eastern peaks, now the western, just revealing the sharp points of the mountains, as in the great western ocean an unlimited expanse of glassy white waves are made by the ' ship-swallowing ' fish when he lifts on high his mane, beats the deep with his dorsal fins, and lashes to and fro his tail as he roams about seeking for prey.   There flew forth four or five small birds from the edge of the cliff whose notes were worth hearing.   The priest said they were called ' Buddha's birds,' and that at the time of his manifestation these birds straightway cried ' Fuh hsien,' — ' Buddha appears.'   I listened carefully, but decided it could not be as he said.   The mountain-top was bitterly cold and entirely destitute of other birds, and for this reason it was very remarkable that they should be here.   The priest said, It will be very bright to-day, and that we should rest until noon, when there would be a manifestation of Buddha.   We rested in the bronze temple, and tarried for it.   This temple was built with money given by the merciful and holy Empress from the royal exchequer to a fendatory of the Peh Sung, who dedicated it to this purpose.   The seven-jewelled terraces are upon the right of Kwang-Siang temple.   The upper pillars are carved with twisted dragons, the front ones beautifully ornamented and minutely fretted. The whole temple is of bronze except in the centre, where there is a shrine of sandal-wood enclosing the golden form of Pu-hsien seated upon a white elephant.   On the four upper walls are engraved lotus-flowers and one thousand Buddhas ; below are carved jasper-like plants and strange flowers, each one of marvellous form.   Back of the two-leaved doors we have carved images of gold, exhibiting the beautiful scenery from Yünchan to Kiacheu.   Upon the outer walls are also engravings of flowers, very delicate, made of gold plaster, and so brilliant as to dazzle the eyes. There is a pagoda on each of the four corners of the temple, and on the left of the front door is a bronze tablet containing a history of Wang Tai. After reading it I repaired at once to Buddha's observatory.

"The white cloud was already spread at the lower boundary, and the red sun was shining above; the thousands of peaks were obscured, and the myriads of gorges covered. I was standing before the tower of the 'Goddess of Mercy' when the priest reported that the 'child glory' had appeared. I made haste to look. It was then below the cliff, suspended within the borders of the 'Emptiness,' large as a chariot wheel, and adorned with five colors. The image of the beholder was within the 'glory' just as in a mirror, each one seeing only himself. If one moved, the 'glory' moved also. It was exactly mid-day, and below the cliff there appeared another 'glory,' and the priest said it was a 'branch glory,' and it was much larger than the 'child glory.' In the centre was a globe of jadeite; around this was a band of bright-red, surrounded by bands of green, white, purple, yellow, and one of scarlet, — each band a marvel of beauty. Its reflected rays pierced the eyes like arrows. Around this 'glory' was a great halo like a rainbow. The manifestation remained stationary, and in this respect differed from the 'child glory.'

"The priest now reported the appearance of the 'Pu-hsien glory,' and I hurried up to the terrace for observation. It was stationary and strangely beautiful. As compared with the divergent 'branch glory' it was much larger, and showed layer upon layer, and was encircled with a red halo.

"We bowed down and worshipped; all of our followers were greatly moved and also fell down and worshipped. Standing, as we did, upon the highest peak, the mountains in every direction were visible. On the west and north the mighty crags pierced the clouds.

"I saw the Wa-wu, and still farther west were the Snowy Mountains, running athwart like a long city wall, and looking like festoons of white silk. West of this was India and the mountains of Karakorum, and all the barbarous kingdoms. On the south were the Shai-king mountains as plain as a screen before me. Small and near at hand were second and third 'Omeis,' as in the attitude of devotion. The great Fu River and the streams of Kia-Lyng, Lu, and Ya Cheu, with all their windings and girdlings, were before me. The Advocate and I clapped our palms and cried out, 'The grandest view of a lifetime!'

"The great display was over; the morion cloud vanished by degrees, and the 'glory' also faded away. I turned to go to the tower 'Beautiful' to consult with the Advocate about the causes of this manifestation. We came to no conclusion. Shu-Kang-Tang says, 'The god Pu-hsien is infinite; of a hundred thousand colors and of fifty glories.' Our eyes are screened; we cannot even comprehend the broad waters of Shantung; our knowledge is that of the Yu fang [a mere trifle]; how can we reason about the Kwun Lun [mountains of Thibet]? I wished to ascend again to see the holy lights, but the priest said there was a moon, and they would not be visible. I remarked that the 'glory' is made visible by the sun, and the 'lights' are obscured by the moon. I asked how the 'lights' appeared. He said they floated out of space, — at first one or two, which separate by degrees to above a hundred. They can be caught in the hand and crushed like dry leaves. Perhaps some one will say, 'Fire-flies,' metamorphosed from rotted particles of plants, and that the ruined leaf has light. Nay, in this place there are no dry leaves. Whether they are 'lights' or not I cannot say. I have repeatedly reflected upon the spiritual mountains of Ch'an-tan [China] and the underground dwellings of genii and Buddhas. All have 'lights,' and the 'lights' of each are different.

"The immortals are generally very merciful to the mortals who have fallen into black crimes and darkness, so they divide themselves into luminous substances, and thus the 'merciful lights' of 'Pu-hsien' arrest our attention. If we can by our own help break forth from our dark prison houses, wherefore then the necessity of illuminating our eyes with these merciful lights?

"Ta Wei says: 'We are all human, and are we going to alter by thought and scheme? Last night at the third watch I was tossing to and fro on my couch, when I fancied "Pu-hsien" had dismissed me to the "kingdom of no birth" [Western heaven], and in an instant I perceived it was day.' In the morning he went visiting, telling his dream to everybody. Alas! although I have caught a sight of 'Pu-hsien's glory,' and I cannot deny what my pen has registered, it is more than likely it will be pronounced a dream."

The journey is greatly broken by the presence of temples every two or three miles, and in places much more frequently. The temples are hotels as well, and almost any of them can accommodate a hundred or two pilgrims without inconvenience. After toiling up a mountain-side for half a mile, exposed to the rays of the sun, we were sure to find a forest of lofty trees, good tea or cold water, and a hearty welcome from the priests.

We had started with a cloudless sky; but at 1.30 P. M., when we reached the famous temple of Si-Siang, "Elephant Bath," we found ourselves suddenly enveloped in a dense fog. The aneroid registered eight thousand feet above the sea. The abbot who had entertained Mr. Baber ten years before was, for some unexplained reason, averse to our stopping with him for the night. We, however, overcame his objections, and took a room on the second floor. I found him an intelligent man, and if possessed of prejudices he was wise enough to conceal them in his conversation.

The temples are commodious. They are filled with costly images, some of which are peculiar in form and adornment. Owing to the great depth of snow which falls upon the mountain, the roofs are built uncommonly strong, and are covered in some instances with thick planks half-a-dozen deep; some have iron convex tiles a foot or more in length, very heavy and durable I noticed that some of the temples have zinc and tin coverings, of such excellent workmanship that I concluded they were of foreign manufacture ; but the priest assured me the material was from Yun-nan, and made up not far from Omei. Copper and iron are found in abundance not far away. The river which flows at the foot of the mountain and empties into the Min below Kia-ting is called " Copper river."

Where there are no forests on the mountain there is a dense jungle of undergrowth, — a tangled mass of flowering shrubs, creepers, and vines. The temple in which we are lodged is surrounded by a fine old forest of the sha-trees. They tower up to one or two hundred feet, and are covered with a thick growth of ferns half-way to their tops. The ten miles we have made to ascend six thousand feet were through a veritable park. No spot on the globe can boast a greater variety of vegetation, or scenes more beautiful. There is not a barren acre, nor a peak bereft of verdure. I estimate we have seen fifty varieties of trees on the ascent ; flowers without number and of all hues ; ferns everywhere ; black currant bushes of immense size growing from steep declivities, their trunks covered with green moss, and branches laden with well-flavored berries. The insect life is marvellous. Butterflies and moths fly recklessly around and above us, as if inviting capture ; bees and flies of colors black, green, brown, and yellow, hum in the thickets.

In the temple of Kai-san-tsin I found a very peculiar stone with an altar before it. The priests declared they did not know its age, whence it came, or its use. It is called the " sacrificial tower ; " this was all they knew about it. Upon one edge of the stone were carved thirteen characters, now nearly obliterated, but which

were deciphered after several attempts. They are as
follows : "Fu-shun-hsien-tung-hsia-hsiang-hwang-shi-shi-
hsiang-tai-yih tso," "The sacrificial altar of the Hwang
family in the eastern part of Fuh-shun-hsien" (near
the salt-wells). Near this was a board where the daily
offerings are made by the worshipping priests to the
departed priests, called Ku-hwen, and to Fu-tsz, the head
or chief devil, with whom Buddha had a sore contest at
death, and promised him that he should be remembered
in the meal offerings. This tablet before or near the
ancient stone is like that found in all well-regulated
temples, and is called the "Cold Grave Association," —
"Society of the Burial Ground," dedicated to the departed spirits of the five sects of Buddhists, and Fu-tsz,
chief of evil spirits. On either side are tablets, — one
to the four orders of animal life gone to the " precious
land," the other to the " three possessions " metamorphosed in the " lotus pool." I would here say that the
five Buddhist sects are called *Tsui-tan*, followers of
S'âkymuni ; *Lien-tsi*, followers of Wen-chu of Tai-san ;
Tsao-tung, followers of Pu-hsien of Omei ; *Yun-Mûn*,
followers of Ti-tsang of Kiu-hwa ; *Ku-san*, followers of
Kwan-yin of Puto.

While these different sects have their peculiarities,
they differ little in doctrine. It is a custom among
priests, before meals, to make offerings of rice from a
bowl, lifting it from the bowl with a bamboo fork made
in the shape of a hand ; a knife of same material and
size is used to slay any evil spirits who may hover about
to catch the offering. In one temple we saw an idol
covered from head to feet with little saucers, about two
inches in diameter ; these saucers are filled with oil at
night, and lighted. He thus might well be called the
god of light.

It is wonderful what columns of pilgrims there are coming and going; and fully one half of them are women. Later in the day we wandered around the base of a forest-crowned peak, over which we must journey to-morrow. Near the path was a stream of pure water. The path took us to the verge of a great precipice, and far down its side were wood-choppers and medicine-root diggers. The farther we strolled the prettier became the views, until we reached a priestly burial-ground, and an almost impassable brush bridge over a sharp ledge which descended into an uninviting gorge.

I was this evening shown the pool at the foot of the temple where tradition says Pu-hsien bathed his white elephant. There are two of these cisterns, one being of comparatively recent age, but already claimed as the original pool. My baggage carrier said the small pentagonal one covered with moss was the real pool, and I have no doubt it will be some years before the priests will be able to convince the pilgrims to the contrary. I am now told that Pu-hsien came to China as a spirit, seated upon a spiritual elephant, guarding the sacred documents which were brought to the Emperor Minti, second century B. C.

At this altitude we found the temperature very cold; we were obliged to have a large charcoal fire in our bedroom.

The following morning we were up before daylight, and after a cup of coffee started upon the last stage of our journey. Ere we reached the top of the mountain spur, which rose abruptly from the temple, we saw the sun rise over Kia-ting. A heavy dew lay on the tangled vegetation which towered above our heads on either side of the path, and the uneven limestone steps were saturated with moisture. Ascending through a dense grove of the sha, we came to a ridge which afforded us. a view of fully forty miles into the valleys on the southeast. Away on the horizon we could see the Min flowing through its alluvial bed, and uniting with the Tung and Ya Rivers. Clouds covered nearly all the surface of the intervening valleys, but not so dense as to resist the subtle shafts of light. By degrees they were divided and subdivided, and long, wide rents were opened sufficiently to show in the distance the wonderful windings of the small but furious Ya, as it debouched with the Tung. At their junction they shone like burnished brass between banks of snow-white clouds.

> "The clouds were far beneath me ; bathed in light,
> They gathered midway round the wooded height,
> And in their fading glory shone
> Like hosts in battle overthrown,
> As many a pinnacle, with shifting glance,
> Through the gray mist thrust up its shattered lance,
> And rocking on the cliff was left
> The dark pine, blasted, bare, and cleft ;
> The veil of cloud was lifted, and below
> Glowed the rich valley, and the river's flow
> Was darkened by the forest's shade,
> Or glistened in the white cascade."

Nearer to the base of the mountains the view surpassed, in delicate combination of color and form, any picture of fancy. We were seven thousand feet above the lower end of the valley, and between us, above the hovering clouds, were every diversity of form in mountain and valley, — the broad, gently rolling peak, the sharp diamond points, the narrow defiles and eccentric cliffs, all covered with forests of coniferous, with many nuciferous and bassiferous, species. Over this incline of mountain we gazed upon the nebulous billows, snow-white and almost ethereal, broken up here and there, as the strengthening sun pierced through to glassy river or glimmering vale. The little rivers, winding seemingly at our very feet, glittered and gleamed like the phosphorescence of the ocean. When shall another such morning, with such views, greet my eyes? After an ascent of one thousand feet we called a halt for breakfast. As the old monastery came into view, with its roofing of tree limbs, thatched and cemented by grass and ferns, another scene, and one more grand, if possible, than hitherto seen, lay quietly before us in the west. A large company of pilgrims on the descent stood before the temple, and on the roadside a bevy of ladies, dressed in many quaint ways, carrying birch sticks and large fir cones, halted as they saw us, and remained as statues for some time. I stood upon the verge of a gentle crag looking down a thousand feet upon a land-locked lake of yellowish-tinged cloud ten or more miles away. The sun had not yet reached its troubled surface; it was broken like the ocean after a storm, and the sides of the mountains appeared as if laved with angry, foaming billows. Could it be a lake? I soon discovered this to be impossible, yet it was so much like one that an elderly lady cried out in the ecstasy of delight, " The Fu-ho! " Farther to the south, piercing through heavy clouds, shone in majestic grandeur the snow-and-ice-covered peaks bordering Thibet. As I stood wrapt in awe while gazing upon these displays of omnipotence, an old priest came to my side and said, " Those mountains are in Thibet, and thirty days' journey hence."

We breakfasted on this pinnacle of glory, and finally, although unwillingly, we turned our backs upon this picture of supreme beauty, and struggled up the rugged path amidst thorns and briers. As in many scenes in

life's changing experiences, we turn away from present
pleasure, and brave fatigue and sorrow, enter cloud and
storm, with a prospect of yet greater glories to be revealed.   An hour's hard climb brought us to a level belt
rich in forests, shrubs, and flowers.   We sauntered
slowly through this fairy-like dell, screened most completely from the sun's rays; we halted frequently to
gaze about us, or stepped aside and grasped the strong
twigs growing from a cavernous ledge, and peered into
chasms of fathomless depths, where the swollen torrents
looked no wider than the hand.   Near one of these
chasms, and within sound of a silvery bell, beaten at regular intervals, and the noise of merry wood-choppers, we
came upon a garden of wild strawberries.   We had seen
many isolated plants since reaching the crest, and had
tried the fruit and found it the genuine article,—like
those I stained my hands with forty years ago.   The
pilgrims passed by and scorned the queen of fruits, and
laughed as we tore the bright-red clusters from their
downy beds.   I could not stand the temptation longer,
and fell to serious work.   I cast aside my umbrella, and
spread my silk handkerchief upon the light-green moss.
It was not yet ten o'clock, and the dew shone as crystals
upon the delicate ferns and lichens which grew from the
mossy carpet; and here, shaded by forest-trees, a space
fifty feet square was covered with luscious strawberries.
We gathered more than a quart, besides those that fell
into our mouths, and I need not say Mount Omei had
one peculiar attraction that evening.

Hastening on we came to a very large temple, which
had an unusually fine statue of Omito in a glass case,
and over it written in large characters, "This is the
boundary of the ' Western Land '" (Paradise).   One
could almost believe himself in Edenic glory and on the

very threshold of heaven, surrounded by such natural beauties, fanned by cool breezes just strong enough to bend the slender grass, and dazzled by bright rays, which shed a genial warmth over all they touched. We may now reckon ourselves as within the terrestrial limit of the "Happy Land." Farther on, passing a stone tunnel, I observed over the archway that I was only "one step from heaven."

Up we go, resting occasionally after a hard pull. All is life and bustle; people of diverse habits and looks rush up and down, excited by what they have seen and hope to see. We are now very near to the mighty head cliff; we shall soon leave behind us the highest trickling rill and living spring; the trees have already lost half their size and height, and look shrivelled with age; the bamboos are not above five feet in height, — scrubby little things. I have not seen an animal in all the mountains larger than a squirrel, and few of these; no snakes, lizards, or toads. There is much animal life in the distant gorges and forests, but that which we see is of bird and harmless insect.

The aneroid stopped at eight thousand feet above sea-level. Two hours more of hard climbing brought us to a cluster of temples and "the cliff," which raises its proud head over eleven thousand feet above the ocean. Here we are, after severe exercise for a portion of two days, tired, yet exultant; but in our exultation we are again humbled, for the wonderful prospect is obliterated by the swiftly speeding mist, and so far as view is concerned, we might as well stand upon a granite peak in the centre of the Indian Ocean.

Our first night's lodging in the great temple on the verge of the crag was not a success. Our servant had been ruthlessly thrust aside by a priest while inspecting a room for our accommodation, and we received some slight abuse from this proud son of humility in our endeavor to secure a suitable room. My teacher, who in temper is a veritable Peter, withstood him to his face, and wrangled him out of countenance within five minutes. The priest was so much cowed before I could reach the scene of dispute, that he beat a hasty retreat, leaving the settlement of the question to his better-disposed brethren. Some days after, an official happened to come up for worship, and hearing the story from my teacher, and that we had sought quarters in a more retired place, he ordered the priest to make the journey of two miles with one of his soldiers, and ask pardon of the strangers. I feel it a duty I owe to the officials of Sz-Chuan to say that from beginning to end of my journey and residence in the province I met nothing but fair and generous treatment at their hands.

When we were finally admitted to a room, it was dark and gloomy, and dirty beyond an excuse. Then there was a constant tramp of pilgrims, and a room crowded full of them next us, with such large cracks in the boards as to admit all their nonsensical jabber and the fumes of their opium-pipes. They laughed, talked, and smoked till past midnight, and then were up watching for cock-crowing before three o'clock. Life in this *seventh heaven* had no brilliant opening for us. The only pleasure I extracted from the night was in trying to decipher the four languages scribbled in charcoal over the board walls. There were Thibetan, Mantsz, Cashmere or Karakorum, and Chinese. Lolo there was none. A priest said: " Lolos can't write, have n't any classics, have n't any gods, have n't any laws; bad men; they rob and kill, and they never come here."

The place we occupy is to the Chinaman the most

exalted in the empire, not only in height, but in religious
importance. For hundreds of years the stream of religious humanity has here flowed and ebbed without
diminution. They flock like doves to the window. This
Mecca is now at the height of its season, and thousands
crowd around the rocks to gaze into the awful abyss
where they hope to catch a view of Buddha. Upon the
highest point a few years ago stood the wonderful bronze
temple, which for centuries had been the pride of Western China, and we might say of the empire, for it was
built from subscriptions of fifty taels and five taels from
the officials of each of the ancient thirteen provinces. It
was a work like that of Solomon's temple, — not large,
but costly, and showed the best resources of the nation
in means and art. This unique structure was merely
sixteen feet square, — or about that size, — thirty feet
high, and of three stories. It now lies a heap of twisted
and broken bronze, excepting a few perfect panels and
doors which are wrought into the new building; but
even in its ruins it strikes the beholder as something
exquisitely beautiful and sacred. The great wooden
buildings which formerly enclosed the monument were
twice burned and once struck by lightning. From foundation to topmost ball it was made of pure bronze and
gold, and in its perfection must have been the most
dazzling monument of ancient or modern times.

I cannot do better than give my readers an account of
the temple engraved upon a bronze tablet, which we
found secreted in an outbuilding, and covered with
boards to hide it from pilgrims. The tablet itself is a
marvellous work, being of pure bronze, eight feet high,
three feet wide, and nine inches thick, with a finely
carved pedestal, and a cap of no mean workmanship.
The same plucky man who cowed the priest, and flung

open the yamen doors of Tsz-liu-tsin with his own hands, uncovered this monument and copied the fourteen hundred characters engraved upon its face : —

Tablet of the bronze temple of the great Omei, written by Fu-kwang-tseh, of the city of Lian, Doctor of Philosophy, an official of the third grade, Judge of the Supreme Court, Assistant Commissioner, Provincial Literary Chancellor, and formerly a censor of the province Honan.

I have read in the Miscellaneous Flowery classics that there were three great altars bestowed upon the kingdom Chén Tan : Wu-tai of Tai-cheu, Pu-tan of Min-cheu, and Omei of Kia-cheu.

Wen-chü, teacher of wonderful merit, resides at Wu-tai ; Kwan-yin, sovereign contemplator of sounds, at Pu-tan ; Pu-hsien, the " wide-spreading sage " and " king of vows," at Omei. These three great teachers, with the millions of Pu-sa connected with them, dwell forever at these altars, rescuing mankind with great generosity. Now Pu-hsien was the eldest son of Buddha, and Omei the most beautiful mountain. It was produced by the pulsations of Kwun-lun, passing on beyond the Karakorum Mountains and congealed into these lofty eyebrows ; thence dividing itself formed the Five Peaks.

This mountain westward looks out upon the Spiritual Vulture (or Holy Mountain of India), and they appear to be bowing to each other like persons giving and receiving, like master and pupil, or like father and son, — three acts equally dignified.

Wen-chü is infinite in wisdom, consequently nothing further to desire, without end of existence.

Kwan-yin is mercy revolving, destitute of desire, and absolutely no end to his work.

Suppose the three sages were to become as heaven, which is passionless, yet Pu-hsien in the fitness of things would occupy his august throne in Shuh. Further, this place is one of the cardinal points of the earth, and Omei like the earth's axis, where all the gods must rest in passing, and dwelling here they will manifest their forms. Here priests shall be renovated, and abiding in this mountain shall rest their hearts. All those coming to pay court to his majesty, no matter old or young, Chinese or barbarians, looking up expectantly, shall behold his beautiful form and gem-like glory, and they must inevitably turn from the sordid world and its trials to meditate upon this altar. Those who in the silence of their hearts enter the sphere of true reason, sacrificing the desirable things of this life, shall repose in the true realities. Possibly they may see Pu-hsien on his white elephant coursing through space, and he may stretch out his hand and anoint their heads, and straightway voyaging, with desire to bring them to that Other Shore,[1] he returns to his resplendent and august city.

Again, who is able to measure, who can think or compute by deliberation, or understand the amazing height of this mountain? It rises strata upon strata to the highest region of the air, — a neighbor of the sun and moon, and polished hard by the wind.

Therefore the tiles of the temple were made of bronze and iron; still they have a tendency to fly away; even the beams, corner-posts, and rafters move and shake. In 1601 A. D., the end of spring, I ascended to worship and view the snowy peaks. It was very cold; the brooks were frozen hard, and at night I lodged upon the very top. The temple quaked as if ocean billows lashed it round; it was as if the temple flew into space. I was terrified in my dreams, and cried out, saying, "Where can gold be had to build a temple?" I found it stated in the Tai-ho-chen-wu [holy classics] that the noble-minded, heavenly king of the priest had long ago made a temple of gold; how much more should it be used for the gods! A short time after this the honorable Miao-fung-tun came to Shuh from Tsin. He brought several thousand pieces of gold, the gift of the ruler of the kingdom of Shen. He consulted with the viceroy, who was Sir Wang, of Tsi-nan (Shantung), who delegated certain officials to exchange it for copper at Fung-teu, Shih-chü, and other

____
[1] Paradise.

places. The noble Kiu, a feudatory prince, who had enriched himself, also contributed to the building of the temple, which was begun in the spring of Yun-yin, A. D. 1602, and completed in the autumn of Kwei-mao, A. D. 1603. It was twenty-five Chinese feet high, fourteen feet five inches wide, and thirteen feet five inches deep. The roof was in layers and the ridges carved. It was encircled with windows minutely carved and beautifully fretted, and the great sage sat within surrounded by ten thousand Buddhas, and the empty spaces by the door-posts were carved and ornamented with clouds in relief.

The dangerous places on the road from Kin-ko (Hang-chung to Sz-Chuan) into this mountain were delineated, tortuously twisted and broken. It was gilded with pure gold, was wonderfully grand and dazzling, mirroring the glories of heaven and earth. When it was completed the clouds and vapors were most lustrous, and the mountains emitted precious light. The streams, ravines, peaks, and cones were all of one color like the To-lo-min. The gods came faintly into view as their forms filled space. Oh, how wonderful to rely upon the hearts of mortals to perfect the altars of the gods! In the works of Pu-hsien are evidences of the works of Yulai, who is and is not, with form and without form. The great sage is not the only sage; a myriad of Buddhas do not constitute all the Buddhas.

Pihluche-yulai produced the great lotus-flower with a thousand leaves; each leaf has three thousand great thousands of worlds, and each world has a Buddha to teach the Law, and each Buddha has a Pu-hsien for an elder son. Further, Pihluche-yulai has the strength of his vows, and can fulfil the great vows of Pu-hsien; moreover, he can produce all Buddhas. The guest and host are untrammelled; the first and last are harmoniously blended; the ten worlds and the three ages down to the consummation of all things are also unshackled. Entering the ten worlds and three confines we find T'sa-hwa rules the realm of Law, and it is perfectly governed.

In the form of this one temple all things are brought

together in completeness, and all honor is due to the great teacher. We dare not say a cash or a kernel of rice is fruitless as a cause of blessing; one prostration, one chant with faith, how mighty!

The teacher was a man from Lien-fen in Shansi, a priest in the temple of Wan-ku of Pu, who afterward dwelt at Fan-cha of Lu-ya. He built a pagoda and a bridge several tens of chang long at Shang-ku.

. After this temple was finished he went south to Pu-tan, and north to Wn tai. With all this dignity of work upon him he was not fatigued or remiss, and his heart was not filled with vanity; the meritorious deeds he brushed off as dust from his robes, and they filled no space in his heart. Perhaps he was Pu-hsien divided, seated upon his revolving wheel and came hither. I have honored and had faith in this teacher for a long time, and this temple was the perfection of his work. His desires for good works were limitless as the ocean. I rejoice and am moved, and for this reason offer this mead of praise.

Omei is exceeding fair and distinguished for its great glory.
It has a myriad of gods who rest their hearts in journeying by.
Here is the great sage Pu-hsien, who is Buddha's eldest son,
With ten vows to redeem the world, without beginning and without end.
Here is a golden temple raised to space, an antechamber to Heaven's palace.
Here sun and moon invert their shadows, while bells and cymbals sigh in the wind.
A myriad of Buddhas encompass it around, majestic and of lovely mien;
It is a godly net of shining pearls, from story to story most brilliant.
On the west joined to the "Spirit Vulture," to the east it looks upon Pu-tan,
Northward saluted by Wu-tai with a harmonious sound of bells.
It is one in three, and three in one,
Divided yet united in length and breadth, the three of mystery yet unrevealed;
It exhibits the forms of priests, illustrious as the persons of lords.
The aged men and retired scholars, kings and ministers great,

Together mount the wheel of vows, together course the sea of
    faculties.
The mountain whirlwind ever blows, but this temple changes not;
It shall endure with Pu-hsien, pure as a lotus-flower.
Here lives the six-toothed fragrant elephant, ever coursiug the
    arid desert (of the world),
His majestic sound is not distant, and the flowery dragon near at
    hand.
Lofty space may be dissolved; my desire is to be eternal.

This temple was ornamented with ten thousand small
Buddhas cast upon the bronze plates and covered with
gold, while without were the large flowers described by
the Chinese writer. The present temple, instead of
facing the east and the cliff, as one would expect, faces
the west and the country of the Mantsz; and I am told
that when they come to the mountain peak, they make
all their offerings in this temple, and alone to Pu-hsien.
If this be true, it would seem to indicate that they claim
a peculiar interest in the ancient monument, and that
the statement of an old Chinese writer, that it was built
by one of the feudatory kings under the patronage of a
Chinese empress of the Sung dynasty, may be founded
on fact. The temple was totally destroyed by fire in the
reign of Hienfung.[1]

This truly wonderful mountain, and the cliff upon
which a cluster of rough wooden temples stands, is of
more than ordinary interest. The topmost point is
nearly ten thousand feet above the plain, twenty miles
distant, and quite five thousand feet above the mountains
around its base. It has an almost perpendicular fall of
one mile on the east.

The day after our arrival we strolled along the crag to
the south a mile or two until we came to a new temple,
perched upon the verge of the precipice; thirty feet from

[1] 1851 A. D.

the back door was a head-rock from which we could gaze down into the echoless deeps. There was one young priest in the temple, and we soon bargained for a week's lodging at half a dollar per day, including board for two servants, and any vegetables we might desire, besides a charcoal fire day and night. It was a glorious retreat in the grand park extending south and west. We transferred our effects in a drenching shower, but we were nothing daunted, for the sun came out in half an hour, and revealed countless objects of interest which were screened from us at the other lodging by temples and forests. Here was a mile of wild grassy prairie surrounding us on three sides, and literally filled with red, blue, pink, and white flowers, with occasional clumps of low bushes, and strawberries almost pure white. Our priest was very industrious with the hoe and sickle. Every day after prayers — which were cut short till an older priest came and lengthened them one half — he put on his large bamboo hat, short coat, and heavy boots, and strolled down to his potato patch. He owned a farm-house in the hollow at the foot of the first slope, and around it had an acre of Irish potatoes in full bloom, seeming as much at home as in Erin itself. They were planted in rows and hilled, just as in New England, and seemed to be the staple vegetable on top of the mountain; there were turnips, spinach, and a few cabbages near the temple, which were placed at our disposal, but the main dependance seemed to be upon potatoes.

There were depths of forest and dense jungle into which we dared not go, for the weather was not to be trusted; now a perfectly blue sky and the warm sun smiling into the darkest gorge, then a dense mist sweeping up from the mountain gulf and enveloping heaven and earth. It was most impressive when we realized that

the artillery of heaven played below us instead of above."
There was a great rolling and crashing until, finally, a
fierce wind swept over us. I fell to calculating the force
of resistance there would be in the shell-like house we
occupied, and in case it were to start on a voyage over
the cliff, how I could escape; for I must say I had no
wish to take a mile trip down in so disjointed a balloon,
especially when the lightning seemed to play up from
below. Dr. Morley calculated that it would take but
nineteen seconds to make the descent. The temple has
two wings, perhaps for this very purpose !

On one hand we have an unrestful sea of mist and
cloud at times, and again, such sweeps of vision as stag-
ger the imagination ; on the other side are forests and
ever-rising mountains, even up to the snow line. I am
surprised to find such luxuriant foliage and so many
varieties of birds and insects at this height. The spring,
summer, and autumn are crowded into four months, but
the almost total absence of cold winds makes the short
summer here a perfect paradise.

From our front door we look over mountain and valley, on, on, past the Wa-wu and other lofty ranges, to the
snow caps on the borders of Thibet, quite one hundred
and fifty miles distant. With the help of a priest I have
been able to locate the countries of many of the wild tribes
who live within a few days' journey of the mountain.

In the early morning, from the head-rock at the verge
of the precipice, is spread out before me mountain,
valley, plain, labyrinth of river and silver stream, the
city of Omei, the white pagoda, Kia-ting, and a hundred
towns and hamlets, almost to Chenteu, one hundred and
thirty miles to the northeast. I have not been able to
see into India or to Canton, as some Chinese visitors
have believed they did. Into these depths come daily

white feathery clouds, floating from north to south, and passing the out-jutting points until the broad expanse directly below us is completely filled; not a peak remains unveiled; then the gauze-like clouds float higher and higher, until early in the afternoon (from two to four o'clock) the cliffs are mirrored upon these bright, white walls. Then if the observer stands upon the edge of the precipice, and the sun shines brightly upon him, he will see his dark shadow away off upon the white clouds, with an exceedingly bright and sometimes large halo around it, which changes in size and brilliancy every moment as the mists rise, recede, or advance. Stretch forth your hands, and the giant shadow does likewise. Now the mist rises and dances about your feet, and finally obscures the sun's rays, and the " glory " is gone.

It is while thus gazing that many pilgrims in their ecstatic frenzy, either intentionally or not, throw themselves over into the abyss. Our monk tells us that there are many tens of pilgrims who annually throw themselves over to Buddha. Another monk said that the act was not intentional; that they are dazed, and leaning too far over fall down. My own experience was that as the gulf filled up with clouds swaying to and fro, and rising almost to the level of the rock on which I stood, the giddiness which follows looking into the open gulf left me, and I could stand within a foot of the edge of the precipice as easily as by the seashore. I also found myself when the aureola was brightest making insensible advances toward the image in it. All the temples except this provide walls and iron railings along the edge of the crag, to prevent persons falling over; and yet, with such precaution, many lives are lost. I discovered an old proclamation upon one of the temples forbidding people to throw themselves over ; so the priest's story that they do so with the expectation of going direct to Buddha may have some foundation in fact. This natural phenomenon, which is common to some other peaks and mountains, such as Adam's Peak, in Ceylon, and the Spectre of the Brocken in the Hartz Mountains, is considered by the devout Chinaman the manifestation of Buddha's spiritual presence, and an object of worship. Neither of the mountains mentioned is so lofty as Omei, Adam's Peak being 7,420 and the Brocken merely 3,417 feet. Those desiring further information can find an interesting article on Shadows by William Acroyd in " Science for All."

There is a similar phenomenon in the Wa-wu range, which lies fifty miles southwest of Omei, but not equal to the views here obtained.

The proclamation of which I speak read thus :—

" Those visiting the mount to make offerings to Buddha and the Queen of Heaven (Teu-lao) who sacrifice their bodies are surely exceedingly ignorant. Our bodies are difficult of attainment, and fortunately for us born in the ' Middle Land.' Riches and honors, poverty and affluence, are wholly under the control of High Heaven. Your bodies, even to hair and skin, are the gifts of your parents. In perfection they were received, and in perfection they should be returned. Do not dishonor your ancestors. In an instant the body is destroyed, and below are wolves and tigers. How can Yien Wang help railing at you, seeing you thus mutilated in death? I would exhort the people of this world to be filial betimes to their parents, and let there be harmony among brothers. Choose to make your habitation among the humans. Great Heaven knows not partiality. The virtuous only are helped.

" What goodness ! What goodness ! What misery to him who sacrifices his body !

" Hail, Amita Buddha ! "

The shrines and idols found in these plain board temples are made from elaborate designs, and are far richer in appearance than usually found in Chinese temples. They are so arranged as to exhibit the different divisions of the " Happy Land," such as the shrine of the " Silver Boundary," of the " Porcelain Boundary " and the " Gold Boundary."

The temple in which Pu-hsien is enshrined is new and costly; it is really a brick temple within an immense wooden building. Into the square brick building are set a dozen or two large bronze plates from the old bronze temple. The god occupies the centre of the windowless brick building, seated upon a standing bronze elephant. He is dressed in rich flowing pink satin robes embroidered with many devices, and has a diadem upon his head, and from behind the great altar would be easily mistaken for the Goddess of Mercy. Here men and women gather after their long journeys, and for half a day pour out their souls in chants and prostrations, and in leaning over the chain fence to catch if possible a glimpse of his daily manifestation to the benighted world.

While viewing the wonderful altar and striving to get a good view of the most holy recess in which the god is enthroned, a band of pilgrims came and knelt upon the mat before the high altar, men and women side by side, and followed their precentor as they poured out their hearts in exciting chants. It is a solemn sight to look upon a score of these footsore, fatigued creatures, engaged in an act which has cost them so much effort. Many long miles have been traversed, many cash laid by for this one hour, the grandest of a life-time.

Think of the Arabian entering the Caaba and approaching the holy stone, and you have a picture of these poor creatures before the sacred shrine.

The natural glories to be seen would well repay any effort; but the poor devotees are not concerned with these grand exhibitions of divine power, and the beauties of plant and flower stir little emotion in their phlegmatic natures. Their hearts are centred upon the god of vows, Pu-hsien. A mistaken idea is that held by some philosophers in France in reference to the Chinese, that they are greater lovers of Nature than Christian nations, and that Fetichism brings a people nearer to the beautiful productions of Nature than does Theology. We grant that the Chinese as a people do admire shrubs and flowers, as they do music and painting and sculpture. Who has not observed, however, that it is the fantastic and unnatural in shrub, flower, and painting which captivates their sense of beauty? Who sings of violets, pansies, forget-me-nots, daisies, and buttercups? Not the Chinaman. A thousand Chinamen ascend this lovely mountain, and will ten take any particular notice of the large white clematis by the roadside? Who steps aside to examine the dozen varieties of bramble in flower and fruit, or who enters the bowers to make a nosegay from the half-dozen varieties of roses? Here we have the beautiful hydrangea, laburnum white and blue, several kinds of clerodendron, five kinds of rhododendron, the several kinds of primula, the acanthus, oxalis, geranium, the delicate begonias, the saxifragious plants, the polygonums, the many kinds of lilies, the numerous corydalis, with many small and large plants unknown to me. Do the Chinese poets sing of them? Do artists paint them on porcelain to any extent? Do pilgrims arrange them in bouquets and enjoy their fragrance as they descend from this heaven of beauty? Nay. A birch staff, a few pine cones, a few medicinal roots, fill their hands.

August 2. A heavy thunderstorm raged during the night, with grand displays of electricity, accompanied by an infantile cyclone, " The sky in pieces seeming to be rent." On presenting myself before the gods, as is now the custom, when leaving my bedroom, a strange incident occurred, such as one living in the flesh could scarcely expect to behold. It was not the great plain covered with spotless white billows, nor the mighty snow range stretching from due north to west-southwest in an almost unbroken arc, with the giant peak near the centre quite twenty-five thousand feet high, clothed for eight thousand feet with snow and ice, and glistening in the first beams of morning; nor was it the jasper sky beyond and between the wide cleft peak,— none of these which I expected to see. It was a scene which will live in memory to the last, and a fitting climax to my already eventful journey.

As I entered the hall filled with the fragrance of early incense, I drew my great coat closely about me, and gave my red wool cap an extra pull, for the morning was bright and chilly. Two blue pilgrims were prostrating themselves to Ta Mo, Kwanyin, and Pu-hsien, when, seeing me, they wheeled about and prostrated themselves at my feet, knocked their heads several times upon the hard floor, crying continually, "Omito-foo! Omito-foo! Amita Buddha! Amita Buddha!" What unexpected honors come to the humble-minded! A crowd of pilgrim women looked at me one day as I descended a sharp peak, and as I drew near they cried out, "Holy Sage!" I comforted their troubled minds with mortal words, and strode on.

At sunrise we had our best views of the far-away snow peaks and the rich valleys of the Fuh, Ya, and Tung Rivers; then on till noon the ever-shifting clouds and different shades upon the green valleys, the lowly peaks, the rivulets, the caverns 'neath the proud cliffs, and the mists of purple, yellow, pink, and fading hues combined their beauties below us. It was, however, after the glories of the " Buddha manifestation," in the afternoon, that the full grandeur of the day was revealed. At six P. M. the plains, the hills, and even the mountains were covered with a sea of white billows; not one peak pierced through. Later on they settled, and one by one the peaks arose as islands in the ocean, until the valley came out clear, even to the distant pagoda of, Omei.

> " The fairest, brightest hues of ether fade;
> The sweetest notes must terminate and die.

> " Lo, in the vale, the mists of evening spread ;
> The visionary arches are not there,
> Nor the green islands, nor the shining seas;
> Yet sacred is to me this mountain head,
> From which I have been lifted on the breeze
> Of harmony above all earthly care."

In the west, as the sun hung in a dark crimson cloud over the highest snow-covered peak, one by one, white and yellow tinged, billow-like clouds settled into the vast mountain ranges between us and the snow-covered arc. Little by little the low mountains were covered ; the clouds expanded and rolled above the higher ranges to the northwest, rising and falling by turns until every mountain peak, even to the snow range, excepting the Wa-wu and nine others out of the hundreds, just peered out of this cloud-ocean which rolled at our feet. As twilight deepened it seemed as if these fleecy billows nestled into gorges and vales, there to await the coming of the sun. At length the moon shone on this silvery carpet of glory, and I watched until but a few long belts of white remained to screen the deepest vales.

One morning we sauntered down a beautiful combe to a fairy dell called " White Dragon's Pool." The cool dew-drops hung as pearls from the feathery grass-tufts, and the birds warbled in the birch and pines. At the bottom of the combe there issued from the rock a large fountain, with force enough to form a sprightly brook. To this fountain many pilgrims come to catch and carry away a large lizard six or seven inches long, with a flat head. A little shrine stands near the pool, and three ancient bronze gods. One has lost a leg, but still manages to balance himself; the best is seated upon a white elephant, and the third upon an animal neither elephant nor tiger. It once had a horn, which was broken off in some conflagration.

The stream from this fountain joins another a little way off, and lower down will leap in cascades into the Ya; it then rolls on, broken into fierce rapids, until it reaches the Tung and Min, and lower down the Golden Sands; again it speeds through orange-groves, deep gorges, and broad rivers, at last reaching the mighty sea.

In one of our tramps we succeeded in following a lumberman's trail over the south side of the crag; and for a time the zigzag path, though very rough, was such that we managed to follow it. At length we scarcely had a foothold on the rocks; sometimes the loose earth had been partially banked up with half-decayed sticks and spruce boughs; below us were only yawning chasms. We reached one ledge where a ladder rested, the other end being on another ledge which descended several hundred feet; we passed over and reached the outjutting wall of solid rock on the opposite side of this chasm. It now became a subject of serious debate whether a thousand feet of such climbing, done principally on all fours, or by hanging to twigs and roots above us, would pay for the ferns we might get. The coolie we had picked up at the temple advised us to return. However, we went on, led by Dr. Morley. The path grew worse and worse, until the descent was made upon two logs placed together, with holes chopped in them for the feet. I felt quite ashamed of my nervousness upon meeting two brawny lumbermen, carrying heavy planks up this almost perpendicular road. .Each man carried three planks fourteen feet long, one foot wide, and one to two inches thick. The planks were lashed to a yoke three feet long, which rested upon the shoulders. On our way back we found it almost impossible to pull ourselves up over places which they scaled with seeming ease. Reaching the lumbermen's forest we had an hour of unalloyed bliss searching for flowers and rare ferns, and were rewarded by finding some beautiful specimens. I am inclined to think that one could descend the mountain upon this side, but the priests say " no."

August 14th we were back again in the " Monastery of a Myriad Ages," and it was Sunday morning, bright and cool. I had read thirty pages of Bunsen's Life of Martin Luther, while keeping up a skirmish with a score or more huge brown mosquitoes. At length I entered the quiet temple, — for now few pilgrims come, — and found the old priest fast asleep, while " Everlasting Wisdom " — for so the boy priest is named — was just coming down from the throne of the great bronze idols. He came toward me smiling, and I made the round of the temple with him, trying to tell him how foolish and wicked is idolatry. He gravely assented to all I said, and accompanied me to my room, where I gave him Matthew's Gospel, fully illustrated, and a " History of Moses." I told him that he could read them to the old priest, which he did.

A priest called " Perfection of Truth " came and accepted two books; and on the last morning of our stay Weiching, " the one made upright," who was the abbot, came in after our prayers and made an informal address in praise of Saint Matthew's Gospel, which he had read, declaring that " the doctrines are true, and able to perfect the conscience."

The time had now come for us to leave this sacred retreat, where we had been kindly and hospitably entertained for a month. Farewell, temples, priests, pilgrims. I shall see you no more, but you will ever be fresh in my memory; and I trust that remembering our words, you may reflect upon that " Prince of Peace " whose yoke is easy, and whose burden is light.

On Wednesday we descended to the city of Omei, where we passed a comfortless night, and early the next morning, in dilapidated sedans, borne by old opium-smokers, we passed out at the East Gate. The populace came in crowds to get our illustrated books.

I had heard much of the " thousand eyed and handed Goddess of Mercy," which was near this gate, and had determined to see her if possible. The coolies knew all about it, and were ready to guide us and to act as interpreters if necessary. We left our chairs on the main road, and made our way through fields of ripe rice to a group of lofty temples.

The first and second buildings were fine. They were filled with what would be considered costly images in other provinces, but in this district they were of little account, so rich is it in bronze statues. The third temple has three lofty stories; in the centre is a grand stone platform six or seven feet high and twenty square; upon this costly carved dais rises the most imposing bronze statue it has ever been my privilege to see, —

more imposing than the famous Buddha of Japan, although not quite so large. It is a well-proportioned standing image of the goddess, thirty-six feet high, and with many half-outstretched arms, measuring from hand to hand, in the widest place, not less than twenty feet. Covered with bright gold, and towering into the third story, it presents an awe-inspiring object. In this and the fourth temple there are many other. bronze statues, but none to compare in size with this one. Weito — the Protector of the Law — is the most symmetrical statue I have seen, and, possibly, of the richest bronze. The goddess was cast in the Min dynasty, under the superintendence of a famous priest called Wu Kiung. How many more famous gods and goddesses there are in this part of the province I cannot say. It is truly wonderful what treasures those old priests were able to extract from imperial coffers.

While wandering about the grounds and the now familiar courts, I happened upon a stall where odds and ends peculiar to a religious establishment were exposed for sale. Among other things a very thin book attracted my eye, and I purchased it. The book turned out to be an interesting description of the mountain and temples, written by a scholar, — an enthusiastic disciple of Buddha.

It is of quite recent date, no longer ago than 1844, and in some respects is a faithful description of what may be seen at the present time. It is in poetic form, and exhibits the exaggeration expected from a writer of Cathay. With the Chinese writer, thousands and ten-thousands are round numbers, and express better the author's exuberance of feeling than exact numbers.

Measurements in time and space give free play to the imagination, and it is hard work for the " Vermilion pen" to come into the region of exact statement. A lizard becomes a huge dragon, and a pool fifty feet in diameter is a great lake with high waves.

Notwithstanding some high soaring and considerable hyperbole, the little poem contains so much that is faithful to Nature, and affords such an insight into religious life in China, that I am impelled to give my readers the benefit of the poet's musings, although in blank verse. In many instances it must necessarily be very obscure to those not acquainted with Chinese Buddhism or the folk-lore of this peculiar people.

Omei, the Divine Mountain of Sz-Chuan.

It is said that this celebrated mountain was bestowed by the Emperor upon the great scholar, Pu-hsien, who, in the reign of Minti, about B. C. 146, came from the Western Land to select a holy mountain in which to dwell. His first choice was Tieh-Ping, " Iron Plateau." The water of this mountain was not clear, and he could not effect his purification. He afterward selected Wa Mountain upon which to enthrone himself in the lotus seat, but it shook so dreadfully he left it, and selected Kún-lún peak of Omei. This mount is one thousand li (three hundred miles) in circumference, has more than a hundred large caves and twelve small ones. The streams coursing from foreign lands — from nine mountain ranges — gather here in China, and flow thence through the thirteen provinces.

From here the merciful light of Pu-hsien shines upon all the world ; the mountains are always green, and the waters clear. The spirits of immortals, made perfect, rise sphere above sphere. . . . Below his lotus throne the drums are beaten, the bells are rung. The star of Felicity shines above him, for the everlasting protection of all people and for the salvation of the world. It is here that all petitions are answered.

When the clouds divide, the mists vanish and the golden light
    appears ;
Mount Omei is wondrous clear and beautiful from afar,
For it is exalted of Heaven and the veins of Kúu lún [1] are there.
Hither from all quarters the pilgrims are hastening,
For there is the Emperor [2] of Great Peace, the equal of Yao and
    Shun, [3]
And the gods of mountains, streams, and earth, with the Unicorn,
    are seen.
The people are happy, the winds are tempered, and rains propitious;
The four Oceans sing ballads and chant litanies of peace.
I cannot narrate the generations of emperors and kings.
I pray you, noble gentlemen, be seated upon the divan ;
No matter from what city or town,
Listen while I sing of the divine beauties of Omei,
And tell its wonders one by one.

We have heard it is said Mount Omei has a wonderful god,
And thither we determined to come.
Although we had a sincere desire to visit this mount,
One day was prolonged to three, and three to nine;
Finally the right time came and the propitious day chosen,
The money and the clothing for the journey were collected.
We fasted and bathed and longed to be on the way.
The golden hen [a cock] announced three times the morning
    dawn,
And ere we were aware the daylight had come;
Upon Mount Omei the white clouds were dissolving.
But to visit the mount and see Buddha the heart must be true.
We threw umbrellas of fragrant woods over our backs,
And left our homes with incense burning ;
Making the journey with considerable difficulty,
Straight to city of Omei we came,
And within its walls took lodgings in an inn.
The master brought forth tea and tobacco;

[1] A high mountain in Thibet, said to contain the sources of the Yellow River; it is now usually applied to the almost unknown range,
Koul-Kun Mountains, lying about latitude 85 degrees north, between the
desert of Gobi and Thibet.

[2] A reference to the god Pu-hsien.

[3] The two greatest emperors of antiquity, who reigned respectively
B. c. 2357 and 2255, nearly coeval with Terah.

Furnished with these, we went sight-seeing.
Here were guilds from the thirteen provinces ;
Of merchandise a hundred kinds, and all things pleasing to men.
The camps of the frontier are here,
With yamens, civil and military, six in number,
While of soldiers and horsemen there are full five hundred,
And viands of all kinds and flavors unnumbered.
The temple to Pisces [1] is wonderful to behold.
If the gods you would see, out of the city go,
For without the East Gate is a remarkable temple to Fuh,[2]
And out of the small South Gate are altars to I. K. A. in the paw
    of the Great Bear.
At the West Gate is Money Transmuting temple upon Si-Po,
And out of the North Gate is the temple which flew from heaven,
That was so wonderful in ancient times.
Who dared to enter its courts ?
Those who came to worship and pay vows
Burnt their sacrifices without its gates.
Of this temple we cannot speak in detail.
But now return into the walls of Omei,
For the red sun has sunk in the west and the glow begun.
We returned to our inn and sat down for a chat,
First having offered incense-sticks and paper money,
Then we supped and made peaceful our hearts.
It were vain to detail our talk in the inn;
Ere we perceived it, daylight had appeared,
And from the forts the great guns resounded.
The black-haired race awoke in a daze.
Lo! there were the guests all trembling with fright,
While each one was endeavoring to open the doors.
We bathe our faces with clean water and purify our hearts,
We bid farewell to our host, and commence the ascent.
Each one bearing upon his hip a bag
Filled with incense of Chen-tan and Kwang,
We slowly traverse the crowded streets and hastily pass through the
    lanes,
Until we stand before the city temple.[8]
Again we bathe our hands, offer incense, and pray,

    [1] Temple to learning.
    [2] Buddha.
    [8] A temple where officials worship the tutelar or palladial god. It
answers to the Greek Rhadamanthus.

Register our names, and proceed out of the South Gate;
We pass over the bridge of the Dragon made holy,
Where people learn how to be gods.
Now at the court of Shih-fang we burn incense.
Not more than a hundred steps further
We come to Pi Mountain, where dwells a mighty spirit.
Here the Boddhistava, holy and magnificent, is enshrined,
And here a multitude of learned priests meditate and pray.
There is to be seen the footprint of an ancient empress,
And in the middle of the path the footprints of a god;
Below the temple called "Precious" is a marvellous bell,
Whose sound is heard three days' journey away.
There is the seven-storied pagoda, a wonderful sight,
And pomegranates laden with flowers and cypress ever green;
Yu-lai,[1] the progenitor of all Buddhas, is revered in this place.
We worship Pu-hsien, the honored by Sâkyamuni,
And Pao-lin, the ruling prince of the bright law throne,
Where the light is so lurid the bravest dare not go.
Next we repair to the Protector of the Kingdom and Helper to the
    gods of the earth;
Then to the temple of the God of War, where we burn incense.
After crossing the bridge Hsien-lung we
Now come to Yung-Chen, the gate of the mountain possessed of a
    fearful spirit.
It was here that Chao, the great warrior, humbled
The dragon and made tigers lie prostrate,
And caused those slain in battle to become gods.
To right and left are the eighteen Lo-han,[2]
Above them are written Hsien-Ang; no two better characters
    are found;
These Lo-han fixed all the dwellings of the caves,
And folded them round with sages and heavenly hosts.
It was here that the laughing Buddha, made from three slain gods,
Did first manifest his dread spiritual power.

  .   .   .   .

On both sides of the temple great pines and evergreens rise;
In front are verdant mountains and pure, running rivulets,
While the dagobi-triumphal arch is at the foot of the hill,

---

[1] "Thus coming Buddha." The highest appellation given to any
Buddha. A Buddha who reveals perfected human nature.

[2] Disciples of Sâkyamuni, who stand next in order to Buddhas. They
stand or sit nine on each side of Buddha.

With " Pao-koh " carved upon its face by imperial decree.
The octagonal tower is in front of the hall,
Where multitudes burn incense, looking up to the skies;
We are soon at Rafterless Temple, where genii dwell;
Then walk over the Bridge of Cool-winds leisurely
And take the new road, not yet smooth.
Here is a temple both quiet and beautiful.
Upon Muh-Yü-Pao we behold the mountain's form,
Where the new-blown lotus-flowers are fragrant and fair;
We now see the crown of Mount Omei lowering over Blackwater
    River,
And at the foot of White-Road Mountain the green dragon is seen;
There also is Pao-ma River, where a chief rebel gave up his life.

We will not sing of this place's olden stories,
But go and look into Hog's-liver cave,
The place where our father, Lü,[1] was made perfect in reason;
His true likeness is preserved in this cave.
Within are two wonderful treasures,
Which always and everywhere have been talked of by men.
Cha Yüen came and seized the precious treasures, —
The hog's liver,[2] which dropped kernels of rice,
And the sheep's liver, from which trickled drops of water.
He bruised the hog's liver, and its virtue was gone,
And now alone remains the sheep's liver dripping water.
We now come to the Tiger's palace, where Lao-tsz is enthroned;
If you would see the caves and the rugged gorges you must climb;
The road to the top of the Hill of Liberation is difficult and
    dangerous,
For kilins[3] and tigers will meet you on the way.
Let us take a seat in the temple-majestic,
Shaded by an umbrella of fragrant woods,
And chant " Omito " a full thousand times.
Here a genuine god may be seen,
Who in ancient days left a memorial, —
A boat made of stone to ferry mortals over.[4]
Fifty-three steps from this place

[1] A noted Taoist recluse.
[2] Tradition has preserved many stories of those miraculous fountains.
[3] Auspicious animals: the male of the Chinese unicorn.
[4] No doubt one which was believed to have fallen from heaven, used to
ferry people over the Bitter Sea.

We come to Tien-tai, where we burn incense;
Thence we walk to the bridge of Wan-fuh for a good view.
Here carved upon a stone is Kwanyin's solemn oath;
In the temple of great Omei we worship the world's Honored One.[1]
So many are the sights they are difficult to remember.
Each stone has some beautiful writings.

. . . .

It was here that Hsiyi,[2] the aged divine, laid down his pen.
At the water pavilion of the genii are the two characters " Fuh"
    and " Sheu; "[3]
Below this pavilion we quaff the waters of the gods,
Which are better than the clear water from the pitcher of Kwanyin;[4]
In the temple of the " middle cliff " there dwells an old priest,
Whom the Min and Tsing dynasties have enrolled as " divine
    Elder; "
They decreed he might live a full thousand years as Elder,
In the enjoyment of blessings without bounds,
And have a throne in Chungbwa [5] a thousand myriad of springs.
On the way to his temple, Kwanyin is revealed everywhere.
Before the hill of " Gauze-net " there was a very subtle serpent,[6]
Which vomited a silken net and swallowed the galls of men.
Who did not dread the bright atoms of mist he breathed out?
This monster had been here a thousand years and more,
Not lightly disturbing and injuring this celebrated mount.
Luckily the Elder saw him with his spiritual eye.
He captured this monster, and he wriggles his body no more.
We now ascend to the top of Dragon's Peak;
Here from a broad space Buddha reveals his precious form,
Next unto the flying bridges, where is the divinest of scenery;
It is here the pilgrims give vent to their feelings.
We reverently enter the temple with clear notes of music,
For the water of this place can wash the heart of an ox into a Buddha.
Here too, is the grotto where the King of Medicine [7] gathered drugs.

[1] A reference to Pu-hsien.

[2] A noted scholar.

[3] Blessing and Longevity.

[4] Goddess of Mercy.

[5] Middle Flowering Land, China.

[6] Not unlike, —

        " And Cerberus' many months do bay
        And bark out flames, as if on fire he 'd fed."

[7] A disciple of Sâkyamuni. In one of his previous forms of existence
he was Sarva Sattva Priya Dars'ana (q. v.); in another he was Vimala-
garbha (q. v.).

Upon the hill of the gibbons and apes the vital fluids are
    overflowing.
We have reached the plateau for allowing living things to go;[1]
Everybody here offers petitions to the gods.
A feudatory king who came to this place found his heart all of a
    shake,
For the fierce tigers kept the night watches with howls.
The pythons are everywhere, but never bite men.
The crows here pay court to Buddha, chanting in the heavens;
They also discuss and settle good and bad omens.
The pools have emys [2] with writings on their backs;
Good men will be able to comprehend the characters.
Turning from thence we enter the forest of Hung-chen-pin;
Within it are a multitude of things beautifully arranged, —
The dragon temple, and phœnix tower some thousands of stories;
Here is Weito, Protector of the Law and ruler of the mountain
    gate,
Who in ancient days was transformed into a priest;
He went to Yao-cheu to beg from the good people;
The good people kept themselves aloof and would not subscribe,
So he suddenly vaulted into heaven and rode upon a beautiful
    cloud.
This priest all at once vanished from sight;
Then the good people knew a god had visited them,
And sent their subscriptions to Hung-chun-pin,
The honored of the world, perceiving him to be the divine Protector
    of Law,
Conferred upon him a throne in Buddha's gate.
Weito was thus crowned a most intelligent god.
Here is Teh-lin, where is seen the white dragon's cave and many
    wonderful sights.
It was here he became divine and would not go away.
When the almond bursts into blossoms the dragon appears;
We circle around the lotus dais and view the writings;
We look aloft to the Lin-kwan;[3] with what may they be
    compared?
They are like the chao-kwan of the city's throne;

---

[1] There are societies called Fan-sen-hui whose object is to release animals which have been captured.

[2] A small species of tortoise, whose shell has twenty-eight plates on its
edges, and is much used in divination.

[3] Spirit officers, of which are reckoned five hundred.

There in the Sz-hui-tin they composedly rest.
Look up and view Tsieh-Yin,[1] which is made of bronze;
Thirty and more feet towers his lofty form.
At Tsz-shen-ang are fairy sights and writings;
Here is kept the genuine likeness of Hung-Wu,[2]
And that seamless robe which the world has heard little about;
The beautiful verses he sung and his martial poems are here,
Also the great bronze bell; none like it can be found,
For into its mould he cast his gold signet for a memorial.
There is the white robe, variegated with emblems from the sea,
And Buddha's tooth, kept here by imperial decree,
Which we begged to view,
And while we gazed we said " Omito Buddha " a thousand times.
Thence to the temple of a myriad ages we climbed.
The first of the temples is called Pi-lu;[3]
Here three holy bronze Buddhas reign on their lily thrones,
And upon a bronze dais the Emperor sits in his court;
Smoking incense from every land fills the urn.
To right and left are rows of golden melons and steel axes,[4]
And double ranks of courtiers and warriors pay him homage.
Upon both sides the royal chariots fill the hall;
In the vermilion court stands the pagoda-shaped transmuting furnace;
It is new and richly carved with dragons and horses.

Let us take leave of temple Pi-lu,
And hasten to the one of brick in the centre of the monastery.
It is the Dragon's place and rich with his veins;[5]
It is encircled with hills and pure streams;
Before it is Mount Poyü peering through Dragon Gate;
Behind is the Dragon-veined peak revealing the heart of Kwanyin;
To the left the Blackwater River and the tracks of Leaping Tiger;
On the right the stone-bamboo growing from the yellow earth.
In the centre of the tower stands a bronze elephant weighing ten
    thousand catties;
Upon it Pu-hsien sits in awful majesty,

---

[1] Amita Buddha is frequently given this title, which means to lead into Paradise.

[2] Founder of the Min dynasty, 1368 A. D.

[3] Dedicated to the trinity.

[4] Insignia: wooden bludgeons with gilt heads like the melons, and axes made of steel.

[5] Spiritual manifestation of the dragon.

And thousands upon thousands of little Buddhas enthroned around,
While myriads of Pusa burst forth from golden lilies;
Awe-inspiring is this priceless temple which rises tier above tier;
Lofty are the towers, and the pavilions charming to view ;
The seven rings have a myriad of Buddhas in rows.
Here we see the eighteen honored ones and Kia-lan;[1]
It was built of brick in the Yüen-yin of Wan-li,[2]
And thither come barbarians and Hans bowing low before his
    majesty.[3]
The royal tablets hang in the lofty space above,
And the incense, gifts of emperors, ever burns upon its altars.
There is seen the ladies' toilet mirror of immaculate reflection,
And two pitchers of pure water to cleanse the defilements of the
    world.

.   .   .   .

All of the Buddhas of Mount Omei were redeemed from the earth.
Before we were aware the sun sunk below the mountain of the
    west,
And the priests had made ready for ns to lodge.
We cannot detail the conversations of the night;
Ere we knew it from the great court came peals from drum and
    bell,
While the priests in the brick temple were reciting their prayers,
And lo! the star of the morning flashed forth in the east.
With a farewell offering to Wan-nien we recommence the ascent.
Near by in a quiet retreat is the renovating temple of Kwanyin;
Above it is a rock bearing the likeness of a prince.
He was without father or mother, and nameless.
At the hill of Inspecting the Heart we took a good look,
And in front of barred Devil Gate we were terrified,
For the sentinels stood in ranks by the gate, fiercely chiding.
The judge and his little devils are never at rest;
The good and evil in men's hearts is here manifest.
The seven-armored spirit-virgins descended to this place;
They came to meet the good and pilot them over the bridge,
And they pass over with joyful steps.
Say not, Here we will have merciful thoughts,
For the bravest are disheartened at this place.
Every year unbelievers come to this spiritual mountain,
Many men and women of insincere hearts;
Of such, some have been bitten of snakes;

---

[1] Name for Buddha.   [2] 1573 A. D.   [3] Pu-hsien.

Others, while on the journey, have been eaten of tigers;
Some have gone mad and thrown themselves over the precipice;
Some have been taken away into space,
Without a trace of their bodies to be found.
At "Restiug the Heart" is Sâkyamuni, the sleeping Buddha, the
    godlike.
In front of "Light-dazzling" Hill is a stone Kwanyin;
If you make an offering of a bowl of clear water,
It will reflect both Nanking and Peking.
To Mount Wo-er the pilgrims come in confusion,
Where everything is talked over clearly.
A day's journey brings us to the "Temple Most Beautiful."
It is here the peak Mount Omei takes its rise;
The mountains are green, the waters pellucid, revealing forms
    spiritual.
Even the true visage of Yü-lai Buddha is manifested.
At Place Peaceful bursts forth the nine-dragon spring,
Where the tired pilgrims allay their thirst;
Thenceforward their journey has unalloyed pleasure.
The lotus-flowers are seen upon the lofty peaks,
And a thousand lilies are carved upon the stones.
Would you look upon the likeness of a true god?
Walk slowly down the front steps
And ask for the one made upright who sits in the grotto;
You will be shown the honored Tsao[1] of the Chen dynasty.
The road is difficult and our heads pierce the clouds,
And the whole company of pilgrims are dripping with perspiration.
Even a serpent would recoil from making the ascent.
The pilgrims plunge into Elephant Pool for a bath;
Here the pure-hearted Ta-chan[2] are seen in the white mists.
There is a proverb about the hill of Lo-han;
Though there are no traces of Buddhas upon the mount,
There are five hundred and fifty O-lo-hau,[3]
Who are always in the road manifesting their spirituality.
Near by is Tartarus quaking with dread frights;

[1] More than a thousand years before Christ.

[2] "Those in the third degree of saintship, — that of Buddhisatwa. Such
an one, like a great conveyance, can transport himself and all mankind to
Nirvana."

[3] Arhats, "a term applied to the famous disciples of S'âkyamuni. Each
of those disciples is expected to reappear on earth as Buddha, each
assuming then the title 'Samanta Prabhâsa.'"

The echoes of fetters and chains are heard in the depths.
The good pass along with great joy,
But when the wicked come they begin to repent;
Say not Lao-Tien [1] will never retribute.
We repair to Light-Appearing terrace for a good view.
From it may be seen the prophet's form divine upon the peak of genii,
And the spirit bell and sword which flew down from heaven;
They are suspended in space from the middle cliff.
Here are the genii, gem virgins, and the dragon's-head stone,
The kingfisher cypress, purple bamboos, and phœnix-tailed pines,
And better than all are the Waters-of-Merit Pool.[2]
Upon the rock is the jadeite fountain which sparkles like stars.
Now if the pilgrims were perfectly sincere and reverent,
All the Buddhas beholding would greatly rejoice,
And the eighteen Lo-han would come and receive them.
Above the temple Rejoicing is the hill of Kwanyin;
No matter how brave, your courage will now vanish,
For never a man who came and did not fear.
When the priests hear the pilgrims coming
They take the royal dragon flag and ornaments, and put them on
　　each side of the door;
Then they beat three times the great drum made of elephant skin.
The pilgrims enter and worship the body of the prince,
Seated now in the temple of Eternal Peace.

.　　.　　.　　.　　.　　.　　.　.　　.

If you would know the history of this great teacher,
Go to the peak of Kún-lún and ask the old priest,
For he knows all about the teacher who opened this mountain.
All within the four seas have heard he has a body of gold,
And that above this place is the agave pagoda,
Also the temple Tsao-ang, — a present from the Emperor.
The Agave-precious pagoda is still in its glory,
And every pilgrim coming thither must spend a few cash;
For whoever gives silver or money to the prince
Will have children to honor his memory,
The god will shine upon his full lighted halls,
And guarded with peace will happily hold his possessions.
The good men and believing women hasten on in the upward
　　journey,
Even to the gate of heaven with hearts sincere,

　　　1 Old Heaven, — ruler of heaven.
　　　2 A wonderful pool, which possesses seven virtues.

For the Peck-measure-mouthed spirit-rulers sit at its gate.
They separate the good from the evil, permitting the good to
    proceed.
Having entered this gate we are in a true Buddha land,
And in a broad way which leads us straight on.
Upon the bridge of the seventh heaven is an image of diamond,
Within heaven-piercing pagoda is the bodily form of Pu-hsien.
We inspect with great care the bronze temple,
For it is much thought of by men.
The bronze tiles shine like pure gold,
The pewter tiles glisten like flowers of silver, white as snow,
 In front is the balcony where the classics are stored.
 Within the ancestral temple we offer our incense,
 Pu-hsien was its founder, and is enthroned in his lotus dais,
Lovely with incense and flowers, and brilliant with tapers.
We made the journey for the purification of our families,
And travelled a thousand li in coming hither,
Hoping this to be the propitious time for the spirits to descend.
We bend humbly according to rites and in sincerity worship,
And wait expectantly for the Pusa to descend to his lotus throne.
If our hearts are for Buddha, his heart is with us,
To-day is the time opportune, and the honored of the world we shall
    witness.
To-day we gaze upon the face of a Pusa,
And the desire of our hearts shall be fulfilled in paying court to the
    mount.
The old add a hundred blessings in burning incense,
The young by their offerings joyful spirits produce.
While worshipping think of your parents with reverence,
Think of your boys and girls and wish them long life,
Pray for yourself that you may be kept from harm,
And beseech for your children that the root of your family be
    continued.
Merchants come to pray for business prosperity,
Officers civil and military make offerings for continued promotions,
And pray for increase of riches by water and land.
Here the hard-worked students pray for fame of the scholar;
With pure hands all place the burning incense in the urns,
And the gold ingots and silver money commit to the flames,
With the hope that old Buddha[1] much assistance will give,

---

[1] A term for Guadama himself as a god. We find from Mr. Mat-
thews's account of the religion of the Hidatsa or Grosventre Indians of the

That the whole family may be unsullied and enjoy perfect peace,
And the vows of the incense be returned to the purified heart.
Repair first to the gold temple, for not on earth is its like found;
The pilgrims never forget the first sight of its beauty, —
The bronze tiles, the bronze pillars, and precious gold cap;
Within are bronze walls, bronze partitions, and bronze doors,
Bronze Buddhas, bronze elephants, bronze tablets and pagodas,
And a mighty bronze urn weighing thousands of pounds.
Would you know in what year this temple was built ?
It has come down from the year Kwei-mao.
Now walk to the precipice for a wide survey.
Look above!   The palace of heaven is there in the clouds;
Look down!   There in the abyss is the gate to hell.
Would you know how an ordinary soul may become a god?
Walk to the front, and I will sing it to you in four lines :
Drop your body down to the depths of the mountain, and your soul
        will uprise to the clouds.
Omito will descend from the west and meet you;
From henceforth your body will remain below,
While the soul enters joyfully the palace of heaven.
The views of the gold temple are beyond all conception.
Regard with silent attention the temple ancestral,
Swept and cleansed every year by the great god of Thunder.
The good from the evil he gathers and locks the gate of the mountain.
At that time the eight genii haunt and commingle,
And through the whole night chant their prayers to the Wise One.[1]
The green dragon and the white tiger come now to worship,
While a myriad of cups and bright lamps illumine the path of Pu-
        hsien.
This is the place where the Wise One became a god.

Missouri, that they have almost the same expressions for God as are here
and elsewhere employed.   They speak of him as "Old Man Immortal"
or "Great Spirit," which correspond very nearly with "Old Buddha "
and "Old Immortal."   Lao Sien really means "Old Man Immortal."
We find a great similarity of religious belief and worship with the Indians of that tribe, who worship not man alone, but the sun and moon,
the stars, all the lower animals, all trees and plants, rivers and lakes,
many bowlders and other separated rocks, even some hills and buttes
which stand alone, — in short, everything not made by human hands
which has an independent being, or can be individualized, possesses a
spirit, or, more properly, a shade.   How strangely like the ancient belief
and worship of China !

[1] Pu-hsien.

Leaving the city of Omei with reluctance, we took the boat from Suchi upon the little Omei River, and gliding down through pleasant vales and rich fields to the Ya and Tung, we reached early in the afternoon the West Gate of Kia-ting, and were within half an hour snugly stowed upon a palatial row-boat, and ready to leave for Chungking, three hundred miles below. Before reaching Kia-ting, the boatmen eyed the white thunder clouds in the east, and made some remarks which led me to question them on their conversation, which proved to be about the images of Omei mountain and the god Pu-hsien upon the white clouds. They said they were often seen in the white clouds at this hour. I was incredulous at this time as to such a phenomenon; but I have noticed that similar phenomena do occur in other parts of the world, and I thus have less reason to call in question the veracity of my informants.

We made some few purchases in the city, such as knives, which are from Chenteu and the best in China, a few pewter ornaments, etc., and by nine o'clock the next morning, 19th of August, were ready to plunge down the great and dangerous rapid just below the great Buddha two miles below our night's anchorage.

Our boat was too light for safety, and had too little cargo for the boatman's purse; so the captain came to anchor at a straggling town twenty li below Kia-ting to take a lot of block salt which is manufactured near by. There are reckoned to be eleven hundred salt-wells large and small between Kia-ting and this place. The lifting frames came out of the ends of the factories, giving the buildings more the appearance of old-fashioned country churches than anything else. We took on board about a ton of dark, hard block salt, each cake or block weighing quite two hundred pounds; the blocks looked much like ice covered with ashes. There are wells on both sides of the river extending over a large territory. Soft coal is used as fuel for the pans, and fills the air with volumes of smoke. We canvassed the town while waiting for the cargo, and made an excellent sale of books.

Below this point an inferior kind of wax-tree is seen upon the hills. Mantsz caves are seen in the steep cliffs, but not in any great numbers. Sü-cheu, like Chungking, is situated upon a promontory between two rivers, — the Golden Sands and the Min. It is difficult to judge which stream has the greater volume of water; probably the Golden Sands, as it is much the longer. Both are fine, wide streams, and full of water in the summer. Sü-cheu is an important city and well located for steamboat traffic, as large steamers could go with ease from Chungking to this point. The country from Kia-ting to Sü-cheu is very romantic, — not so grand as below Chungking, but quite as interesting.

From this point on to Lu-cheu, we swept through a tamer but more fertile country. As we approach Chungking numerous orange-groves occur along the river-banks which produce a most pleasing impression. After nearly five days of rowing and floating (sailing is almost unknown above Chungking), we came in sight of the high rocks of Chungking and the little white pagoda and numerous temples on the opposite side of the river. The four hundred miles from Chenteu to Chungking by water is an uninterrupted succession of natural pictures.

We found all peaceful in Chungking, but hot enough to suit a salamander. After a few days of preparation we started on our return journey to the East, leaving Mr. Cady in absolute possession of the palace of Loh. Our voyage down was not all that could have been desired. The expected five days lengthened to eleven before we came in sight of Ichang. The heavy rains above us sent the river up at the rate of more than a foot an hour, until it had risen in the space of twenty-four hours some thirty feet.

With the floods commenced our difficulties. We broke our rudder in a violent whirlpool, which detained us thirty hours; and our boat was so top-heavy that a head wind was a sure signal for an immediate stop; a fair wind seemed to be dangerous, and a mist was too much for the men. And then they must have from four to five meals per day. Reaching the city of Kwei-cheu we found the gorge below the city so full of water that no boats were allowed to go down, so we had thirty-six hours more of detention.

The boatmen have some very queer ideas; when the boat was caught in a very large and swift eddy, the boatmen all sat down except the captain of the "sweep," who would grasp the bowl filled with dry rice which was always near at hand, and throw some of it into the worst part of the whirlpool on either side of the bow. This was done several times on the downward journey. The object was to appease the hungry spirits who were underneath the swirl, ready to capsize the boat. Rice is often made use of in times of sickness and death. Some one will run out with a bowl of dry rice, and scatter about the house and street, calling loudly for the sick person's spirit, which has wandered out of the body.

We found the gorges very difficult of navigation after the flood, and our men so frightened that it was torturous travelling. We came very near coming to grief in the Wind-box gorge. The current sent us flying into the middle of the stream, a swirl sent us round and round like a top, and at last out of it, to be caught by a very swift current which brought us stern down toward sharp rocks at a speed of ten miles an hour. We just grazed the rocks, and were thrown again, much to our relief, into the middle of the river. I cannot conceive of anything more exciting than making the gorges at high water.

While here we had an episode which came near proving fatal to one of our party. Dr. Morley took books and went to the upper part of the suburbs, where we had made heavy sales on our way up-river. Fortune smiled upon him for a season: a crowd assembled near the bank where he stood, and were as civil as such crowds usually are; but a rowdy spoiled his business, and came near doing worse for him. This man, naked downward to his loins, was brawny and powerful for a Chinaman, and carried a most satanic face. He made some absurd offers for a book, and being refused snatched all the Doctor had. The Doctor endeavored to recover them, and while so doing, the man took advantage of the situation, seized him by the hair, put his arm around his neck, and pulled him headlong into the river, which was swift and deep. A struggle ensued, greatly to the disadvantage of the Doctor, as the man had a firm hold upon his hair, and an arm around his neck, so the Doctor had not only to support himself in the water, but his assailant. He found the man could endure submersion quite as well as himself, and that his blows were unavailing to compel the man to let go his hold. Finally, when nearly exhausted, a terrible effort dislodged his antagonist, and both made for the shore. I cannot describe the Doctor's appearance when he staggered aboard seemingly more dead than alive. Suffice it to say, upon application the foo and hsien acted promptly in arresting the man, and sent him aboard with an old chain around his neck for recognition. He was given five hundred blows that night, and the next morning he was brought to us with a cangue around his neck, and a message that this was the man's sixth offence. During the day the hsien sent us a large piece of beef, two chickens, *et cetera*, with compliments.

We were glad to glide into the Lukan gorge, but the poor sailors were not. The swirls were still immense, and the current, in certain places, so fierce that the stoutest nerves quailed as we whirled and dashed from swirls toward some jagged rocks. The boat stopped, but after a couple of hours started again ; but we soon had occasion to regret our rashness. We dashed down one rapid toward evening, which our men had tried hard to escape by rowing with all their might to the shore ; but all their efforts could not save us, so over we went, but fortunately without accident. A little later I saw a junk rushing down the rapid without a soul upon it, and breaking up rapidly as it flew along. It turned out to be a very large junk that had passed us in the early part of the day, and had anchored a few miles above. Starting again, it was caught in one of the mighty whirlpools, and was dashed upon a sharp rock and thus came to grief. It was heavily laden with salt and medicines.

CHAPTER XIII.

PROVINCE OF SZ-CHUAN.

THE reader will have gathered from the former chapters that this province is not only of very great extent, of exceeding beauty, of salubrious climate, but prolific also in its productions, and the home of a large and pacific population.

It is not my purpose to speak of its eventful history, of its aggressive wars, nor of its heroes and statesmen, painted in rose-colored hues by local chroniclers ; nor of scholars and poets, — of whom it has had its share, — who have been deified by an over-appreciative posterity ; nor of the spirit of art, which has here shown more of the genius of Athens than in some other nations ; nor to do more, in fact, than to speak in a general way of its handicrafts.

It has a history of more than ordinary interest, culminating at the beginning of the third century of the Christian era, when it became the seat of empire for Western China, and was known as the kingdom of Shuh. To unravel the numerous threads woven in so many events as have occurred here, would require an intimate knowledge of Imperial, Provincial, and Local Annals, which fill hundreds, if not thousands, of volumes.

This province has nearly two hundred thousand square miles within its borders, but a large portion of this immense tract is mountainous, and nearly one third occupied by native tribes, under their own chiefs. Four large rivers course through Sz-Chuan from north to south, which unite with the Yang-tsze, or, more properly, the Golden Sands. The Chinese consider the Min River as the main branch, and say that it has its rise in the Min Mountains of Sitsang, Thibet, and flowing through Hwang-shén-kwan enters Sz-Chuan, and divides into ten or more streams, and flows around Chenteu to the southwest, where they reunite; they say that the Min receives in its course the Golden Sands and a half-dozen more streams, until it unites with the Kia-ling at Chungking, from which place it takes the name of Min for Ta, or Great. Of course modern travellers have demonstrated that the Min is a tributary to the Golden Sands, which flows from Thibet almost due south into Yun-nan, and then north and again into Sz-Chuan.

The province is largely made up of mountains, as I have said, but they are of such a character as to afford ample slopes for cultivation. The red sandstone which abounds here is very soft, and by the action of the atmosphere crumbles easily into dust, thus forming a soft, friable covering to the very highest peaks of the mountains. There is comparatively little bottom-land along the courses of the numerous streams, and the rivers, as a rule, have deep channels and abrupt banks of sandstone. Wherever bottom-lands exist, as in some places between Chungking and Chenteu, they are marvellously rich, and produce excellent crops in great variety. The scantiness of the soil is manifest everywhere; even in the lower portions we are constantly coming upon uncovered rock.

The humidity of the Sz-Chuan climate is such that if there is but a few inches of soil, good crops may be obtained in ordinary years. If Sz-Chuan experienced

the droughts of Northern China, or even the sunshine of
Central China, it would be practically a desert. Rains
are frequent, and heavy clouds cover the heavens three
fourths of the year; and in absence of clouds, a smoky
mist veils the earth from the piercing rays of the sun.
The climate is equable, and even the summer, although
long, and severely hot in July and August, is modified,
by frequent showers. The plain in which Chenteu is
situated has less heat than Chungking and some other
parts of the province. The winters are very mild;
white frost is seldom seen, and snow is almost unknown,
except upon the mountains. Experience shows the climate to be fairly healthful, and no more trying than that
of Central China. Taken as a whole, Sz-Chuan may be
called a beautiful province. Its numerous rivers and
small streams and the ever-changing form of mountain
and hill lend grace and dignity to its scenery, despite its
sombre sky. In the great variety of its productions it
excels all other provinces. There is scarcely an article
grown in China which is not found here in great abundance. Rice is a staple product, and in good years the
ample supply allows it to be exported to the East.
Wheat is grown everywhere, and is of the best quality;
barley, pease, Indian corn, and millet grow in vast
quantities. Sugar-cane and sorghum are produced in
sufficient abundance for home consumption, and some
cotton is grown. It produces more silk than any other
province, as well as hemp in large quantities. It raises
the best tobacco, and, in recent years, large quantities of
opium. It has an ample supply of oranges, lemons,
pumalos, peaches, apples, pears, plums, cherries, and
other small fruits. Of medicines it produces enough for
half the empire, and exports great quantities. Its salt-
wells are celebrated all over China, and their products

find their way to several contiguous provinces and to the table-lands of Central Asia. Its minerals suffice for home use, and are exported in small quantities. For the material welfare of its people there are ample resources at home, and with greater encouragement and better facilities for trade, its present productions might be increased indefinitely. The silk industry could be largely expanded, immense quantities of wool could be raised, and would be if there were any opportunities for its manufacture. The soil and climate are well adapted to tea culture, of which a considerable amount is now exported.

There is much tea exported to Siberia *via* Si-ngan-foo. Besides the ordinary tea, which is extensively cultivated for home and foreign consumption I came across two kinds of tea on Mount Omei which are peculiar to that mountain, and sold largely to pilgrims, called "sweet tea" and "white tea." The sweet tea is made from the leaves of a slender growing shrub which is found half-way to the top of the mountain. The leaf is large and thick, and when green has no sweetness; but when dried it has a peculiar, sweet, licorice-like flavor not altogether unpleasant. The white tea is prepared from the leaf of a very peculiar shrub found upon the side of the mountain; it is palatable, and not unlike the genuine tea of commerce in flavor.

Besides these teas, which are never exported, except in small quantities by visitors, I found two kinds of very good tea, grown by the priests and farmers around the monasteries. The tea-shrubs were not unlike those found in abundance in Kiangsi, and the tea is quite as good as that grown in Nganhui.

Thibet and the wild tribes are furnished with tea from the provinces, principally from Kiung-cheu. Abbé Huc says: "You meet every moment on these narrow paths

long files of porters carrying brick tea, which is prepared at Khioung-Tcheou, and forwarded from Ta-
tsien-lu to the different provinces of Thibet. Brick tea
and the *khata*, or ' scarf of felicity,' are the great articles of trade between China and Thibet. It is scarcely
credible what a prodigious quantity of these goods is
exported annually from the provinces of Kan-su and
Sz-Chuan."

The mines are almost untouched. Gold is found in
almost every county, iron ore everywhere, and coal in
nearly all the mountains; but there is little inducement
to mine where there are no paying markets.

The population of Sz-Chuan has been variously estimated. In the reign of Kiaking, about ninety-two years
ago, it was returned at 20,463,904, besides 168,953 families among the forty or fifty different wild tribes in the
west and southwest of the province. Later it was given
as 35,000,000, and recently a writer has placed it as high
as 70,000,000. The Catholic priests of Sz-Chuan, who
ought to be fair authority, give it as 45,000,000. I am
inclined to accept the last as about the present population of the province, inclusive of all the semi-independent
tribes. This province has escaped the cruel devastations
which many others have suffered during the past few
years, — such as the Taiping rebellion, which swept away
countless millions of people from Central China, and the
famine in North China. The whole central part of the
country is fairly populated, and in a few sections it is
densely peopled. We must, however, remember that
only about one half of its area — 100,000 square miles,
twice the size of Ohio — is capable of sustaining a
great population, and that there are large districts occupied by unconquered tribes, who are by no means numerous. Forty-five millions of people sustained almost

entirely from a territory not twice as large as Ohio is a state of things far in advance of Western economy. We must also take into account that millions and millions of acres are devoted to other than food-raising products. Opium is largely grown, while Indian corn and millet are raised in great quantities and used for making intoxicating drinks.

The population was fearfully decimated at the beginning of the present dynasty; and to make good the loss, myriads of people poured into the province from different parts of the empire. The people are now industrious and pacific, milder in disposition than those of the central provinces, and somewhat less manly.

There seems to be a higher appreciation of art here than elsewhere: the houses are in better taste, and the graves better decorated; stone monuments, such as commemorative arches and bridges, are of superior design and more perfectly executed; the work in iron, steel, copper, and brass is much superior to that found in the East; and as a whole the people evince much more artistic taste and genius than in other provinces.

In short, Sz-Chuan is a wonderful section of the empire, — an empire of itself, independent in a great measure of outside help. There is no very great concentration of wealth, as the largest cities are not equal in population and trade to many of the Eastern and Northern cities; neither do we find as much poverty as in other sections of China. There is perhaps a more even distribution of wealth, as some travellers have stated; many millions are engaged in commercial and manufacturing pursuits, yet the larger portion of the population is engaged in the petty agriculture so generally practised in China.

A considerable portion of the west and southwest of

the province is sparsely inhabited by native tribes, under their own chiefs, who are to a certain extent responsible to the provincial government for good behavior. Little is known of them beyond what has been casually learned by visitors. Out of the forty or fifty tribes which are scattered over the vast mountainous tracts, a few only have come in contact with the Europeans, and they in a manner to leave their customs and the character of their civilization almost unknown. Mr. Baber visited a section of the Lolo land and acquired some knowledge of that people, and fortunately was able to obtain specimens of their written language. Some of the tribes are very warlike, and require constant watching and control by the presence of forts and soldiery upon their frontiers; and even then constant depredations are committed upon their more civilized neighbors. While in the temple of Wan-nien a vivacious friend entertained us one evening relating incidents about the Lolos, with whom he had had some association. From his account they must be great experts in hunting and a formidable enemy for the Chinese soldiery to cope with.

They think nothing of pouncing down upon a Chinese village, and carrying off the women and everything found in it. Their territories are wild and almost inaccessible to the Chinese soldier, who finds it a hopeless task to recover the stolen people and property. Many thousands of Chinese are supposed to live among them as slaves, doing the hard work, while their masters hunt and forage. This race of people, the most peculiar and interesting of all the tribes, is divided into what they, or the Chinese, call the " Black-bones " and " White-bones." From the top of Mount Omei a very fair view is obtained of their country, which lies to the south and east, and may be reached easily in two days from the hsien.

No doubt the languages and customs of these different tribes, when fully known to the Western student, will throw no inconsiderable light upon the ancient civilization of all Sz-Chuan.

Missions in Sz-Chuan. — Jesuitism.

The records in regard to the planting of missions in this province are less complete than in more accessible quarters. Whatever progress had been made from the East or South, previous to 1722, then came to an abrupt end. In 1685 six French priests embarked from Brest and landed at Ningpo, July 23, 1687. They soon proceeded to Pekin, ingratiated themselves into favor with the Emperor, and through their influence upon the government, mission work was resumed throughout the empire. It was not long before a reaction set in, and in 1722 every advantage was lost and missions prohibited. Father Gaubil writes of this time, saying: "What we have been dreading for so many years — what we had so often predicted — has at last come to pass. Our holy religion is entirely proscribed in China; all the missionaries, with the exception of those who were in Pekin, have been driven from the empire."

A century of uncertain vicissitudes passed with little systematic proselyting, except at some central points; but in 1822 the Institution for the Propagation of the Faith was founded at Lyons, with the one aim of promoting Roman Catholic Missions.

In reference to this society the traveller and writer, M. Huc, pays the following tribute to the foundress : —

"The great and beautiful association for the propagation of the faith, with the idea of which God inspired a poor

woman of Lyons, has made considerable progress; the Holy
See has erected the eighteen provinces of China into so many
Vicariates Apostolic, in which priests of foreign missions,
Jesuits, Dominicans, Franciscans, and Lazarites labor with-
out ceasing for the extension of the kingdom of heaven.

"Every vicariate possesses, besides a great number of
schools for the education of both boys and girls, a seminary
where young Chinese are brought up to the ecclesiastical
profession; in various parts of the country also pious associations have been formed with the purpose of bestowing bap-
tism upon dying children, or collecting those who have been
abandoned; and nurseries and asylums have been instituted
on the model of those that have prospered so well in
France."

The same writer says of Sz-Chuan in 1850 : —

"At the present time the propagation of the gospel is,
nevertheless, not going on so well as before. The missionaries are no longer at court under the protection of the
Emperor and men of high rank, going and coming with
the ceremonials of mandarins, and appearing in the eyes of
the people in the imposing position of a power recognized
by the State."

In 1844 Dr. Perocheau, Vicar Apostolic of Sz-Chuan,
writes of the Mission : —

"It continues its work of baptizing children in danger of
death, and the Lord continues to bless it. Each year the
number of those whom they regenerate goes on increasing.
It was, in 1839, 12,483; in 1840, 15,766; in 1841, 17,825;
in 1842, 20,068; in 1843, 22,292; in 1844, 24,381."

He remarks that about two thirds of the number of
these children died in the year in which they were bap-
tized. Thus out of the number of 1844, 16,763 "winged
their flight a short time afterward to everlasting bliss."
Thus we find the present society now operating in

Sz-Chuan had its origin in the mind of a devoted Catholic woman of Lyons, France, in 1822; that one of its main objects is education and baptizing infants.

If Abbé Huc's estimate of the number of converts in 1850 be correct, there has been a loss of some thousands since then. I have not been able to procure any statistics showing the growth of the Catholic Mission since its foundation, or any personal reminiscences of its chief founders, or any particulars about the numerous troubles through which it has passed, scattered as it is over a territory nearly as large as France, and larger by many thousands of square miles than Japan.

The most authentic account obtainable is of recent date, and direct from one of the priests at Chungking. There are three diocesan bishops in the province, ninety-six foreign priests, mostly Frenchmen, and eighty-six native priests. Besides this force there are many nuns and nurses, both foreign and native, and a large number of catechists. Each diocese has two seminaries or colleges, — one for Latin and one for Philosophy and Theology. The number of Christians is reported to be 88,445: A statement of the number of churches, schools, and pupils under instruction, the orphanages, and industrial schools would have been interesting items, but could not be obtained.

It would appear from Abbé Huc's statement and the one given me during this year that the past forty years have been sterile of results, if not worse. It would be unfair to judge of the merit of the work without more particulars as to the plans now pursued. Previous to 1844 infant baptisms made up a heavy item of the annual increase ; and if that custom still prevails, —and I have no reason to question its existence, — the increase from adult conversions is insignificant. In whatever light we look at Jesuitism as a factor in the development of the province, it is not an insignificant element to deal with. We have eighty-five thousand individuals under the pupilage of one hundred and eighty-two educated men, presided over by three learned prelates, — men who have grown up with their institutions, — trained in all the etiquette, customs, and literature of China, and fully conversant with every question likely to arise touching their work. Its organization is so complete that questions which greatly embarrass other missions are settled promptly and advantageously with the local officials.

Chenten, the provincial capital, and Chungking are centres of great influence. Two bishops and several foreign priests preside over some twenty thousand Christians in these two cities. Their influence under these learned leaders is out of all proportion to their numbers. Some of the Christians are wealthy men, and occupy, in some instances, important and lucrative positions, which give them considerable power in their immediate localities. Such is the case of the Loh family, the head of which felt equal to coping with the mob in 1886, and slew a large number of the assailants in and around his palace.

About twenty years ago the warrior Li-Hung-Chang was sent to this province with a formidable force, to settle a district feud which had raged for some months between the Catholics and the heathen, and invariably to the advantage of the former. Local officials, always easily approached by a shining bribe, are won at such times; and no one knows better the power of such temptations over the mandarins than the French priest, or has the tact to use it to better advantage, if so disposed.

While the leaders have made the political and wealthy centres strong, as has been their rule from the commencement of missions in China, they have not neglected the less important and sparsely settled regions.

Two by two these indefatigable workers, devoted to one idea, — the extension of Romanism, — have gone into all the cities and towns, and, wherever possible, have gained a firm foothold. While Eastern Sz-Chuan was in tumult, and scores of Catholic buildings were demolished and committed to the flames, in July, 1886, Western and Northern Sz-Chuan remained quiet and Christians were undisturbed.

In each city where their labors have met with success, an institution antagonistic to the political, social, and religious ideas of the Chinese has developed in spite of all opposition. It were needless to point out in what respects Romanism antagonizes society in China. Its assumptions are not less, but rather, more, extravagant here than in Europe. It also comes in contact with elements farther removed from its creed than in Christian lands. It has claimed the right to protect its members before civil tribunals, and in many instances overawed judges or bribed them to the miscarrying of justice, causing thereby much ill-feeling upon the part of the heathen against them. Every priest to some extent takes official standing among his people, and local affairs, which belong purely to Chinese officials, are dealt with as in a mixed court, in which the priest, from his foreign relations, has for many years enjoyed a decided advantage.

These assumptions have been fruitful sources of complications, which have resulted in local disorders in which the Church has frequently suffered partial destruction at the hands of infuriated mobs; but from the wonderful elasticity of the ecclesiastical machinery the wheels are set going with increased vigor.

It is difficult to judge how widely Jesuitism affects society beyond its own followers, and the measure of good they receive from their attachment to it. It is certain their operations are carried on with the most scrupulous secrecy. Their seminaries, schools, and chapels are shut out from the people; the priests are seldom seen in public; and religious books are very rare.

I passed through the best of the province, but did not meet with a priest; no converts came to me; not one of their books was seen. I did not see a school or a chapel after the first day from Chungking. Priests, converts, chapels, and schools exist at all central places, but are largely secluded from the public.

Such an organization, while it develops slowly in silence, by stealth, through wealth gained largely in business projects,— in renting of houses and lands,— cannot become an aggressive spiritual force in society. It cannot gain the confidence of the better classes, and will never be trusted beyond its own membership.

No one would hail with more delight than I any apparent good results from Romanism. I would not depreciate its spirit of sacrifice or the constant, careful oversight seen in the lives of men and women devoted to church work in this province. But it is too sectarian to control public sentiment beyond its immediate followers. China requires open-handed dealing; she demands such help in transforming her decaying civilization as comes from more generous impulses than are found in Jesuitism.

Protestantism. — China Inland Mission.

Previous to settled missionary work in the province by the China Inland Mission, there had been some trips made by missionaries for the purpose of colportage and

inspection for future settlement. The first was made by
A. Wylie, Esq., agent for the British and Foreign Bible
Society, and Rev. Griffith John, of the London Mission, both men of great experience in China, masters
of the language and literature, discreet and wise in their
intercourse with officials and people. Mr. John hoped to
open work in the province soon after his return, which
was in 1868; but from lack of men and money, that most
efficient worker has never yet been able to carry out his
original intention. They spent most of the summer of
1868 in Sz-Chuan selling books and preaching in many
of the principal commercial cities and in Chenteu, the
capital.

Mr. Lilly, agent for the Scotch Bible Society, travelled
widely and sold books. Mr. Molliman, a Russian gentleman, devoted some years to book-selling in all parts
of the province. Later, Rev. Mr. Wilson traversed it
in every direction with the Word of God. Rev. Mr.
Scarborough, of the Wesleyan Mission, went as far as
Chungking with the intention of opening a mission;
unfortunately his Board was not prepared to second his
proposition, and that large society was prevented from
occupying the coveted field.

It was about 1877 that Mr. McCarthy, of the China Inland Mission, travelled through a portion of the province
on his way to Burmah, and rented a house at Chungking,
which was occupied soon after by Messrs. Cameron and
Clark. Since that time the Mission has had one or
more men laboring at Chungking. The results up to
date are meagre, as at other points.

They report twenty-three baptisms, and an orphanage
with seven children, one chapel in the residence, and
another about to be opened. Chenteu, the provincial
capital, was occupied by Mr. Samuel Clark in 1881, and

the work has been continued up to the present, having been quite largely reinforced the present year (1887). The Mission reports thirty-three communicants and two day-schools with twenty pupils. During the present year the city of Paoling-foo on the Kia-ling River has been occupied. The China Inland Mission has at present nine men and eight women in the province.

I am largely indebted to Rev. Spencer Lewis, of the West China Mission, for the following statements.

The needs of the great field of Western China had long appealed strongly to those devoted men who pray, plan, and toil in behalf of missions at home and abroad. At the meeting of the General Committee in New York, in November of 1880, Dr. Fowler, then missionary secretary, advocated the founding of a mission there.

The Committee admitted the great need, but in view of the heavy debt embarrassing the treasury, and the urgent calls from the world-wide field, determined not to risk crippling the missions already established by starting a new one. But just as they were about to adjourn, a note was handed in from Brother Goucher, a Methodist preacher from Baltimore, offering to give five thousand dollars a year for two years, or as much longer as might be necessary, for the support of a Mission to be called the West China Mission of the Methodist Episcopal Church. This seemed so evidently Providential that the generous offer was accepted and the mission determined upon.

In the following spring search was made for a suitable man to lead the new undertaking, and Dr. L. N. Wheeler, who was the former superintendent of the North China Mission, was chosen. Dr. Wheeler was accompanied by his wife and two youngest daughters and Miss Frances, his eldest daughter, who became the first missionary of the Woman's Foreign Missionary Society at Chungking.

Mr. Lewis was selected to go with Dr. Wheeler, and, with his wife, sailed from San Francisco, September, 1881. Illness compelled him to spend five weeks in Japan, and it was the 10th of November when he reached Shanghai. He spent his first year at Chinkiang, which had been recently opened as a station of the Central China Mission. Dr. Wheeler settled his family in Kiukiang, and soon after, in company with Mr. Bagnell, set out to explore the new field. Their boat was wrecked among the rapids of the upper Yang-tsze, but procuring another they proceeded to Chungking, which they reached during the month of January. They found two China Inland missionaries there, and in Chenteu, three hundred miles distant, was Mr. Samuel Clark, of the same Mission.

Mr. Wheeler remained two weeks in Chungking, and was convinced that this commercial centre of Western China ought to be the first station of the new Mission. He succeeded in renting a Chinese house, and returned to Kiukiang. The following autumn both families started on their westward journey, leaving Ichang in native boats on the last day of October, and arriving in Chungking on the third of December. A room was fitted up in Mr. Lewis's dwelling for the reception of Chinese women; and soon after the Chinese New Year they began coming in a ceaseless stream, sometimes numbering a hundred or more in a single afternoon. Miss Wheeler and Mrs. Lewis received them on alternate afternoons. After several months of house-hunting they succeeded, on the 10th of March, in purchasing a large piece of property in one of the most favorable locations in the city.

The place was reputed to be haunted, but they had braved too much already to be daunted by tales of Chinese ghosts. After a few repairs and improvements

Mr. and Mrs. Lewis went to live in the house in May, and Dr. Wheeler and family in June. Mr. Lewis returned to Shanghai the following September to meet Dr. and Mrs. Crews, the round trip being made in three months.

One of the buildings upon the premises was fitted up for a chapel, and on the 17th of February, 1884, it was opened for the first public service with sermon. About the same time a room was opened for street preaching, and a school started for boys. On the second Sunday after the chapel was opened a curious crowd, of nearly a thousand people, swarmed over the whole place, and for several months there was not a Sunday when we could seat all the people. Dr. Wheeler's health had been failing for several months, and in March, 1884, he was again obliged to return to America. Mr. Gamewell, of the North China Mission, was appointed Superintendent, and arrived on the field the following December. Miss Gertrude Howe, from Central China, also arrived, and the ladies secured property near that of the parent board for a residence and a girls' school.

All branches of the work were prospering. In January, 1885, a Sabbath-school was opened, with an attendance of about eighty. Dr. Crews opened a dispensary, which was well patronized. Early in 1886, after negotiations extending over several months, the Mission succeeded in purchasing a fine property in the country, three miles from the city, and upon the main road leading to Chenteu. The plan was to build here two or three residences, a hospital, chapel, and eventually a boys' boarding school, while the ladies were to erect one large building to be used as residence, orphanage, and girls' school.

In March work was commenced upon the residences,

and at the same time upon two small buildings for sanitariums, across the River of Golden Sands and opposite the city. About this time the military students began to come up for their triennial examinations, and soon set afloat all sorts of absurd rumors about the Mission. The houses were said to be forts from which cannon would be turned on the city to destroy it and its inhabitants. They pretended to find a book which told of a dragon, whose head was in one river and his tail in the other a mile away. Our residences were said to be upon his neck and crushing him, and if the building did not cease dire calamities would follow, such as drought, famine, and pestilence.

The Catholics are very strong in Chungking and throughout the province, and by meddling in civil matters had stirred up jealousy and ill-feeling. Two years before they had built a fine cathedral and covered it with yellow tiles. It was then threatened by a mob, which the officials dispersed at once. It was said, "Wait till the military students come, and we will burn it down." The feast of the fifth day of the fifth moon happened to fall upon Sunday, the 6th of June. All the missionaries were in the city attending the Chinese and English services except one lady. An idle crowd of fellows of the baser sort gathered in front of our residences in the country and demanded admittance. Being refused, they proceeded to batter down the gate. They were met by this lady, who successfully defended the place against them.

Soon after this the district magistrate asked us to stop the work until the military students went away, and for the sake of peace we agreed to do so. Work still went on at the sanitarium, as that was not objected to. Later placards suddenly appeared in all parts of the city, in which the military students called upon the people to rise and destroy all foreign property and drive away the foreigners. The date fixed was the 2d of July. Still the work went on as usual upon the buildings. Such placards had appeared before, and we did not believe they would do what they threatened. The girls' school closed, after three very prosperous years, on the last day of June. On July 1, one day earlier than the time fixed in the placards, the storm burst.

The residence of a Bible colporteur in the country was looted, then one house rented by the China Inland Mission in the city was looted and torn down, and another simply looted. The house of the British Consular Agent was looted also, and he narrowly escaped with his life, receiving two wounds upon his head. The Catholic cathedral and residences were burned to the ground. Lastly, our residences were looted, torn down, and carried away. The sanitariums were burned. The Consular Agent and the Catholic priests took refuge with the taotai, and the Protestant missionaries with the magistrate.

The riot lasted two or three days in the city, thence spreading into the country for many miles, and continued for some weeks. The Romanists lost a few cathedrals, colleges, nunneries, and other buildings. Many Catholic Christians were robbed, their residences burned, and if resistance was offered they were put to death. After our missionaries had taken refuge in the magistrate's yamen they were intimidated by the official, who, to carry his point, gave out that the mob would burn his residence if the missionaries did not accede to his demands, — a trick often resorted to by native officers to frighten foreigners who have taken refuge with them in times of trouble. Here the missionaries remained fif-

teen days in " durance vile." No one unacquainted with
a magistrate's yamen can fully appreciate the lamentable
condition of the refugees. They had scarcely room to
spread their beds at night; husbands and wives were separated; some were ill, and others suffering from fright and
exposure. They had saved little beyond what they had
upon their persons, and that was little enough; for the
heat was intense at the time, and they were thinly clad.

The river was flooded, so that no boat could go down
with safety; and when the waters subsided they were
compelled to await the tardy movements of the unfeeling
mandarins, who would not consent to their departure
until they had agreed to exchange the property in the
country. They were subjected to many indignities from
the official in charge, who, as a matter of policy, laid all
the troubles at their door, and missed no opportunity to
taunt them for their indiscretions.

After repeated delays, the pain of which was intensi-
fied by physical and mental suffering, they were permitted to leave their prison. It was on the night of the
15th of July that the astute city fathers had arranged
everything to their liking. Their purpose was to impress upon the victims, who were wholly at their
mercy, the intense hatred and excitement which existed
in the city against them; that their lives were not safe
for a moment among the populace without the interven-
tion of military force.

Midnight came, and yet it was not late enough to convey them in safety to the river's bank. The night wore
on till three A. M., when the half-naked, sad, and half-
sick missionaries were hustled into sedans and borne
swiftly through the tomb-like streets to the river's side.
Bands of soldiers guarded the forlorn company, and es-
corted it to three small, dirty, mat-covered boats. The

mats were so old and scant that they afforded little protection from rain or the fierce rays of the sun. Thus terminated the work of five years, and the faithful laborers were forced to leave a field which they had already consecrated by their prayers and labors.

The reader having followed my footsteps over comparatively unbeaten paths in this marvellously interesting empire cannot have failed to form a very high estimate of the province of Sz-Chuan, for its natural resources, for its almost tropical luxuriance, and unrivalled beauty. In one other feature, to the mind of the Christian philanthropist, it possesses remarkable interest, — as a missionary field. It has not been my aim to speak largely of this feature, or to deal in problems connected with the evangelization of its peoples.

While of no greater present importance than many other portions of China, to the prophetic mind it possesses latent possibilities which enlarge its consequence and make it a peculiarly interesting section of the empire. Secluded as it has been by natural barriers from that free intercourse with other provinces which electricity and steam are about to remove, it has remained up to the present time a sort of wonder-land, an undefined territory to the average Chinaman. The past year has seen it introduced to North, East, and South by means of the electric wire, thus giving it politically all the privileges enjoyed by other provinces. Steam will tame the wild rapids of its mighty river, and bring an unimagined commercial prosperity to its wealthy centres. Railroads will convey its rich products safely and quickly into Kansu and Thibet. All Central Asia will hold out eager hands for its multifarious productions, and thus it will become a highway of nations. Here we find more than an eighth of China's population engaged in the peaceful pursuits of civilized life.

Looking at this province in its present and possible future relations, it challenges the world for a grander field in which to test the heroic spirit of modern Christianity.

It presents to the eye of faith a picture of sublime grandeur, the realization of which must come through devotion at home and stubborn conflicts there; through gifts and prayer by those who would support so good a cause, and by more than ordinary sacrifice by those called to enter this distant field.

In whatever sense we may look upon this or any other portion of China, the interest must increase the longer we consider the hoary customs and institutions, which, like worn-out garments or cruel fetters, are still cherished. To those Christians who think they have discharged their obligations to the heathen world when Christ has been preached in the ear of every individual, China — and especially these western and southern portions — presents most fascinating fields; for here untold millions have never listened to the voice of the Christian herald. To those who believe duty demands systematic and long-continued efforts, employing every available means to plant a new and better civilization, the picture is no less attractive. Mighty evils are to be eradicated, which now, as leprous spots or ugly ulcers, are poisoning the life of each generation as it arises. Such evils as few nations are weighted with rise up before the vision of the intelligent Christian; among them are the universal custom of female foot-binding, infanticide, and slavery, besides opium-smoking and many revolting social festers, with which the people themselves are unable to deal.

There is no short road to the coveted goal; it will only

be reached through sore trials, such as come to every ardent and successful worker of reform, in sacrifices not to be weighed in the little balance which determines the value of separation from country, friends, and Christian civilization. Here, as elsewhere, we have presented problems which require mature thought from gifted men and women, to solve which will demand long and patient endurance in well-doing. To plan, to work, to pray, is the lot of the intrusted ambassador, even when the heart is bursting with grief at the indifference around him, at the stolid stubbornness and hatred manifested on every face.

We shall see the consecrated task borne in light and darkness alike, the worker now lifted up by hopeful prospects then as surely cast down, abased, and humbled in the dust in presence of the self-imposed task.

> " But noble souls, through dust and heat,
> Rise from disaster and defeat
> The stronger.
> And conscious still of the divine
> Within them, lie on earth supine
> No longer."

I see the grand picture of the fifty millions of people in this province brought under the benign influences of a higher life unknown to their fathers, by the power of a love such as has consecrated the path to the cross in every age, by that love which burns in the soul of the ideal missionary of modern times, which is a fixed principle of his spiritual life, which no circumstances can suppress, — a perennial stream flowing into a spiritual desert.

How hard to love without some response! There is encouragement in the faintest echo; but the pioneers of the gracious work set before the Christian world are called upon to lavish untold riches of love upon millions of unresponsive people, yet firmly believing that in the fulness of time it will bear fruit in the lives of other millions of true believers.

The great question for those interested in the welfare of such a multitude of men and women as exist in Sz-Chuan — one twenty-eighth of the human race — is, How can we best reach them; how administer to them such aid as shall help them to throw off the iron fetters of superstitions, out of which grow innumerable cruelties; how teach them to overcome the slavish vices which have eaten up all manhood, and sustain their weakened moral energies until they are competent to help themselves?

Self-sacrifice is written on every feature of Christian labor which may be carried on in that distant field. The very character of the province and its people calls for heroism. It is distant from other mission centres and the encouragement and indirect aid afforded by semi-Christian communities, such as exist at Shang-hai and Hankow; the missionaries are called upon to meet all difficulties, and brave all dangers incident to any field, without having the supports granted workers in many more favorable locations.

If we are to do what the manifest importance of the province demands, the present conditions are such that there must be some modification of former plans. Single men are needed there; for we must not attempt to plant Christian families, to any great extent, with modern houses, at this stage of affairs. Our plans, while comprehensive and liberal, must be as simple as efficiency will admit. Christian charities are not for the purpose of founding large institutions to be controlled by foreign boards, — engines to be guided at will by home corporations, — even when wholly sanctified to the generous purpose of developing churchly orders among the heathen. They are rather intended to open paths in which new generations may walk; to throw a clearer light upon the people, that they may extricate themselves from their evils; to alleviate sorrow, and give object lessons for the millions; or, in other words, to establish new institutions or germs of institutions, which may be eventually taken up and developed by the people themselves. Let us away with the idea that organizations here are to govern there, and church forms which have answered to our wants here are to be recast there. The grand idea is to give light, give life, and as quickly as possible. Several important centres should be opened, from which may be worked a number of harmonious enterprises. Each station should be supplied with an experienced physician and sufficient funds to start both dispensary and hospital. We have come by long experience to appreciate this branch of mission work in China at something like its true value, but it has taken many years to bring it into its legitimate position. Schools are great factors after the hospital has softened the hearts of the masses. The Press and every conceivable element should be laid hold of to awaken, enlighten, and attract the people.

A few words as to candidates. Much has been written and more said about the proper gifts required for success in foreign fields. I have little doubt that the standard should be as high for China as for first-class pulpits in America or England. If the English Government chooses a young man for any post abroad, it is absolutely necessary that he should be proficient as a student, and able to pass a severe test examination, besides bringing the very best testimonials as to character. He goes abroad and does not stand upon the topmost round at once, but begins at the lowest, with a small salary, and by dint of his own energy and talents works his way to the top.

It may seem cruel to hedge the way to so philanthropic a work as educating the heathen with stringent restrictions, to demand high merit in the candidates who are destined to instruct the poor Chinamen in the rudiments of Christianity.

Let us be calm and look the situation in the face. China is a great empire; it has an ancient and voluminous literature; it has a language which it requires brains to master. It has a vast army of literary men, keen and scornful, who will meet the teachers of Christianity at all points. There are ancient systems of philosophy and religion much older than the system you bring to them, and having as many followers. The teacher is brought into contact with a people who reverence to idolatry all that belongs to their great past, or in any way partakes of it. It is not unreasonable to demand that one who undertakes to evangelize such a people should have talent, and be so generously equipped that his superior intelligence may command the respect of those who hear him. The day is past when an indifferent man or woman should be sent to China; the field demands great heads and noble hearts.

There is one requirement of momentous consequence. The candidate should have a conviction that China is a land worthy of his greatest efforts, and the place of all others where he can best serve humanity. Let no one think, because he has been popular in his little sphere at home, that he need only to bring his brightly burning lamp to the shores of China, and thousands will bow down to worship. Your great flood of light will penetrate about as far as the blaze of a tallow candle in a Yang-tsze fog.

The present is an age of wonders, and the spirit which dominates Western lands is rousing sleepy China. The multiplied physical agencies of Christendom are centring in portions of the empire. They will encounter the obsolete methods of an effete civilization; and who can doubt the result? Should not the endeavor be made, that moral and spiritual progress shall keep pace with the physical and material?

INDEX.